"Few things are as shockingly repugnant as reading bold [illegible] slavery written by those who claim the name of Jesus Christ. How could anyone transformed by the gospel advocate human trafficking, captivity, forced labor, and the destruction of families? Some have argued that a Christian vision of gender complementarity will one day seem as horrifying as antebellum slavery views. In this careful scholarly work, Ben Reaoch examines this trajectory hermeneutic as it relates to slavery and to gender. The contemporary generation of Christians should pay close attention to this debate."

—**Russell D. Moore**, Dean, Southern Baptist Theological Seminary

"*Women, Slaves, and the Gender Debate,* from the pen of Benjamin Reaoch, presents orthodoxy in doctrine and clarity in polarizing positions, together with a cogent reminder of exactly what is at stake in the gender debate. He recognizes that the debate over roles in marriage and family structure tears away at the warp and woof of who God is and what he had in mind for the man and woman created in his image, since the creation order is his tool for revealing himself through the metaphor of the family and familial relationships. Reaoch harmonizes and interfaces appropriately faithful exegesis and consistent hermeneutical methodology so that there is no question of authority or the nature of truth. Whether complementarian or egalitarian, you need to read this book. The complementarian author interacts with egalitarians respectfully by letting them speak for themselves and responsibly by pointing out the underlying issue for all: does God say what he means and mean what he says? For Reaoch, nothing trumps the written Word of God—not modern-day prophets or learned theologians, not new cultural values or human philosophies presented through innovative trajectory hermeneutics. I thank God for raising up men such as Benjamin Reaoch to hold the standard high and refuse to compromise for convenience or culture."

—**Dorothy Kelley Patterson**, Southwestern Baptist Theological Seminary

"Ben Reaoch has given us a well-researched, well-written, and well-reasoned resource on the issue of slavery and gender in the New Testament. As our society becomes more and more polarized on issues of sexuality, race, and gender, Christians need significant guidance in navigating what the Bible says and does not say about these issues and how we are to understand and interpret them. This book provides such guidance and should become a standard in this area of study. It already has a place my library. I highly recommend it to yours."

—**Tony Carter**, Pastor, East Point Church, East Point, Georgia

"In this very useful study, Benjamin Reaoch adds his voice to the growing chorus of those who have raised concerns with William Webb's 'redemptive movement hermeneutic,' including eminent evangelical scholars such as Wayne Grudem, Thomas Schreiner, and Robert Yarbrough. Reaoch does not merely repeat these critiques, however, but excels in providing an incisive and comprehensive assessment of a hermeneutic that has the appearance of sophistication but in the end is found wanting when examined in light of the biblical teaching and subjected to judicious analysis."

—**Andreas J. Köstenberger**, Senior Professor of New Testament and Biblical Theology and Director of PhD Studies, Southeastern Baptist Theological Seminary

"Benjamin Reaoch carefully sets forth and analyzes the views of those promoting development in a redemptive-historical hermeneutic. Not only does Reaoch fairly and accurately describe the position, but he also conducts a careful evaluation in which the exegetical and hermeneutical weaknesses of the view are unfolded. I enthusiastically commend this major and convincing treatment of one of the central hermeneutical debates of the day."

—**Thomas R. Schreiner**, James Harrison Buchanan Professor of New Testament Interpretation, Southern Baptist Theological Seminary

WOMEN, SLAVES, AND THE GENDER DEBATE

WOMEN, SLAVES, AND THE GENDER DEBATE

A Complementarian Response to the Redemptive-Movement Hermeneutic

Benjamin Reaoch

P&R PUBLISHING
P.O. BOX 817 • PHILLIPSBURG • NEW JERSEY 08865-0817

Italics within Scripture quotations indicate emphasis added, unless specified otherwise.

ISBN: 978-1-59638-401-9 (pbk)
ISBN: 978-1-59638-567-2 (ePub)
ISBN: 978-1-59638-568-9 (Mobi)

Printed in the United States of America

Library of Congress Cataloging-in-Publication Data

Reaoch, Benjamin, 1976-
Women, slaves, and the gender debate : a complementarian response to the redemptive-movement hermeneutic / Benjamin Reaoch.
p. cm.
Includes bibliographical references (p.) and indexes.
ISBN 978-1-59638-401-9 (pbk.)
1. Women in the Bible. 2. Slavery in the Bible. 3. Equality--Biblical teaching. 4. Bible. N.T.--Hermeneutics. 5. Bible. N.T.--Criticism, interpretation, etc. 6. Christianity and culture. I. Title.
BS2545.W65R43 2012
225.8'305--dc23

2012006205

To Stacy

"Her children rise up and call her blessed;
her husband also, and he praises her."
Proverbs 31:28

Contents

FOREWORD

One of the most sobering verses in the Bible is Psalm 50:21, where God accuses Israel, saying, "You thought I was just like you" (HCSB). We are shaped and molded by our culture in more ways than we recognize and even imagine. We have presuppositions, beliefs, and values that later generations will disparage. More important, we have beliefs, practices, and presuppositions that are repugnant to our sovereign, holy, and good God.

Our culture congratulates itself on being more compassionate and caring and gentle than previous generations. After all, our ancestors in the United States practiced slavery. They treated black human beings like property and degraded and dehumanized them. And we rightly see from our social location and place in history that American slavery was a horrendous evil. We see the evil of how we treated Native Americans in the United States, and acknowledge the atrocities committed by some soldiers in wars. We study marriages from a previous era and recognize that too often men have abused their wives and treated them like their property.

We see many of these things clearly and want to avoid the sins of earlier generations. We may secretly congratulate ourselves that we are kinder and gentler than those who preceded us. As Christians we may have grown up with fundamentalist parents who were exceedingly strict and, recognizing their harshness and rigidity, we see ourselves as more like Christ because we are forgiving, tolerant, and compassionate in ways that contrast with them.

In accord with our cultural context and way of perceiving reality, a new hermeneutical approach has arrived. It argues that we need to go beyond the Bible in constructing our ethic. If we stick with what the Bible says, we will perpetuate what is unjust and wrong. According to this hermeneutic, if we follow what the NT says about the relationships between men and women and husbands and wives, we will not be doing the will of God, for the redemptive movement in Scripture means we must go beyond Scripture to discover God's perfect will.

What makes me skeptical is that the conclusions reached with this hermeneutic fit so well with our cultural moment. According to these interpreters, the Bible doesn't teach that only men are permitted to serve as pastors. Those off-putting verses that Paul wrote don't apply to us today. When we truly understand the message of Scripture, so it is said, we will acknowledge that women may serve as pastors.

Is the redemptive-movement hermeneutic correct? We don't want to be like the fool in Proverbs who gives an answer before listening to what someone else says. We want to listen patiently to new views so that we are not close-minded traditionalists. Yet it is right to be chary of a view that resonates with our culture and goes contrary to what most Christians have believed throughout history. History isn't the final authority. Traditions can be wrong. Everything must be judged by Scripture, yet the burden of proof is surely on those who argue contrary to the view that Christians have espoused throughout history. And I am happy to commend Ben Reaoch's book, for he has patiently listened to those who advocate a redemptive-movement hermeneutic and found it wanting. Significantly, Reaoch makes his case by thoroughly examining and interpreting the Scriptures.

What is worrying is that we tend to think God agrees with our cultural values. We are prone to thinking God is just like us. And if we throw radical postmodernism into the mix, the brew can be quite toxic. I am not saying that the redemptive-movement advocates are postmodern. I am only saying that it fits with the postmodern turn. I just read recently someone who took exception to the command that we should be baptized, for such a hermeneutical conclusion was far too definite and imperious. If God's clear commands are vacuumed into the abyss of postmodern relativity, the Word of God is swallowed up in a philosophy that is contrary to the teachings of Christ (Col. 2:8).

The above comments could be misunderstood. The hermeneutical issues are complex, and those who advocate a redemptive-movement hermeneutic raise matters that must be carefully considered. Ben Reaoch's insightful evaluation of the hermeneutical and exegetical questions is precisely the kind of work we need. The issues raised can't be examined thoroughly in a brief essay or a foreword! The question is whether the redemptive-movement hermeneutic is itself hermeneutically persuasive and exegetically faithful. Reaoch demonstrates that it falls short on both levels. The author's work is marked by careful exegesis, hermeneutical awareness, and charity toward those with whom he disagrees. I am grateful for this book, for Reaoch believes that God's final and definitive Word is found in the NT, and that the ethic of the NT does not need to be improved upon, for it is the living and abiding Word of God.

Thomas R. Schreiner

Acknowledgments

Working on this project has been a joy, and finally bringing it to completion is an occasion for much thanksgiving. God has been very good to me, and I am grateful to him for so many individuals who have blessed my life. My parents, Ron and Barb Reaoch, have been a great encouragement and inspiration to me since I was young. They instilled in me a love for the Bible and a passion for Bible teaching, ministry, and missions. In God's good providence, I have been fortunate to develop many friendships that have spurred me on in my love for the Lord and for his Word. Noah Toly, John Kimbell, Jason Meyer, Dustin Shramek, and Doug Wolter are among these. Additionally, God has graciously given me the opportunity to sit under many godly mentors and teachers. Mark Talbot at Wheaton College inspired me to think deeply and clearly about theological matters. John Piper, Tom Steller, and Sam Crabtree at Bethlehem Baptist Church continued to feed this passion and imparted to me a love for the church.

This book began as my doctoral dissertation under the supervision of Tom Schreiner at Southern Seminary. Tom has been for me an exemplary teacher, pastor, and friend. I have learned much from his classes, sermons, and books, from his insightful feedback during the process of this project, and from his wise counsel in various matters of life and ministry. Bruce Ware, Bill Cook, and Andreas Köstenberger also read this material, and I thank them for their valuable feedback. It has certainly improved the final product.

I also want to express my gratefulness to all those at P&R Publishing who have been involved in bringing this work to publication. Marvin Padgett, John Hughes, and Brian Kinney have all been a great help and encouragement to me in this process.

It's a great privilege to be serving as pastor of Three Rivers Grace Church in Pittsburgh. I serve alongside elders and deacons who have made many sacrifices to help me complete this book, and the entire congregation has encouraged me and prayed for me throughout the process. I count it a tremendous blessing to be part of this congregation.

Finally, I want to express my profound gratitude for the precious family that God has given me. Our children, Milaina, Noah, and Annalyse, are a joy to my heart. My wife, Stacy, has been an amazing support and encouragement to me through all the ups and downs of school, ministry, and family life. She is a passionate follower of Jesus, an excellent wife, a loving mother, an organized and efficient homemaker, an example and mentor to other women, a joy to share life with, and my dearest friend. In many ways, Stacy is responsible for this writing project, for she was the one who suggested that I write a dissertation related to biblical manhood and womanhood. This has been a topic that is near and dear to Stacy's heart, and we have had the joy of seeing its fruit in our own marriage, in our family, and in ministry. I am very fortunate to be married to a woman who joyfully embraces the biblical vision of womanhood. It is therefore with much joy that I dedicate this work to her.

Abbreviations

AB — *Anchor Bible*

ABD — *Anchor Bible Dictionary*

BDAG — Walter Bauer, Frederick William Danker, William Arndt, and F. Wilbur Gingrich, eds., *A Greek-English Lexicon of the New Testament and Other Early Christian Literature*, 3rd ed. (Chicago: University of Chicago Press, 2001)

BDF — Friedrich Blass, Albert Debrunner, and Robert W. Funk, *A Greek Grammar of the New Testament and Other Early Christian Literature*, rev. ed. (Chicago: University of Chicago Press, 1961)

BECNT — Baker Exegetical Commentary on the New Testament

BZNW — Beihefte zur Zeitschrift für die neutestamentliche Wissenschaft

CGTC — Cambridge Greek Testament Commentary

CSR — *Christian Scholar's Review*

DLNTD — *Dictionary of the Later New Testament and Its Developments*

EQ — *Evangelical Quarterly*

HCSB — Holman Christian Standard Bible

HNTC — Harper's New Testament Commentaries

ICC — International Critical Commentary

IVP — InterVarsity Press

JAAR — *Journal of the American Academy of Religion*

JBMW	*Journal for Biblical Manhood and Womanhood*
JETS	*Journal of the Evangelical Theological Society*
JSNTSup	Journal for the Study of the New Testament—Supplemental Series
LCL	Loeb Classical Library
LXX	Septuagint
NAC	New American Commentary
NIBC	New International Biblical Commentary
NICNT	New International Commentary on the New Testament
NIGTC	New International Greek Testament Commentary
NIVAC	The NIV Application Commentary
NTS	*New Testament Studies*
PNTC	The Pillar New Testament Commentary
SBLDS	Society of Biblical Literature Dissertation Series
SBLMS	Society of Biblical Literature Monograph Series
SNTSMS	Society for New Testament Studies Monograph Series
TLNT	*Theological Lexicon of the New Testament*
TNTC	Tyndale New Testament Commentaries
TrinJ	*Trinity Journal*
WBC	Word Biblical Commentary
WTJ	*Westminster Theological Journal*

INTRODUCTION

The current debate over the role of women in the home and in the church shows no signs of diminishing.[1] Egalitarians continue to present arguments against role distinctions, while complementarians still argue that the Bible presents men and women as equal in essence and distinct in role. An egalitarian argument that is gaining support is known as the redemptive-movement hermeneutic, or trajectory hermeneutic.[2] Advocates of this approach concede many of the exegetical conclusions made by complementarians concerning the relevant biblical passages, but then they argue there are indications in the Bible that move us *beyond* the specific instructions of the Bible and toward an ultimate ethic. For instance, the Bible commands slaves to submit to their masters, and yet basic principles in the Bible point toward the abolition of slavery. The issue of women's roles is very much the same, these writers assert.[3] The Bible

1. In 2004, two significant books on this topic were published. From the egalitarian position came Ronald W. Pierce and Rebecca Merrill Groothuis, eds., *Discovering Biblical Equality: Complementarity without Hierarchy* (Downers Grove, IL: IVP, 2004). From the complementarian position came Wayne Grudem, *Evangelical Feminism and Biblical Truth: An Analysis of More Than 100 Disputed Questions* (Sisters, OR: Multnomah, 2004). More recently, Grudem has published another book on this subject, *Evangelical Feminism: A New Path to Liberalism?* (Wheaton, IL: Crossway, 2006).

2. Most notably, William Webb, *Slaves, Women, and Homosexuals: Exploring the Hermeneutics of Cultural Analysis* (Downers Grove, IL: IVP, 2001). Also R. T. France, *Women in the Church's Ministry: A Test Case for Biblical Interpretation* (Grand Rapids: Eerdmans, 1995); David L. Thompson, "Women, Men, Slaves, and the Bible: Hermeneutical Inquiries," *CSR* 25 (1996): 326–49; I. Howard Marshall, "Mutual Love and Submission in Marriage: Colossians 3:18–19 and Ephesians 5:21–33," in *Discovering Biblical Equality*, ed. Pierce and Groothuis, 186–204; idem., *Beyond the Bible: Moving from Scripture to Theology* (Grand Rapids: Baker, 2004). Prior to these evangelical feminist writings, a similar line of argumentation is found in Krister Stendahl, *The Bible and the Role of Women: A Case Study in Hermeneutics*, trans. Emilie T. Sander (Philadelphia: Fortress, 1966).

3. For example, Kevin Giles, *The Trinity and Subordinationism: The Doctrine of God and the Contemporary Gender Debate* (Downers Grove, IL: IVP, 2002), devotes an entire chapter to this, "The Parallel Exhortations to Slaves and Women to Be Subordinate," 251–58. Also, one of David Thompson's three major theses is as follows: "The church's experience in discerning the will of God

places women in a subordinate role in the home and in the church, yet there are also principles in the Bible that point toward their full liberation.[4]

THESIS

On the one hand, the redemptive-movement description of the slavery issue may prove to be helpful. We must not be too quick to forget how adamantly our evangelical forefathers argued from the Bible for the continuation of slavery,[5] and complementarians may benefit from insights the redemptive-movement hermeneutic offers in arguing against slavery from the Bible.[6]

However, there are some key differences between the slavery issue and the gender issue in the Bible, and the redemptive-movement hermeneutic overemphasizes the similarities between the two. The analogy between slaves and women is a foundational assumption for this hermeneutic,

regarding slavery provides a hermeneutical paradigm sufficiently parallel to instruct its processing of the biblical material on the relationship between men and women" (Thompson, "Women, Men, Slaves, and the Bible," 327).

4. The verse most commonly cited is Gal. 3:28. F. F. Bruce, *Commentary on Galatians* (Grand Rapids: Eerdmans, 1982), 190, comments, "Paul states the basic principle here; if restrictions on it are found elsewhere in the Pauline corpus, as in 1 Cor. 14:34f. . . . or 1 Tim. 2:11f., they are to be understood in relation to Gal. 3:28, and not *vice versa*" (italics original). Similarly, Paul Jewett, *Man as Male and Female: A Study in Sexual Relationships from a Theological Point of View* (Grand Rapids: Eerdmans, 1975), 148, says, "Had the church, through the centuries, interpreted 'neither slave nor free' in Galatians 3:28 in terms of the explicit implementation in the New Testament, the institution of slavery would never have been abolished. The same is true of women's liberation." Also see Richard Longenecker, *New Testament Social Ethics for Today* (Grand Rapids: Eerdmans, 1984), who deals with the cultural (Jew/Gentile), social (slave/free), and sexual (male/female) aspects of Gal. 3:28.

5. See Willard M. Swartley, *Slavery, Sabbath, War and Women: Case Issues in Biblical Interpretation* (Scottdale, PA: Herald Press, 1983), 31–64. A notable defender of slavery was Charles Hodge. See his essay, "The Bible Argument on Slavery," in *Cotton Is King, and Pro-Slavery Arguments Comprising the Writings of Hammond, Harper, Christy, Stringfellow, Hodge, Bledsoe, and Cartwright on This Important Subject*, ed. E. N. Elliot (1860; reprint, New York: Negro Universities Press, 1969), 841–77. Also see Allen C. Guelzo, "Charles Hodge's Antislavery Moment," in *Charles Hodge Revisited: A Critical Appraisal of His Life and Work*, ed. John W. Stewart and James H. Moorhead (Grand Rapids: Eerdmans, 2002), 299–325.

6. Wayne Grudem does not think a redemptive-movement hermeneutic is needed in order to oppose slavery from the Bible. The abolitionists, he asserts, "*did not advocate modifying or nullifying any biblical teaching*, or moving 'beyond' the New Testament to a better ethic. They taught the abolition of slavery from the Bible itself" (italics original) (Grudem, *Evangelical Feminism and Biblical Truth*, 614). He cites Theodore Weld, *The Bible Against Slavery*, 4th ed. (New York: American Anti-Slavery Society, 1838), and Mason Lowance, ed., *Against Slavery: An Abolitionist Reader* (New York: Penguin Books, 2000). I agree with Grudem that we do not need to move "'beyond' the New Testament to a better ethic." However, I am open to learning from trajectory egalitarians as they have wrestled with the complex biblical and historical data on slavery.

and therefore we must closely scrutinize it. It may be appropriate to see a "trajectory," in some sense, in the biblical statements on slavery, whereas the instructions to women do not allow this. My thesis is as follows: The significant differences between the New Testament instructions to slaves and to women seriously undermine the conclusions made by the redemptive-movement hermeneutic. The fact that the New Testament "points beyond" the institution of slavery does not indicate that it likewise points beyond God's design for gender roles.

The crucial distinction between the two issues is seen in the fact that no biblical writer advocates for slavery based on the order of creation. In this way the slavery passages are significantly different from the instructions concerning the roles of men and women, which are explicitly rooted in creation. The issue of slavery in the Bible is not an easy one, however. The New Testament does not explicitly condemn slavery or clearly command masters to release their slaves. Is the absence of a clear denunciation of slavery because the New Testament contains a less-than-ultimate ethic, as trajectory advocates would suggest? Or is there a more accurate way to understand the New Testament statements in light of their cultural context?

This book will thoroughly investigate the exegetical and hermeneutical questions related to the issues of slavery and women in the New Testament. I will seek to demonstrate that a trajectory approach is not a viable solution to these complex questions and is not justified in its conclusions with regard to the gender debate.

The Redemptive-Movement Hermeneutic

This book will be a combination of exegetical study and hermeneutical analysis, with an emphasis on the latter. Chapter 1 will begin with a description of the redemptive-movement hermeneutic, including a brief discussion of complementarian responses to this hermeneutic, and finally a section on the nineteenth-century slavery debate.

Exegesis

Chapters 2 and 3 will examine the passages that pertain to slaves (chapter 2) and women (chapter 3). The detailed exegesis of these passages is a crucial component of this study. Kevin Giles asserts, "The reasons given for slaves to be subordinate are more consistent and weightier than those to women, for there is a repeated Christological appeal (Eph. 6:5; Col. 3:22; 1 Peter 2:18–21)."[7] These kinds of statements must be evaluated carefully. I will attempt to conduct a detailed exegetical analysis of each passage in the hope of clarifying the distinctions between the two kinds of texts.

Chapter 2 will begin with a section on slavery in the first century. Then the exegetical discussion will be organized by focusing on the passages where specific commands are given to slaves, first examining the passages that contain a ground for obedience (Eph. 6:8; Col. 3:24; 1 Peter 2:19–20) and then the passages that attach a purpose clause to the imperative (1 Tim. 6:1; Titus 2:10). Other relevant passages will then be covered (Philemon; Gal. 3:28; 1 Cor. 12:13; Col. 3:1; 1 Tim. 1:10; 1 Cor. 7:21). The chapter will conclude by addressing the question, "Why does the New Testament not condemn the institution of slavery?"

In chapter 3, a similar format will be used in the examination of the New Testament commands to women, first discussing those commands that contain a ground clause (1 Cor. 11:8; 1 Tim. 2:13; Eph. 5:23; Col. 3:18; 1 Cor. 14:34), and then the two passages in which exhortations to women are followed by a purpose clause (1 Peter 3:1; Titus 2:5). Chapter 4 will be a comparison of the data gathered in chapters 2 and 3. I will observe that similarities are evident between the slavery passages and women passages when we look at the purpose clauses, but a comparison of the ground clauses reveals significant differences. Chapter 4 also contains a discussion of the Household Codes.

Hermeneutics

The other significant component of this study will be hermeneutical. The exegesis is crucial to demonstrate clearly the similarities and differences between the texts, but the hermeneutical questions are the determining factor in this debate.[8] Much of the hermeneutical discussion will involve responses to William Webb, since his book and articles contain the fullest expression of a redemptive-movement hermeneutic.[9] Other

7. Giles, *Trinity and Subordinationism*, 257.

8. Marshall, *Beyond the Bible*, points to the difference between his own commentary on the Pastorals and William D. Mounce's commentary on the Pastorals, even though the two scholars share "much the same exegetical environment." He then states, "Something more than exegesis is at work" (36).

9. William J. Webb, *Slaves, Women, and Homosexuals*; idem, "A Redemptive-Movement Model" in *Four Views on Moving Beyond the Bible to Theology*, ed. Gary T. Meadors (Grand Rapids: Zonder-

trajectory advocates will enter the discussion at various points, but the structure of chapters 6 and 7 will be organized around eight of Webb's hermeneutical criteria that he presents in *Slaves, Women, and Homosexuals*. Chapter 5 will include a discussion of theological analogy, preliminary movement, seed ideas, and purpose/intent statements. On these points, there are certain similarities between the slavery issue and the issue of women's roles.[10] However, there are also important differences. Chapter 6 will deal with the issues of original creation, primogeniture, creation versus redemption, and specific instructions versus general principles.

The redemptive-movement hermeneutic seeks to wrestle with some difficult interpretive questions, and helpful observations are made. However, the conclusion these authors reach, that we must move beyond the specific biblical instructions concerning manhood and womanhood, is not warranted. I will seek to demonstrate that it is unwarranted through the detailed exegesis of the slavery passages and women's passages, and then by interacting with the hermeneutical points that have been presented.

---

van, 2009), 215–48; idem, "Balancing Paul's Original-Creation and Pro-Creation Arguments: 1 Corinthians 11:11–12 in Light of Modern Embryology," *WTJ* 66 (2004): 275–89; idem, "Bashing Babies against the Rocks: A Redemptive-Movement Approach to the Imprecatory Psalms" (paper presented at the annual meeting of the Evangelical Theological Society, Atlanta, November 20, 2003); idem, "The Limits of a Redemptive-Movement Hermeneutic: A Focused Response to T. R. Schreiner," *EQ* 75 (2003): 327–42; idem, "A Redemptive-Movement Hermeneutic: Encouraging Dialogue Among Four Evangelical Views," *JETS* 48 (2005): 331–49; idem, "A Redemptive-Movement Hermeneutic: Responding to Grudem's Concerns" (paper presented at the annual meeting of the Evangelical Theological Society, San Antonio, November 17, 2004).

10. I will use the phrase "the issue of women's roles" to refer to the group of issues that come under one umbrella in biblical teaching, namely, husband-wife role relationships and the question of women teaching or having authority over men in the context of the church.

1

The Redemptive-Movement Hermeneutic

This chapter will summarize the views of several scholars who have advocated a trajectory hermeneutic and have drawn a close parallel between the slavery issue and the gender debate. This summary will contain a comprehensive history of neither the slavery debate nor the gender debate, but rather will focus on the redemptive-movement hermeneutic and the relationship between slavery and the issue of women's roles in the New Testament. The chapter will conclude with a section on the nineteenth-century slavery debate, because some aspects of the redemptive-movement hermeneutic find antecedents in abolitionist arguments.

Krister Stendahl

In his 1966 book, *The Bible and the Role of Women: A Case Study in Hermeneutics*, Krister Stendahl presents a hermeneutical model very similar to the trajectory approach advocated by evangelicals today.[1] He writes in the context of the debate over women's ordination in the Church of Sweden, and he acknowledges that the real issue in the debate is the *application* of Scripture. Both sides agree concerning the original meaning of the texts,

1. Krister Stendahl, *The Bible and the Role of Women: A Case Study in Hermeneutics*, trans. Emilie T. Sander (Philadelphia: Fortress, 1966). Originally published in Swedish in 1958.

but they disagree as to how the texts should be applied today.[2] Stendahl advocates moving beyond the practices of the first-century church and following the trajectory set out for us in statements such as Galatians 3:28 and 1 Corinthians 11:11–12. He refers to the "breakthrough" of Galatians 3:28, and he sees in 1 Corinthians 11:11–12 a "glimpse" of that breakthrough.[3] He stresses the need to apply Galatians 3:28 in all its dimensions and all its fullness. Each pair (Jew/Greek, slave/free, male/female) must be worked out in the life of the church and not restricted to "the realm *coram deo*."[4]

Stendahl also emphasizes the newness of this "breakthrough," stating that "something has happened which transcends the Law itself and thereby even the order of creation."[5] These radical principles obliterate the traditional distinctions in each of the three pairs, and point beyond them to a higher ideal. Therefore, we must no longer enforce the specific instructions concerning women's subordination. Those instructions *describe* the situation of the early church, but they are not *normative* for the church today.[6]

Concerning slavery, Stendahl gives slight preference to the following translation of 1 Corinthians 7:21: "but even if a chance of liberty should come, choose rather to make good use of your servitude."[7] In other words, Paul was probably not encouraging emancipation, but rather calling individuals to remain in their current positions. Stendahl briefly discusses Philemon and writes, "The tone of the letter is best understood as a plea for having

2. Ibid., 8.

3. Ibid., 32, 35.

4. Ibid., 34.

5. Ibid. Earlier, he stated, "It should be noted that [Gal. 3:28] is directed against what we call the order of creation, and consequently it creates a tension with those biblical passages—Pauline and non-Pauline—by which this order of creation maintains its place in the fundamental view of the New Testament concerning the subordination of women" (32).

6. Ibid., 35–36: "[The 'realistic interpretation'] does not see that the correct description of first-century Christianity is not automatically the authoritative and intended standard for the church through the ages. . . . [B]y making their description normative, they neutralize the power of the new and contribute to a permanent 'holding minus *x* minutes' in the drama of the launching of the kingdom."

7. Ibid., 33. Stendahl makes reference to the two renderings of the verse given in the New English Bible. The one he favors is found in a footnote of that Bible. For a full discussion of the difficulties here, see S. Scott Bartchy, *MALLON CHRESAI: First Century Slavery and the Interpretation of 1 Corinthians 7:21* (Missoula, MT: Scholars Press, 1973). He does not think this verse makes a judgment one way or the other on slavery. He translates the verse this way: "Were you a slave when you were called? Don't worry about it. But if, indeed, you become manumitted, by all means [as a freedman] live according to [God's calling]" (183). For a defense of the view that Paul is encouraging emancipation, see Gordon Fee, *The First Epistle to the Corinthians*, NICNT (Grand Rapids: Eerdmans, 1987), 315–18. So also David E. Garland, *1 Corinthians*, BECNT (Grand Rapids: Baker Academic, 2003), 307–14.

Onesimus set free."[8] But then he asserts, "Whatever the implications of such texts, there can be no doubt that the New Testament shows no urgency in the matter of emancipation of slaves."[9] He points to the history of the debate over slavery as an indication that we must move beyond biblical proof texts and apply Galatians 3:28 more broadly to political and social matters.[10]

In summary, these "trajectory" arguments from Stendahl have been around for almost half a century. Stendahl maintains that the real issue in the debate over women's ordination is how the texts should be applied. His assertion is that the "breakthrough" texts such as Galatians 3:28 and 1 Corinthians 11:11–12 should point us beyond the specific instructions we find elsewhere in the New Testament. These passages point to something new, something beyond the order of creation. Stendahl also uses the uncertainty of the New Testament's stance on slavery as an indication that we cannot limit Galatians 3:28 to the level of individual salvation, apart from political and social issues. This "breakthrough" must trump other New Testament statements.

R. T. France

R. T. France comments on the similarity between the slavery debate and the debate over the ordination of women. Concerning the slow process that brought about the abolition of slavery, he writes,

> It was only gradually that Christians were led to realize that Scripture speaks with more than one voice on the issue, and that the simple appeal to the cultural pattern which appears on the surface of the biblical text may need to yield to more fundamental ethical principles which, while not explicitly applied to slavery in Scripture, must ultimately lead to its abolition.[11]

He also observes the male-dominated nature of first-century society and comments, "it remains, like the institution of slavery, a part of the given scene which is neither commended nor directly disputed, but which will

8. Stendahl, *The Bible and the Role of Women*, 33.
9. Ibid., 34.
10. Ibid.
11. R. T. France, *Women in the Church's Ministry: A Test Case for Biblical Interpretation* (Grand Rapids: Eerdmans, 1995), 16–17.

in due course be undermined as Christian people are enabled to apply the wider principles of New Testament ethics in the context of a changing world-order."[12]

At the end of the book, France cites F. F. Bruce's comment that Galatians 3:28 is the basic principle by which the other Pauline statements must be interpreted.[13] France agrees with this principle, which rests not on a small number of texts, "but in a *trajectory* of thought and practice developing through Scripture, and arguably *pointing beyond itself* to the fuller outworking of God's ultimate purpose in Christ in ways which the first-century situation did not yet allow" (emphasis added).[14]

Richard Longenecker

In his book *New Testament Social Ethics for Today*, Richard Longenecker sets forth a "developmental hermeneutic." He upholds the proclamation and principles of the New Testament as normative, and then clarifies, "The way that proclamation and its principles were put into practice in the first century, however, should be understood as signposts at the beginning of a journey which point out the path to be followed if we are to reapply that same gospel in our day."[15]

In the rest of the book, Longenecker seeks to embark on that journey, and he organizes his discussion around the key passage, Galatians 3:28. First he deals with the social ramifications of Jew and Greek, then slave and free, and finally male and female. In his chapter on the male/female compo-

12. Ibid., 36.

13. F. F. Bruce, *Commentary on Galatians* (Grand Rapids: Eerdmans, 1982), 190. Luke Timothy Johnson, commenting on 1 Tim. 2:12, expresses the same sentiment: "I find the statements [in 1 Tim. 2] to be in sharp tension with other Pauline declarations of a more egalitarian character, above all Gal. 3:28. . . . I agree that our growth in understanding of the human person, partly guided by the Holy Spirit, and partly driven by the resistance of brave women to these strictures, makes it impossible to regard the statements disqualifying women from public speech and roles of leadership as either true or normative." Luke Timothy Johnson, *The First and Second Letters to Timothy*, AB (New York: Doubleday, 2001), 208–9. On the other hand, Judith Gundry-Volf, in an essay dealing with Gal. 3:28, writes, "In Paul we are witnessing a model of thought in which equality does not presuppose all-out sameness (dissolution of femininity or/and masculinity) but sameness *in some respects*—with respect to sin and with respect to the way of salvation" (italics original). Judith M. Gundry-Volf, "Christ and Gender: A Study of Difference and Equality in Gal. 3, 28," in *Jesus Christus als die Mitte der Schrift*, ed. C. Landmesser et al., BZNW 86 (New York: Walter de Gruyter, 1997), 476.

14. France, *Women in the Church's Ministry*, 94–95.

15. Richard Longenecker, *New Testament Social Ethics for Today* (Grand Rapids: Eerdmans, 1984), 27. Idem, *Galatians* (Nashville: Thomas Nelson, 1990), 156–59.

nent of this verse, he points out two key categories that the apostle Paul was dealing with: creation and redemption. The focus on creation emphasizes "order, subordination, and submission," while the focus on redemption stresses "freedom, mutuality, and equality."[16] "What Paul attempted to do in working out his theology was to keep both categories united—though, I would insist, with an emphasis on redemption."[17] Thus, there are still differences between men and women (e.g., Paul condemns homosexual behavior). But the emphasis is on redemption, so that "what God has done in Christ transcends what is true simply because of creation."[18]

This emphasis on redemption over against creation is closely related to the principle of following the perceived path of the *general* principles in Scripture (which are the redemptive, forward-looking, liberating statements) rather than some of the *specific* instructions (which seem restrictive, emphasize order, and may be rooted in creation). Like France, Longenecker cites Bruce's comment on Galatians 3:28. This seems to be a basic presupposition for these scholars, namely, that their understanding of Galatians 3:28 takes ultimate priority in the discussion. This implies a tension between the general principle in Galatians 3:28 and the specific instructions in other passages.

David Thompson

In his 1996 article, "Women, Men, Slaves and the Bible: Hermeneutical Inquiries," David Thompson develops a system that is similar to what Webb would present five years later.[19] "One attends especially to two matters in discerning the direction of the canon's dialogue: 1) the relationship of the particular passages to their cultural environment, i.e., the direction in which the passages themselves in their historical contexts are already pointing, and 2) the relationships between the passages involved."[20]

16. Longenecker, *New Testament Social Ethics for Today*, 84. A similar sentiment is shared by J. A. Ziesler, *Pauline Christianity* (Oxford: Oxford University Press, 1983), 121: "So, the state and society remain, but the theological realities of the New Age are already undermining their *inequitable, discriminatory, and hierarchical* foundations. To change the metaphor, within the old society is a new one, built on quite different foundations of *love, equality, and unity*" (emphasis added).

17. Longenecker, *New Testament Social Ethics for Today*, 92.

18. Ibid.

19. David L. Thompson, "Women, Men, Slaves, and the Bible: Hermeneutical Inquiries," *CSR* 25 (1996): 326–49.

20. Ibid., 332.

Here we see a foreshadowing of the cultural analysis conducted by Webb. Thompson also capitalizes on the comparison between slavery and the gender debate. The abolitionists, he writes,

> saw a trajectory leading beyond the canon and its unresolved dialogue to the abolition of slavery. . . . This is important history, for few if any present evangelicals would want to defend slavery as acceptable Christian teaching. This means we have already accepted the hermeneutic entailed in the egalitarian position regarding men and women.[21]

Thompson observes a close parallel between the issue of slavery and the issue of women's roles in the home and church. He also advocates a trajectory hermeneutic that analyzes the relationship between biblical commands and the cultural setting in which they were written.

William Webb

Slaves, Women, and Homosexuals has been a significant addition to the trajectory hermeneutic;[22] William Webb also refers to it as a redemptive-movement hermeneutic. It becomes much more complex and detailed in the way he formulates it. He presents eighteen criteria by which we can determine whether a command is limited to the original culture and setting, or whether it transcends culture and is applicable to all times and places. As the title indicates, he analyzes the three issues involving slaves, women, and homosexuals, and the method is to compare what the Bible says about these issues with the cultural contexts in which the biblical statements were written (either ancient Near Eastern or Greco-Roman). When the biblical commands can be seen against the backdrop of their cultures, a trajectory can be discerned that is either more liberating or more restrictive than the original context. Webb sees the commands concerning homosexuals moving in a more restrictive direction, whereas

21. Ibid., 344.

22. William J. Webb, *Slaves, Women, and Homosexuals: Exploring the Hermeneutics of Cultural Analysis* (Downers Grove, IL: IVP, 2001); idem, "The Redemptive-Movement Hermeneutic: The Slavery Analogy," in *Discovering Biblical Equality: Complementarity without Hierarchy*, ed. Ronald W. Pierce and Rebecca Merrill Groothuis (Downers Grove, IL: IVP, 2004), 382–400; idem, "Gender Equality and Homosexuality," in *Discovering Biblical Equality*, 401–13; idem, "A Redemptive-Movement Model," in *Four Views on Moving Beyond the Bible to Theology*, ed. Gary T. Meadors (Grand Rapids: Zondervan, 2009), 215–48.

he sees the commands for slaves and women moving in the direction of complete liberation. Thus, on the one hand, he concludes that the biblical prohibitions against homosexual behavior are still authoritative. On the other hand, we are encouraged to move beyond the specific instructions that condone slavery and male headship.

Webb repeatedly likens the issue of women's roles—the combination of biblical issues such as a wife's role in marriage and women teaching and having authority over men in the context of the church—to the slavery issue, and this correlation is foundational to his hermeneutic. Under the criterion of "seed ideas," Webb discusses the social implications of Galatians 3:28 (also 1 Cor. 12:13; Eph. 2:15; Col. 3:11). He states,

> One must now ask if the "in Christ" formula should carry social implications for the equality of women. It certainly did in Paul's day for Gentiles. And, it did over the course of church history for slaves. Why should it not today for females? In this manner Paul's sociological outworking of the Galatians 3:28 text becomes a paradigm of equality for these other categories of social inequality.[23]

The parallel that is drawn between the slavery texts and the women's texts has a great deal of persuasive power. Virtually all agree that slavery is wrong and that abolition is an appropriate application of the Bible's teaching. But the question Webb raises in the above quote is crucial: Why shouldn't the social implications of Galatians 3:28 be applied in such a way that male headship is abolished just as slavery has been abolished in this country?

Webb is keenly aware of the apparent difference between the two issues. "Obviously there exists a crucial difference between slavery and patriarchy. The former is not found in the creation story, while the latter, perhaps in implicit ways, is."[24] Therefore a significant piece of Webb's argument has to do with original creation. Criterion 6 and criterion 7 are devoted to this issue, and they fall under the designation "Moderately Persuasive Criteria." Webb states, "A component of a text may be transcultural if its basis is rooted in the original-creation material."[25] He then discusses various components of Genesis 1–2, seeking to demonstrate

23. Webb, *Slaves, Women, and Homosexuals*, 87.
24. Ibid., 248.
25. Ibid., 123.

that certain aspects are transcultural (e.g., lifelong marriage as opposed to divorce) while others are not (e.g., farming as an occupation, ground transportation, vegetarian diet). Concerning the roles of men and women, he admits that there are "hints of patriarchy" in the creation narrative. But since there are several cultural components in the garden, these "quiet whispers" of patriarchy cannot be conclusive.[26]

In criterion 7, he moves to a discussion of primogeniture, the rights of the firstborn. The importance of this discussion is found in the debate over the correct interpretation and application of 1 Timothy 2:12, where the following verse (v. 13) grounds the instruction in the order of creation. "For Adam was formed first, then Eve." Webb is sympathetic to the complementarian interpretation of this verse, which acknowledges the aspect of primogeniture. However, he then marshals an argument against the continued application of this principle. Several biblical examples are given in order to show that primogeniture is often overturned. Primogeniture is also an ancient practice, and it is no longer enforced by Christians. Therefore, since primogeniture is a cultural component of the text and no longer applicable today, Webb concludes that we should only apply the underlying principle of "granting honor to whom honor is due."[27] In relation to 1 Timothy 2 specifically, he says we should apply this principle to both genders: "Choose teachers/leaders who are worthy of high honor within the congregation."[28]

Pivotal to Webb's conclusions are the following assumptions: (1) the issue of gender roles is closely analogous to the slavery issue, and (2) patriarchy's basis in original creation does not conclusively differentiate the two. If, in fact, basis in original creation is more than "moderately" persuasive, and thus sets apart the women's texts from the slavery texts, Webb's egalitarian position based on a trajectory hermeneutic would be severely weakened.

KEVIN GILES

Kevin Giles is more explicit than Webb in drawing a parallel between slavery and the gender debate.[29] He strongly emphasizes the biblical support

26. Ibid., 130–31.

27. Webb, *Slaves, Women, and Homosexuals*, 145.

28. Ibid.

29. Giles's overall emphasis is slightly different from Webb's. Whereas Webb stresses the redemptive movement in the Bible, Giles stresses the difference between our culture and the ancient cultures

for slavery, and rehearses the arguments that have been used to defend it. His point is to show that slavery is a cultural aspect of the Bible just as male headship is. In fact, he says, "The 'biblical' case for slavery is far more impressive than the 'biblical' case for the permanent subordination of women."[30] The tendency is to read the slavery texts in a negative light, which is then presented as a conclusive argument for moving beyond the Bible's instructions.

Giles also attacks the assumption that the slavery issue and the gender issue are supported differently in the Bible. He writes, "The assertion by contemporary hierarchical-complementarians that these parallel exhortations to women and slaves to be subordinate are to be contrasted is an entirely novel idea, never heard before the 1970s and rejected universally by critical scholarly studies of the Household Codes or Rules."[31] He proceeds

---

represented in the Bible. Giles comments on Webb's claim concerning the redemptive movement anticipated in the Bible, "There is much in Webb's book with which I would agree, but to prove his point he would have to show that the moderating comments on slavery and women in Scripture were unique to the Bible. . . . In any case, I cannot see how this argument really helps on its own. The primary question is, why did Christians not see this redemptive motif in Scripture on slavery for eighteen centuries and on women for twenty centuries? Was it not a change in culture that allowed Christians to see in Scripture what had hitherto been hidden to them? The redemptive motif did not bring the change, it was the change that brought to light the redemptive motif." Kevin Giles, *The Trinity and Subordinationism: The Doctrine of God and the Contemporary Gender Debate* (Downers Grove, IL: IVP, 2002), 244n29. Giles has also written "The Subordination of Christ and the Subordination of Women," in *Discovering Biblical Equality*, 334–52.

30. Giles, *The Trinity and Subordinationism*, 230. Craig S. Keener also discusses the relevance of the slavery issue in his book, *Paul, Women, and Wives: Marriage and Women's Ministry in the Letters of Paul* (Peabody, MA: Hendrickson, 1992). Concerning Ephesians 5–6 he writes, "Those who wish to save this passage's power structure in the home regarding wives and children but not regarding slaves will have a difficult time. It is true that the Bible enjoins children's obedience more clearly than it does that of slaves; but it also *enjoins the submission of slaves more clearly than it does that of wives*" (italics original) (Keener, *Paul, Women, and Wives*, 188). Keener also writes, "Those who today will admit that slavery is wrong but still maintain that husbands must have authority over their wives are inconsistent. If they were consistent with their method of interpretation, which does not take enough account of cultural differences, it is likely that, had they lived one hundred fifty years ago, they would have had to have opposed the abolitionists as subverters of the moral order—as many Bible-quoting white slave owners and their allies did" (Keener, *Paul, Women, and Wives*, 207–8). In a similar way, J. Albert Harrill, in his Epilogue, criticizes the Southern Baptist Convention for the inconsistency between its "Resolution on Racial Reconciliation" and the article on the family in *The Baptist Faith and Message*, which says, "A wife is to submit herself graciously to the servant leadership of her husband." Harrill writes, "This amendment on women, which explicitly affirms the inerrant and timeless truth of the household duty codes, contradicts the resolution on slavery, which implicitly denies their moral relevance today. The contradiction exposes the specious argument present in the amendment" (J. Albert Harrill, *Slaves in the New Testament: Literary, Social, and Moral Dimensions* [Minneapolis: Fortress, 2006], 195).

31. Giles, *The Trinity and Subordinationism*, 253.

by comparing the exhortations to wives and the exhortations to slaves and concludes that "the appeal to creation is *the exception to the rule*, not the pattern" (emphasis original).[32]

This gets to the heart of the question I will be dealing with in this book. What, in fact, are the similarities and differences between the slavery texts and the women texts? Giles emphasizes the similarities and minimizes the differences, and thus builds a case for viewing the biblical instructions as remnants of an ancient culture. They no longer apply in our day. If a careful study of the two issues demonstrates significant differences, Giles's conclusions will lose much of their force.

I. Howard Marshall

I. Howard Marshall can also be placed in the category of those who advocate a trajectory hermeneutic. He argues that the New Testament commands concerning women are no longer applicable. Paul was speaking to his cultural context, and those details have little or no relevance for us now. In his book, *Beyond the Bible: Moving from Scripture to Theology*, Marshall sets forth a program similar to although not as comprehensive as Webb's.

Marshall refers favorably to Webb's work: "[Webb] is able to show how there is a tendency toward a fuller liberation in the ongoing history of redemption, . . . and he argues that this can and should be carried further in the church."[33] In Marshall's chapter in *Discovering Biblical Equality* he sounds very much like Webb when he says, "The concept of marriage between equal partners is just beginning to be perceived in the New Testament, and Paul should not be expected to step outside his time and see the consequences of his teaching any more than he is to be faulted for not commanding the abolition of slavery."[34]

32. Ibid., 256. Giles bases his comparison on the tables found in David C. Verner, *The Household of God: The Social World of the Pastoral Epistles* (Chico, CA: Scholars Press, 1981), 88.

33. I. Howard Marshall, *Beyond the Bible: Moving from Scripture to Theology* (Grand Rapids: Baker, 2004), 38. Marshall also refers to the hermeneutical principles set forth in C. H. Cosgrove, *Appealing to Scripture in Moral Debate: Five Hermeneutical Rules* (Grand Rapids: Eerdmans, 2002). And, interestingly, he states, "The idea of a 'redemptive trajectory' is not original with Webb" (Marshall, *Beyond the Bible*, 38n7), and references R. T. France, *Women in the Church's Ministry*.

34. I. Howard Marshall, "Mutual Love and Submission in Marriage: Colossians 3:18–19 and Ephesians 5:21–33," in *Discovering Biblical Equality*, 195.

Complementarian Responses

Wayne Grudem and Thomas Schreiner have both critiqued Webb's system in a detailed manner. On the issue of slavery, Grudem criticizes Webb for assuming that the Bible condones slavery: "The NT never commanded slavery, but gave principles that regulated it and ultimately led to its abolition."[35] The important question is whether or not the statements in the New Testament can be taken as an endorsement of slavery. If so, either slavery is in fact justified, or the redemptive-movement model seems to be a necessary and plausible tool in showing why it is not justified. But if the New Testament simply regulates slavery and points toward its abolition, then the perceived need for the redemptive-movement hermeneutic evaporates.[36]

Thomas Schreiner's main criticism of Webb is that he does not deal sufficiently with redemptive *history*. There is a tremendous emphasis on redemptive *movement*, but it lacks an explanation of redemptive *history*.[37] This results in confused comparisons between certain Old Testament statements and New Testament instructions. For instance, since many of the practices in the garden of Eden are seen as cultural (vegetarianism, walking as the only mode of transportation, farming as the only occupation), Webb relegates his sixth and seventh criteria (basis in original creation, and primogeniture) to the level of only "moderately persuasive." Since we do not continue to enforce many aspects from the garden, neither should we continue to enforce the instruction from 1 Timothy 2:12, which is based on truths from the garden.

When we let Scripture interpret Scripture, though, we can see fairly easily what aspects of the garden have an enduring significance. As Schreiner notes, it is clear even in the book of Genesis that God did not intend for all humans to limit themselves to walking or farming or a vegetarian diet.[38] When we come to 1 Timothy 2 we should see the weight of Paul's argument from creation. Not everything in the creation

35. Wayne Grudem, "Should We Move Beyond the New Testament to a Better Ethic? An Analysis of William J. Webb, *Slaves, Women and Homosexuals: Exploring the Hermeneutics of Cultural Analysis*," *JETS* 47 (2004): 313.

36. Grudem concludes, "Once we remove his claim that the Bible condones slavery, Webb's Exhibit A is gone, and he has lost his primary means of supporting the claim that we need his 'redemptive-movement hermeneutic' to move beyond the ethic of the Bible itself," ibid., 314.

37. Thomas R. Schreiner, "Review of *Slaves, Women and Homosexuals*," *JBMW* 7 (2002): 46.

38. Ibid., 48.

account is to be applied today, of course, but the inspired apostle uses this pivotal aspect of the creation order in his instruction for the ministries of women. Schreiner writes, "When it comes to divorce, homosexuality, and the women's issue, the NT argues from the created order."[39] Slavery, in contrast, is not supported in this way in the New Testament. "Nowhere does Paul justify slavery by referring to a particular OT text or the created order, as he does the relationship between men and women."[40]

Robert Yarbrough also critiques the redemptive-movement hermeneutic, responding to Webb as well as Stendahl, Bruce, and Giles.[41] First, Yarbrough responds to Webb's critique of his chapter in the first edition of *Women in the Church*.[42] Webb speaks unfavorably of Yarbrough's "static hermeneutic," and contends that it should not be labeled "historic" or "traditional," for the redemptive-movement hermeneutic has also played a major role in the history of interpreting the Bible.[43] Yarbrough agrees that the redemptive-movement hermeneutic has been used throughout the centuries in various ways. "But," he says, "I continue to maintain that my hermeneutic, which affirms some form and degree of male headship in home and church, is the 'historic' one compared to [Webb's]."[44] He goes on to say, "How can we call Webb's approach 'historic' when it demands that we change the general understanding of biblical teaching on men and women that prevailed for nearly twenty centuries?"[45]

Later in the chapter, Yarbrough interacts with Krister Stendahl and F. F. Bruce, who both used Galatians 3:28 to effectively silence other gender passages. Yarbrough concludes:

> The problem with Bruce's and Stendahl's method is not that it recognizes tension in the Bible. The Reformation principle that Scripture interprets Scripture (*sacra scriptura sui interpres*) implies the presence of obscure or ostensibly conflicting passages. The problem lies in the recourse to

39. Ibid., 49.

40. Ibid.

41. Robert W. Yarbrough, "Progressive and Historic: The Hermeneutics of 1 Timothy 2:9–15," in *Women in the Church: An Analysis and Application of 1 Timothy 2:9–15*, ed. Andreas Köstenberger and Thomas R. Schreiner, 2nd ed. (Grand Rapids: Baker Academic, 2005), 121–48.

42. Robert W. Yarbrough, "The Hermeneutics of 1 Timothy 2:9–15," in *Women in the Church: A Fresh Analysis of 1 Timothy 2:9–15*, ed. Andreas Köstenberger, Thomas R. Schreiner, and H. Scott Baldwin, 1st ed. (Grand Rapids: Baker, 1995), 155–96.

43. Webb, *Slaves, Women, and Homosexuals*, 35 (including both footnotes); 256n3.

44. Yarbrough, "Progressive and Historic," 122.

45. Ibid., 123.

> a distinctly modern consciousness to adjudicate Scripture's meaning. This is to step outside the horizon of Scripture to determine Scripture's significance. It is to imperil the *sola scriptura* doctrine of the Reformation and similar affirmations of earlier periods.[46]

Finally, Yarbrough critiques the view of Kevin Giles. He states that "Giles too facilely equates biblical teaching on slavery and its teaching on male-female relations,"[47] and goes on to delineate some of the key differences.

The complementarian position observes a fundamental distinction between the slavery issue and the issue of women's roles. The Bible does not, in fact, condone slavery. Rather, it regulates it and points to its demise. Regarding women, on the other hand, we find instructions that are rooted in the creation order and therefore transcend culture.

Nineteenth-Century Slavery Debate

Can the redemptive-movement hermeneutic be traced back to the abolitionist arguments of the nineteenth century? This interesting question has been raised by those involved in the current discussion.[48] A multitude of arguments were formulated against slavery in the 1800s, and some of them were similar to the trajectory approach. I will paint a general picture of the nineteenth-century slavery debate, in which I will describe some of the abolitionist arguments. In this way I hope to show that some abolitionist arguments were similar to the trajectory hermeneutic, but others

46. Ibid., 139.

47. Ibid., 141.

48. In various places, Webb points to ways in which the abolitionist arguments are similar to his, and how the pro-slavery arguments are similar to a "static hermeneutic." For instance, in his discussion of specific instructions and general principles, he writes, "Slave owners in the United States valued the concession-based *specifics* of Scripture and argued their case primarily from those verses. . . . Abolitionists, on the contrary, began with the *broad principles* of Scripture and showed that slavery should be repealed on the basis of love and the ethics of equality in God's kingdom and in Jesus' new community" (*Slaves, Women, and Homosexuals*, 180). Also see pages 33–34, 91, 104, 186. The quote above from David Thompson is another example of this. More recently, Carl Sanders has written a paper titled, "The 19th Century Slave Debate: An Example of Proto-Redemptive-Movement Hermeneutics?" He seeks to show that there are many parallels between the abolitionist arguments of the nineteenth century and Webb's hermeneutical criteria. Sanders provides examples of the following criteria found in Webb's book: preliminary movement, seed ideas, breakouts, specific instructions versus general principles, competing options, penal code, closely related issues, contextual comparisons, appeal to the Old Testament, and opposition to original culture (paper presented at the annual meeting of the Evangelical Theological Society, San Antonio, November 18, 2004).

were not. Thus, an appeal to redemptive movement was not necessary to formulate a valid biblical argument against slavery.

The Biblical Debate over Slavery

Mark Noll delineates four positions that were held in the antebellum slavery debate. The first group abandoned the Bible because they viewed it as sanctioning slavery.[49] The second group agreed that the Bible sanctioned slavery, and thus used the Bible to justify slavery in the United States. A third group "conceded that, while the Bible did indeed sanction a form of slavery, careful attention to the text of Scripture itself would show that the simple presence of slavery in the Bible was not a necessary justification for slavery as it existed in the United States."[50] Finally, there was the position that distinguished between the letter and the spirit of the Bible. The letter may condone slavery, but the spirit of the biblical message was clearly against it.[51] This final position resembles facets of the trajectory hermeneutic, for it rests on the distinction between specific instructions and general principles.

Looking at the antislavery arguments, J. Albert Harrill provides an assessment of how these arguments evolved over the course of the debate. The earlier abolitionists, he says, used a more literal and "anti-intellectual" approach to Scripture. For instance, some argued that Jesus never condemned slavery because he never met any slaves, asserting that the Greek word *doulos* simply means "servant."[52] Others even appealed to the translators of the King James Version of the Bible, who always rendered *doulos* as "servant" rather than "slave."[53]

49. Mark A. Noll, "The Bible and Slavery," in *Religion and the American Civil War*, ed. Randall M. Miller, Harry S. Stout, and Charles Reagan Wilson (New York: Oxford University Press, 1998), 43.

50. Ibid., 44.

51. Ibid. Interestingly, Noll later notes, "This move led directly or indirectly to the theological liberalism of the last third of the twentieth century" (Noll, "The Bible and Slavery," 51). Harrill also makes this observation: "The antislavery and abolitionist interpretations of the New Testament during the American slave controversy also pushed biblical exegetes toward a critical hermeneutics, preparing the way in the United States for the eventual reception of German higher criticism" (Harrill, *Slaves in the New Testament*, 166).

52. So Albert Barnes, *An Inquiry into the Scriptural Views of Slavery* (Philadelphia: Perkins and Purves, 1846), 242–49.

53. Harrill quotes from a debate in which it was said, "*If they were slaves, the translators* of our Bible *would have called them so*" (emphasis in original; Harrill, *Slaves in the New Testament*, 167, quoted from J. Blanchard and N. L. Rice, *A Debate on Slavery Held in the City of Cincinnati, on the First, Second, Third, and Sixth Days of October, 1845, upon the Question: Is Slave-Holding in Itself Sinful, and the Relation between Master and Slave, a Sinful Relation?* [Cincinnati: Wm. H. Moore, 1846], 336).

Still others, however, presented a more reasonable rationale for why Jesus did not directly denounce slavery, namely, that he did not speak out against *every* evil he encountered. We do not find any record of him condemning practices such as "sodomy, polygamy, infanticide, idolatry, or blasphemy,"[54] but we cannot conclude that Jesus did not think these were sins.

Nevertheless, when the pro-slavery arguments seemed to be winning the exegetical battle, other abolitionists made a dramatic shift toward "immutable principles." "The exact opposite of the earlier plain-sense approach, the hermeneutics of immutable principles claims that biblical interpretation must look beyond the flat reading of the text."[55] This took various forms, including appeal to the Golden Rule (Matt. 7:12 and Luke 6:31) and to Colossians 4:1, "Masters, treat your slaves justly and fairly." "Because Col. 4:1 cohered with the Golden Rule, it must be the privileged text that exercises hermeneutical control over the interpretation of other, more difficult Pauline passages."[56] Thus, the general principles of love and equality achieved priority over the specific instructions that seemed to condone slavery.

Still, there was the question of why the New Testament does not speak out openly against slavery. Harrill says that among the earlier antislavery arguments, *expediency* was offered as the reason for this.[57]

54. Harrill, *Slaves in the New Testament*, 167. George Cheever wrote, "It is averred that Christ's own silence on the subject of this sin gives consent to it. Christ was silent in regard to the sin of sodomy, in regard to infanticide, in regard to idolatry; and by this method of reasoning, not only is the law of God against these crimes abolished, and the crimes themselves made innocent by such silence, but he that speaks against them, when Christ did not, is himself guilty of a presumptuous sin, and may think himself happy if he is not struck with some divine judgment" (George Cheever, *The Guilt of Slavery and the Crime of Slaveholding: Demonstrated from the Hebrew and Greek Scriptures* [Boston: John P. Jewett, 1860], 332–33).

55. Harrill, *Slaves in the New Testament*, 169–70.

56. Ibid., 172–73.

57. Ibid., 173. He says that William Ellery Channing was the main proponent of this view. Channing was professor of theology at Harvard Divinity School and was a Unitarian. This argument is similar to that used by trajectory advocates today who appeal to evangelism as the apostle's reason for teaching wifely submission. Webb cites Titus 2:5, "that the word of God may not be reviled," and 1 Peter 3:1, "so that even if some do not obey the word, they may be won without a word by the conduct of their wives," demonstrating the purpose for wifely submission. He goes on to say that a wife's submissive spirit may no longer serve those same purposes in our culture (*Slaves, Women, and Homosexuals*, 107–8). Peter H. Davids also takes this approach in his chapter, "A Silent Witness in Marriage: 1 Peter 3:1–7," in *Discovering Biblical Equality*. He writes, "Ironically, interpretations that focus on the unilateral obedience or submission of wives to husbands, regardless of cultural context, achieve the opposite of Peter's intention. Rather than promoting harmony with culture, they set Christian marriage partners

It was thought that if Paul *openly* condemned slavery, it would be so countercultural that it would cause more harm than good. Indeed, an outright attack on the institution of slavery in the first century could have incited the anger of the Roman Empire and brought an end to the burgeoning Christian church.[58] Therefore, it was thought that the seed of abolition grew *secretly*.

Later abolitionists, though, rejected this reasoning in favor of the idea that the seed grew *openly*.[59] Paul was not, in fact, secretive about his position on slavery. He made it clear in 1 Timothy 1:10 (KJV) that "manstealing" is wrong and in 1 Corinthians 7:21 that slaves should seek freedom if the opportunity presents itself.[60] However, when these arguments did not seem to be effective, the abolitionist cause turned to another hermeneutical approach, namely, moral intuition. This position emphasized the ascendancy of personal conscience as a way of discerning God's law.[61] In this way, the abolitionist arguments took a further step away from a "plain sense" reading of the Bible.

Specific Instructions versus General Principles

With this background in view, let us focus on one similarity between nineteenth-century abolitionist arguments and the current trajectory model. Mason Lowance compares pro-slavery and antislavery sermons, and writes of the latter, "Their emphasis was less on the exegesis of text and more on the moral application of the spiritual principles inherent in the text to the social and political issue of slavery in America."[62] Lowance points out this tendency in a sermon by Alexander McLeod, who began with Exodus 21:16 as his biblical text, "Whoever steals a man and sells him, and anyone found in possession of him, shall be put to death." But

at odds with culture and thus heighten the tension, and Christianity is perceived as undermining culture in a retrogressive way. That is precisely what 1 Peter is seeking to minimize" (Davids, "A Silent Witness," 236).

58. William E. Channing, *Slavery*, 2nd ed. (Boston: James Munroe, 1836), 122.

59. Harrill, *Slaves in the New Testament*, 173.

60. The meaning of 1 Cor. 7:21 is debated, as discussed above.

61. Harrill points to the Second Great Awakening and the moral philosophy of Common Sense Realism as two forces that brought rise to this hermeneutic of moral intuition. William Lloyd Garrison took this position to its extreme, for he thought the Bible should not even play a role in moral debates (Harrill, *Slavery in the New Testament*, 175–76).

62. Mason Lowance, ed., *Against Slavery: An Abolitionist Reader* (New York: Penguin Books, 2000), 49.

then McLeod's sermon turns quickly to general principles, and he appeals to the "natural rights of man."[63]

Willard Swartley makes a similar observation of abolitionist hermeneutics and commends this practice to his readers.

> Abolitionist writers gave priority to theological principles and basic moral imperatives, which in turn put slavery under moral judgment. The point we should learn from this is that theological principles and basic moral imperatives should be primary biblical resources for addressing social issues today. These should carry greater weight than specific statements on a given topic even though the statements speak expressly to the topic under discussion.[64]

This emphasis on principles seems to be one of the most apparent parallels between nineteenth-century abolitionism and the contemporary trajectory hermeneutic.

Emancipation of Slaves and Women

The next question is how the abolitionists viewed the relationship between the emancipation of slaves and the emancipation of women, for this connection forms a critical piece of the foundation for the trajectory hermeneutic. On this question we find an interesting difference between nineteenth-century abolitionists and the redemptive-movement hermeneutic today. As noted above, the contemporary trajectory approach appeals strongly to the parallel between the slavery texts and the women's texts. But in the nineteenth century, it was the pro-slavery position that assumed a parallel between the two issues, and abolitionists differentiated them.[65]

Albert Barnes, an abolitionist, writes, "But it is not true that in any sense the apostles 'legislated' for slavery as they did for the relation of

63. Ibid., 73, writing of McLeod's sermon, "The Practice of Holding Men in Perpetual Slavery Condemned."

64. Willard Swartley, *Slavery, Sabbath, War, and Women: Case Issues in Biblical Interpretation* (Scottdale, PA: Herald Press, 1983), 61.

65. See Swartley, *Slavery, Sabbath, War, and Women*, 49, 52. This was not true of all abolitionists. Theodore Weld was an abolitionist as well as an egalitarian and saw some parallels between the two issues. See Donald W. Dayton, *Discovering an Evangelical Heritage* (New York: Harper & Row, 1976), 32–33. Also Robert H. Abzug, *Passionate Liberator: Theodore Weld and the Dilemma of Reform* (New York: Oxford University Press, 1980), 175–78.

husband and wife, and parent and child. It is not true that they ever represented those relations as parallel, or as equally desirable and acceptable to God."[66] Then he demonstrates how they are different,

> (a) they uniformly represent servitude as a *hard* condition, and as in itself undesirable. . . . But where do they represent the condition of a wife or child as necessarily a *hard* and *undesirable* condition? (b) They enjoin on slaves submission *to* their condition as a hard one, and one in which they were constantly liable to suffer wrong. . . . (c) The principal virtue which the apostles enjoin on slaves to cultivate, is that of *patience under wrong*. . . . (d) They represented it as desirable to escape from servitude if it could be done; or as more desirable to be free than to be in that condition [cites 1 Cor. 7:21]. But where is any thing like this said respecting the condition of a wife or child? (italics original)[67]

These observations demonstrate the difference between the way the Bible treats slavery and the way it treats marriage and family matters. The Bible points toward the demise of slavery but does not call for an end to role distinctions in marriage or the end of role distinctions in the parent/child relationship.

The pro-slavery position denies this distinction. George Armstrong writes, "With civil government, marriage, the family, and slavery [the Apostles] dealt in the same way. All that was sinful, contrary to the laws of God, in each, as then actually existing, they clearly and unequivocally condemn. . . . But they touch not the institutions themselves."[68] Pro-slavery arguments viewed the slavery issue as analogous to the gender issue, whereas abolitionist arguments did not. Presumably, since male headship was so ingrained in the social structures of the nineteenth century, the pro-slavery advocates tried to use patriarchy in their defense. The abolitionists had to distinguish slavery from the instructions for women so they could show that the slavery passages needed to be applied differently.

In a review of Swartley's book, Stephen Mott observes the connection between these issues. "That the pro-slavery debaters saw that the hermeneutics condemning slavery could support the emancipation of women

66. Barnes, *Inquiry*, 276.

67. Ibid., 276–77.

68. George D. Armstrong, *The Christian Doctrine of Slavery* (1857; reprint, New York: Negro Universities Press, 1969), 57.

is also striking. Opponents of slavery rejected the connection. History, as well as hermeneutical insight, fortunately appear to be with the fears of the former."[69] This statement assumes the pro-slavery arguments were correct in viewing the two debates as parallel. However, the arguments for the pro-slavery position are not necessarily valid. Abolitionists presented some sound arguments for viewing the two issues differently.

Biblical Arguments against Slavery

Certainly many arguments against slavery were based on immutable principles, and other arguments were weak and misguided. But we must not minimize the value of other solid, biblical arguments that arose out of the texts themselves. For instance, the appeals to Exodus 21:16, 1 Corinthians 7:21, 1 Timothy 1:10, and Philemon[70] are powerful arguments that come from what the Bible itself teaches. One need not pit immutable principles against specific instructions. Rather, these verses speak for themselves. The observation that Jesus did not condemn *every* wrong he encountered is also helpful in refuting the claim that Jesus implicitly *endorsed* slavery.

In these ways, abolitionist arguments were presented that make legitimate appeal to biblical texts. Even in the Old Testament, and especially in Paul, a foundation was laid that would reform slavery and eventually lead to its demise. The fact that the pro-slavery position offered alternative readings of these passages does not diminish these verses as significant statements that undermine the entire slave enterprise. I will further discuss the exegetical issues of the debated passages later in the book. At this point I simply want to assert that some of the abolitionist arguments were sound and biblical, without appealing to immutable principles.

Racism and Slavery

The question then arises, Why did the arguments from Scripture not succeed? Why did abolitionism have to move to immutable principles and

69. Stephen Charles Mott, review of *Slavery, Sabbath, War, and Women: Case Issues in Biblical Interpretation*, by Willard M. Swartley, *Horizons in Biblical Theology* 7 (1985): 120.

70. Barnes writes, "The principles laid down in this epistle to Philemon, therefore, would lead to the universal abolition of slavery. If all those who are now slaves were to become Christians, and their masters were to treat them 'not as slaves, but as brethren beloved,' the period would not be far distant when slavery would cease" (*Inquiry*, 330, quoted in Swartley, *Slavery, Sabbath, War, and Women*, 46).

then even to a hermeneutic of moral intuition? Mark Noll writes, "The main reason, however, that alternative hermeneutics failed, as well as the main reason for the conceptual confusion on Scripture in the division between North and South, was race."[71] The reason the Southern exegetes could not see the hypocrisy of their "exegetical" conclusions was that they were blind to the blatant racism they simply presupposed. Although the slavery advocates may have shown a higher level of exegetical sophistication, their moral blindness kept them from seeing the perversity of their endeavor. Noll notes the disconnect: "On slavery, exegetes stood for a commonsense reading of the Bible. On race, exegetes forsook the Bible and relied on common sense."[72]

Charles Hodge is a prime example of an excellent exegete and theologian who could not see that his racial presuppositions radically affected how he applied Scripture. He believed that the Christian life must be guided by the Bible alone.

> But so pervasive was the instinct of racism, even in his guileless soul, that he could not see how thoroughly he intertwined conclusions about what the Bible taught and opinions about the nature of African Americans that arose from no text of Scripture. The Bible was a lot clearer on slavery than on the enslavement of one race only, but Hodge could not tell the difference.[73]

The debate would have been much different if it were not for this moral blindness. The abolitionist arguments likely would have been received with less hostility and suspicion. There would have been more open-mindedness

71. Noll, "The Bible and Slavery," 61.

72. Ibid., 63.

73. Ibid., 64. It should be noted, however, that Hodge advocated gradual emancipation of slaves. "In a series of learned works, he conceded the biblical grounding for slavery as an institution, but argued that a proper understanding of Scripture, as well as a right judgment on American circumstances, should move toward the amelioration of slavery and then its effacement. Unfortunately for Hodge's later reputation, his attack on the biblical exegesis of abolitionists has been remembered more clearly than his defense of gradual emancipation" (Noll, "The Bible and Slavery," 59–60). See Charles Hodge's essay, "Slavery," *Princeton Review* 7 (1835), reprinted in Hodge's *Essays and Reviews* (New York: R. Carter, 1857), 573–611; idem, "The Bible Argument on Slavery," in *Cotton Is King, and Pro-Slavery Arguments Comprising the Writings of Hammond, Harper, Christy, Stringfellow, Hodge, Bledsoe, and Cartwright on This Important Subject*, ed. E. N. Elliot (1860; reprint, New York: Negro Universities Press, 1969), 841–77. Also cf. Allen C. Guelzo, "Charles Hodge's Antislavery Moment," in *Charles Hodge Revisited: A Critical Appraisal of His Life and Work*, ed. John W. Stewart and James H. Moorhead (Grand Rapids: Eerdmans, 2002), 299–325.

toward the biblical arguments against slavery, rather than the dogmatic assumptions that arose from racism.

Conclusion

The two foci of this study (slavery and women's roles) have been related to one another in fascinating ways throughout the years. The nineteenth-century debate reminds us that we all have presuppositions, and we ought to be mindful of the effect those presuppositions can have on our exegetical conclusions. A reflective and self-critical spirit is needed in dealing with these sensitive issues.

In the nineteenth century, some already observed a tension between specific instructions and general principles, and they asserted that the general principles must take precedence. In modern scholarship, Stendahl applied this method to the debate over women's ordination. Others have adopted this position and have developed it in a much fuller way (mainly Webb). My desire is to take a fresh look at the exegetical and hermeneutical questions related to slavery and women's roles and to bring some clarity to the assumed tension between general principles and specific instructions.

2

NEW TESTAMENT STATEMENTS CONCERNING SLAVERY

Kevin Giles compares the biblical statements concerning slavery and the biblical statements concerning the subordination of women, and he states, "The 'biblical' case for slavery is far more impressive than the 'biblical' case for the permanent subordination of women."[1] He is referring to the "biblical" arguments that have been produced to support the institution of slavery, especially those crafted by the well-respected Reformed theologians of the nineteenth century. And, of course, Giles's point is not to endorse slavery, but to show that the statements about slavery *and* the statements about the subordination of women are *both* obsolete. They are time-bound instructions that applied to the original readers of the New Testament, but they do not apply to us today.

The aim in this chapter is to examine closely what the New Testament says about slavery, and in the next chapter the same will be done with respect to the instructions for women. This chapter begins with a brief description of slavery in the first century, and then analyzes the NT passages that deal directly with slavery. The following questions will guide the

1. Kevin Giles, *The Trinity and Subordinationism: The Doctrine of God and the Contemporary Gender Debate* (Downers Grove, IL: IVP, 2002), 230.

study. What is commanded of slaves? What are the stated grounds for their obedience? What are the stated purposes of their obedience? What other passages are relevant to this discussion? Finally, I will raise the question of why the NT does not explicitly condemn the institution of slavery. Thus, it will be possible to assess what is the NT stance toward slavery. Is there a strong "biblical" case for slavery, as Giles asserts? Or is there a better way of understanding this complex issue? In chapter 4, this data will be compared and contrasted with the NT statements concerning women.

Slavery in the First Century

The experience of slaves in the first century varied greatly. On one end of the spectrum, to be a slave in a good household could be a position envied by some free persons.[2] Epictetus, although he acknowledges that "it is the slave's prayer that he be set free immediately,"[3] goes on to say that freedom will not bring the happiness that the slave expected. The freed slave will eventually say, "Why, what was wrong with me? Someone else kept me in clothes, and shoes, and supplied me with food, and nursed me when I was sick; I served him in only a few matters. But now, miserable man that I am, what suffering is mine, who am a slave to several instead of one!"[4] Thus, there were potential advantages of being a slave, if one belonged to a benevolent master.[5]

On the other end of the spectrum are reports of horrible abuse. For example, Vedius Pollio intended to throw his slave into a pond of huge lampreys for the minor offense of breaking a crystal cup. Fortunately, the slave was spared.[6] In another account, 400 innocent slaves were executed because one of the slaves in that household murdered the master.[7] There is also the sad reality that many slaves were used as sexual objects. The master assumed ownership over the slave's body as well as the slave's work.[8]

2. "How much better it is to have a good master than to live a free man in sordid humiliation!" Menander, *Fragments* 1093 (LCL 132 [1921]: 534). See also S. Scott Bartchy, *MALLON CHRESAI: First Century Slavery and the Interpretation of 1 Corinthians 7:21* (Missoula, MT: Scholars Press, 1973), 75n264.

3. Epictetus, *Discourse* 4.1.33 (LCL 218 [1928]: 253).

4. Ibid., 4.1.37–38 (255).

5. Bartchy, *MALLON CHRESAI*, 75–77.

6. Seneca, *De Ira* 3.40.2 (LCL 214 [1928]: 347–49).

7. Tacitus, *Annals* 14.42–45 (LCL 322 [1937]: 174–81). There were some who protested the execution, but those advocating it prevailed.

8. S. Scott Bartchy, "Slavery (New Testament)," in *ABD*, ed. David Noel Freedman (New York: Doubleday, 1992), 69. Murray J. Harris, *Slave of Christ: A New Testament Metaphor for Total Devotion*

J. A. Harrill describes the use of the Roman whip (*flagellum*) in slave abuse, stating, "The evidence proves the torture of ancient slaves to have been far more severe than the punishments sanctioned by the law in the slave society of Brazil, the most brutal of the modern world."[9] He goes on to say, "Despite claims by some NT scholars, ancient slavery was not more humane than modern slavery."[10]

Indeed, the abuse of slaves in the first century (e.g., unjust punishments, use of the *flagellum*, and sexual abuse) might have been as bad as or worse than modern slavery. However, several facets of Greco-Roman slavery differentiate it from slavery in the New World. Murray J. Harris states the differences succinctly:

> In the first century, slaves were not distinguishable from free persons by race, by speech or by clothing; they were sometimes more highly educated than their owners and held responsible professional positions; some persons sold themselves into slavery for economic or social advantage; they could reasonably hope to be emancipated after ten to twenty years of service or by their thirties at the latest; they were not denied the right of public assembly and were not socially segregated (at least in the cities); they could accumulate savings to buy their freedom; their natural inferiority was not assumed.[11]

These differences mitigate the offensiveness of ancient slavery; however, slavery in any form is an offense to human personhood. When one human being owns another human, it is inherently degrading. Still, it is important to distinguish the slavery of New Testament times from the slavery that ravaged our own country not so many years ago.[12]

In the first century, slavery was an assumed part of the Greco-Roman culture. In some places slaves may have made up one-third of

to Christ (Downers Grove, IL: IVP, 2001), 25, defines a slave as "someone whose person and service belong wholly to another." See also Orlando Patterson, *Slavery and Social Death: A Comparative Study* (Cambridge, MA: Harvard University Press, 1982), 13. He defines slavery as "the permanent, violent domination of natally alienated and generally dishonored persons."

9. J. A. Harrill, "Slavery," in *Dictionary of New Testament Background*, ed. Craig A. Evans and Stanley E. Porter (Downers Grove, IL: IVP, 2000), 1125.

10. Ibid.

11. Harris, *Slave of Christ*, 44.

12. S. Scott Bartchy, "Slave, Slavery," in *DLNTD*, ed. Ralph P. Martin and Peter H. Davids (Downers Grove, IL: IVP, 1997), 1098, notes the five cultures that have relied heavily on slavery as part of their economic systems: the Greeks and Romans in ancient history, and Brazil, the Caribbean, and the United States in modern history.

the population.[13] This sector of the population was constantly in flux. At any given time, there would be some individuals selling themselves into slavery and others being manumitted. Tenney Frank estimates that 500,000 manumissions took place between the years 81 B.C. and 49 B.C., an average of almost 16,000 per year.[14] The anticipation of being released was an incentive for slaves, something for which they hoped and worked. Bartchy says, "Thus, rather than leading to the gradual dissolution of the slave system, frequent manumissions encouraged its smooth functioning."[15]

The way the system worked, with its rate of releasing slaves, was also a factor that kept any ideas of abolition from entering the scene. When there were slave uprisings, they were not intended to overthrow the institution of slavery, but simply to gain individual freedom.[16] Apparently only two groups objected to the institution of slavery in the first century.[17] Josephus says of the Essenes, "They neither bring wives into the community nor do they own slaves, since they believe that the latter practice contributes to injustice and that the former opens the way to a source of dissension."[18] And Philo says of the Therapeutae:

> They do not have slaves to wait upon them as they consider that the ownership of servants is entirely against nature. For nature has borne all men to be free, but the wrongful and covetous acts of some who pursued that source of evil, inequality, have imposed their yoke and invested the stronger with power over the weaker.[19]

13. Bartchy, "Slavery," in *ABD*, 67. Further, A. A. Rupprecht, "Slave, Slavery," in *Dictionary of Paul and His Letters*, ed. Gerald F. Hawthorne and Ralph P. Martin (Downers Grove, IL: IVP, 1993), 881: "Estimates are that 85–90 percent of the inhabitants of Rome and peninsula Italy were slaves or of slave origin in the first and second centuries A.D."

14. Tenney Frank, "The Sacred Treasure and the Rate of Manumission," *American Journal of Philology* 53 (1932): 363. He comes to this estimate by studying the amount of money in Rome's sacred treasury, based on the fact that there was a 5 percent tax on each slave who was manumitted. This article is cited by Harris, *Slave of Christ*, 40, and A. A. Rupprecht, "Slave, Slavery," in *The Zondervan Pictorial Encyclopedia of the Bible*, vol. 5, ed. Merrill C. Tenney and Steven Barabas (Grand Rapids: Zondervan, 1975), 458. Rupprecht adds, "These figures are all the more startling when one learns that the total population of Rome in 5 B.C. has been estimated at about 870,000."

15. Bartchy, "Slavery," 70.

16. Harris, *Slave of Christ*, 62. He makes the further observation that "when rebel slaves were successful in gaining their freedom, they promptly embraced the ideals and pursuits of their former owners and so perpetuated the *status quo*!" (emphasis original).

17. See Harris, *Slave of Christ*, 61n41. Also, Bartchy, "Slavery," 69.

18. Josephus, *Jewish Antiquities* 18.21 (LCL 433 [1965]: 19). See also Philo, *Every Good Man Is Free* 79 (LCL 363 [1941]: 57).

19. Philo, *On the Contemplative Life* 70 (LCL 363 [1941]: 157).

But in the culture at large, slavery was an accepted norm. Abolition of the institution was hardly conceivable. Bartchy says, "If someone in Greece or Rome in the middle of the first century A.D. had cried, 'Slaves of the world unite!' he would have attracted only the curious."[20]

Slavery, with its benefits and abuses, was a fundamental aspect of the first-century culture in which the New Testament was written. Now we turn to those writings.

New Testament Commands to Slaves

Here I will interact with the five passages in which slaves are directly exhorted to obey, respect, and be subject to their masters: Ephesians 6:5–8, Colossians 3:22–4:1, 1 Timothy 6:1, Titus 2:9–10, and 1 Peter 2:18–25. A discussion of some other relevant passages will be found later in this chapter.

In each passage the imperative is addressed to slaves. Paul uses the term *douloi*, whereas Peter uses *oiketai* to refer to slaves.[21] In Ephesians 6:5 and Colossians 3:22, Paul uses the imperative form of the verb *hypakouō* in his exhortation for slaves to obey their masters. In 1 Peter 2:18 and Titus 2:9, *hypotassō* is used.[22] First Timothy 6:1 does not specifically enjoin

20. Bartchy, *MALLON CHRESAI*, 87.

21. *Oiketēs* literally means "member of the household." It specifically refers to a "house slave, domestic," or can mean "slave" in a generic sense (BDAG, 2000), s.v. "*oiketēs*." J. R. Michaels, *1 Peter*, WBC (Waco: Word, 1998), 138, observes a reason for Peter's choice of this term: "The other NT examples of the household duty code address Christian slaves as *douloi* (Col. 3:22; Eph. 6:5), but because Peter has just referred to all his readers as *theou douloi* (v. 16), he switches to *oiketai* in order to focus on household servants as a particular social group (the same group, presumably, as the *douloi* of Colossians and Ephesians). NT and LXX usage suggests no discernable difference in meaning." Paul J. Achtemeier, *1 Peter*, Hermeneia (Minneapolis: Fortress Press, 1996), 194, agrees that *oiketai* refers to slaves in general, but adds, "That is not to ignore the force of this term, however; it was most likely chosen to emphasize that slaves also belong to the Christian community as members of the household of God."

22. It appears as a participle in 1 Peter 2:18 and as an infinitive in Titus 2:9. The participle in 1 Peter 2:18 should most likely be taken as imperatival. See J. N. D. Kelly, *A Commentary on the Epistles of Peter and Jude*, Thornapple Commentaries (Grand Rapids: Baker, 1981), 116; Michaels, *1 Peter*, 138; Thomas R. Schreiner, *1, 2 Peter, Jude*, NAC, vol. 37 (Nashville: Broadman & Holman Publishers, 2003), 137. Contra Achtemeier, *1 Peter*, 194, who interprets this participle as an "adverbial participle of means," modifying the imperatives of v. 17. The infinitive in Titus 2:9 probably modifies the imperative of v. 6. See William D. Mounce, *Pastoral Epistles*, WBC, vol. 46 (Nashville: Thomas Nelson, 2000), 415; I. Howard Marshall and Philip H. Towner, *A Critical and Exegetical Commentary on the Pastoral Epistles*, ICC (Edinburgh: T & T Clark, 1999), 259. George Knight III, *The Pastoral Epistles: A Commentary on the Greek Text*, NIGTC (Grand Rapids: Eerdmans, 1992), 313, "This section (vv. 9–10) assumes an unstated finite verb and therefore harks back either to v. 1 or to *parakalei* in v. 6." On the difference between *hypotassō* and *hypakouō*, Mounce says, "Any differentiation . . . seems overly subtle" (*Pastoral*

obedience or submission, but exhorts slaves to "regard (*hēgeomai*) their own masters as worthy of all honor."

The mere fact that slaves are addressed directly is significant. In this way Paul and Peter implicitly recognize the personhood of slaves and grant them the dignity of moral responsibility. Andrew Lincoln makes this observation in his comments on Ephesians 6:5–9: "In a fashion unprecedented in the traditional discussions of household management, slaves are appealed to directly. They are treated as ethically responsible persons who are as fully members of the Christian community as their masters."[23]

Ground for Obedience

Attached to each of these imperatives is either a ground clause or a purpose clause. In three of the passages we find a ground clause supporting the command given to slaves. The phrase *eidotes hoti* ("knowing that") introduces the ground clause in Ephesians 6:8 and Colossians 3:24.[24] In each case, Paul instructs slaves to obey their masters, and he describes the nature of the obedience. He makes reference to working as to the Lord/Christ and from the heart. This is contrasted with working for men, as men-pleasers. The causal participle (*eidotes*) follows, indicating a ground for the command. Paul commands obedience, and then gives a reason for this obedience (*because you know . . .*). The content of this knowledge that Paul is using to motivate slaves is the truth that the Lord will reward their faithful service.[25] Future reward is the ground for the command. In Ephesians he emphasizes the positive elements of the coming judgment, namely, that those who do good will be rewarded. In Colossians, Paul emphasizes both the positive and negative aspects of the coming judgment, thus communicating both an incentive for obedience and a warning against disobedience.

In both of these passages Paul gives commands to masters as well as slaves, and in this way challenges the perception that masters had absolute

---

Epistles, 415). He cites 1 Peter 3:5–6, where the two verbs are used in the same context, and seem to carry very similar meaning.

23. Andrew T. Lincoln, *Ephesians*, WBC, vol. 42 (Dallas: Word, 1990), 424.

24. Ibid., 413. He has a helpful comparison of the Greek text of Eph. 6:5–9 and Col. 3:22–4:1 on page 412.

25. Harold W. Hoehner, *Ephesians: An Exegetical Commentary* (Grand Rapids: Baker Academic, 2002), 811: "Slaves are motivated to obey because they know that their Master in heaven is going to reward them."

rights over their slaves (Eph. 6:9; Col. 4:1). Indeed, Paul admonishes masters to treat their slaves "justly and fairly" (Col. 4:1) and to stop threatening (Eph. 6:9). In both verses these commands are grounded in the fact that masters (*kurioi*) and slaves alike have a heavenly Master (*kurios*). Lincoln says, "As in the equivalent Colossians passage, here too the focus on Christ as Lord relativizes the social distinction between slaves and masters."[26]

Like the commands to slaves in Ephesians and Colossians, 1 Peter 2:18–25 contains a ground clause that follows the imperative. Here, servants are commanded to be subject to their masters with all respect. Then the instruction goes a step further. Servants must be subject not only to masters who are good and gentle, but also to those who are unjust. The ground clause is introduced by *gar*. The NASB renders verse 19 in this way: "For this finds favor [*charis*[27]], if for the sake of conscience toward God a person bears up under sorrows when suffering unjustly." Peter is indicating here that God will look kindly on those who suffer unjustly while doing good. The use of *charis* at the beginning of verse 19 and the end of verse 20 forms an inclusio, indicating that these two verses are closely related and should be interpreted together.[28] Suffering unjustly while doing good is a gracious thing, that is, something that finds favor before God (vv. 19, 20b). But, in contrast, there is no credit (*kleos*) for one who suffers because of his own wrongdoing (v. 20a). This contrast sheds light on the meaning of *charis* in this context, for *charis* and *kleos* are used synonymously in the contrasting statements. While there is no credit when one suffers for wrongdoing, there *is* credit/favor for suffering while doing good. These verses convey an incentive similar to that found in Ephesians 6:8 and Colossians 3:24. Peter exhorts servants to endure in their suffering and to continue to do good, because God will look kindly on such conduct.[29]

Kevin Giles correctly observes "a repeated Christological appeal" in these three passages.[30] In Ephesians 6:5–8, slaves are exhorted to serve

26. Lincoln, *Ephesians*, 426.

27. Cf. Luke 6:32, 33, 34, where *charis* is used in the same way. See Michaels, *1 Peter*, 135; Achtemeier, *1 Peter*, 196n98; I. Howard Marshall, *1 Peter*, IVP New Testament Commentary Series (Downers Grove, IL: IVP, 1991), 89n2:19 (In this commentary, Marshall's footnotes are numbered according to the Scripture verses); Schreiner, *1, 2 Peter, Jude*, 140. Also BDAG, "*charis*" 2b, "by metonymy *that which brings someone* (God's) *favor* or *wins a favorable response* fr. God 1 Pt 2:19, 20."

28. So Michaels, *1 Peter*, 142; Achtemeier, *1 Peter*, 196; Schreiner, *1, 2 Peter, Jude*, 138.

29. Schreiner suggests that this *charis* is probably referring to "the reception of the future inheritance described in such detail in 1:3–5," (*1, 2 Peter, Jude*, 139).

30. Giles, *The Trinity and Subordinationism*, 256–57.

as slaves of Christ, as to the Lord. In Colossians 3:22–25, similarly, they are to obey their masters, fearing the Lord, and working as for the Lord. And 1 Peter 2:18–25 provides an extended illustration of suffering unjustly by describing Christ's suffering. Based on these observations, Giles says, "The reasons given for slaves to be subordinate are more consistent and weightier than those to women."[31] This is a bold and provocative statement. However, he fails to see that the references to Christ are related to the behavior of slaves and not to the institution of slavery. Neither Paul nor Peter is seeking to undergird the practice of slavery in their references to Christ. Rather, they are concerned to instruct individuals on how to conduct themselves in a manner that pleases the Lord.

In 1 Peter, suffering is a major theme throughout the letter, slavery being only the first mention of it. I. Howard Marshall makes this point, citing the occurrences of *paschō* in 1 Peter (2:19, 20, 23; 3:14, 17, 18; 4:1, 15, 19; 5:10) as well as the noun form *pathēma* (1:11; 4:13; 5:1, 9).[32] In addition, Marshall says of 1 Peter 2:21–25, "In many ways this paragraph, which stands virtually at the center of the letter, is its theological center."[33] This is noteworthy because Peter is doing far more here than providing an example for slaves who are suffering unjustly. As Marshall puts it so poignantly, "Christ cannot be an example of suffering for us to follow unless he is first of all the Savior whose sufferings were endured on our behalf."[34] In these verses (21–25), Peter rises above the particulars of slaves and masters to the overarching story of salvation—that Christ suffered for us so that we might follow in his steps in whatever suffering may face us.[35]

A similar train of thought is repeated in 1 Peter 3:13–22. Here the application is wider, referring generally to any kind of persecution encountered by Christians. The encouragement is similar: "But even if you should

31. Ibid., 256.

32. Marshall, *1 Peter*, 89n2:19.

33. Ibid., 91.

34. Ibid.

35. Michaels, *1 Peter*, 135: "Although v 20 has domestic servants particularly in mind, neither it nor anything that follows is limited to them. Their experience, whether actual or hypothetical, becomes a paradigm for the experience of all Christians everywhere in the empire." Similarly, Karen H. Jobes, *1 Peter*, BECNT (Grand Rapids: Baker, 2005), 191: "Peter claims that slaves, and by extension all Christians (3:9), are called both to suffer unjustly and to continue to do right as they follow the example of Jesus Christ in his passion. Although this call is embedded in instructions addressed to slaves, Peter has previously referred to all Christians as slaves of God (2:16) and restates the principle explicitly for all his readers in 3:9."

suffer for righteousness' sake, you will be blessed" (v. 14), "For it is better to suffer for doing good, if that should be God's will, than for doing evil" (v. 17). The exhortations are similar: "in your hearts honor Christ the Lord as holy" and make your defense "with gentleness and respect, having a good conscience" (vv. 15–16). And the theological analogy which follows is also similar: "For Christ also suffered once for sins, the righteous for the unrighteous, that he might bring us to God . . ." (v. 18). Based on the reasoning of Giles, it seems that we would need to understand this as a weighty theological basis for any societal structure that promotes the persecution or slandering of Christians.[36] But this is clearly not Peter's intent. The point is to provide suffering Christians with an appropriate perspective on their trials. The same is true in 1 Peter 2:18–25.

William Webb makes a point similar to that of Giles, but in a far more nuanced way. Webb refers to these passages (Eph. 6:5–9; Col. 3:22–4:1; 1 Peter 2:18–25) in his discussion of theological analogies. He mentions the use of these texts by slavery proponents and concludes, "If slavery should be assessed as cultural within Scripture (a position developed above), then obviously theological analogy at times accompanies biblical instructions with a dominant cultural component."[37] Theological analogy is not conclusive in determining whether a text is transcultural. The problem, though, is that Webb fails to notice significant differences between the various theological analogies he discusses. The next chapter will discuss the theological analogies found in Ephesians 5 and 1 Corinthians 11, and I will further interact with this issue in chapter 5. The point to be observed here is that the analogy between obeying one's earthly master and obeying the heavenly Master is not meant to give a theological grounding for the institution of slavery. Likewise, the illustration of Christ's suffering is not given as a basis for slavery. Rather, these analogies are drawn to illustrate

36. The same observation is made by Wayne Grudem, citing Heb. 10:34, "Should We Move Beyond the New Testament to a Better Ethic? An Analysis of William J. Webb, *Slaves, Women, and Homosexuals: Exploring the Hermeneutics of Cultural Analysis*," *JETS* 47 (2004): 314: "The Bible does not approve or command slavery any more than it approves or commands persecution of Christians. When the author of Hebrews commends his readers by saying, 'You joyfully accepted the plundering of your property, since you knew that you yourselves had a better possession and an abiding one' (Heb. 10:34), that does not mean the Bible *supports* the plundering of Christians' property, or that it *commands theft*! It only means that *if* Christians find themselves in a situation where their property is taken through persecution, they should still rejoice because of their heavenly treasure, which cannot be stolen" (italics original).

37. William J. Webb, *Slaves, Women, and Homosexuals: Exploring the Hermeneutics of Cultural Analysis* (Downers Grove, IL: IVP, 2001), 186.

the kind of behavior that pleases the Lord, and these instructions are addressed to believers facing various forms of persecution.

Purpose of Obedience

In 1 Timothy 6:1 and Titus 2:10, Paul expands on the imperatives, not with ground clauses but with purpose clauses. Each begins with the conjunction *hina*, and in each case the purpose is related to the reputation of Christianity. It is stated negatively in 1 Timothy 6:1: "so that the name of God and the teaching may not be reviled." Titus 2:10 presents it positively: "so that in everything they may adorn the doctrine of God our Savior."[38]

In 1 Timothy 6:1–2, Paul addresses slaves in general (v. 1) and then narrows his focus to slaves who have Christian masters (v. 2).[39] It is in the first statement that the purpose clause is found. All slaves are commanded to respect their masters so as to protect the reputation of Christianity. It would be a terrible reflection on the Christian faith if many who claimed to be Christians were also known as rebellious and disrespectful slaves. Paul warns that insubordinate behavior will bring slander on God's name and Christian teaching.[40] William Mounce says of the purpose clause,

> Slaves are to respect their masters not because slavery is a proper institution or because Paul supposedly has no social conscience. Rather, the success of the gospel is more significant than the lot of any one individual, and therefore slaves should behave in a way that does not bring reproach on the gospel.[41]

38. Webb points to these passages (among others) in his discussion of criterion number 4: "Purpose/Intent Statements," in *Slaves, Women, and Homosexuals*, 105–10. I will interact with Webb on this issue in chapter 5.

39. There are various interpretations of the situation of these slaves. C. K. Barrett, *The Pastoral Epistles*, New Clarendon Bible (Oxford: Oxford University Press, 1963), 82, argues that 1 Timothy 6:1–2 is connected to the discussion at the end of chapter 5 and is therefore addressing slaves who are elders. Others assert that verse 1 addresses slaves with unbelieving masters, in contrast with verse 2, which explicitly addresses those who have believing masters; e.g., Knight, *Pastoral Epistles*, 244; Philip H. Towner, *The Goal of Our Instruction: The Structure of Theology and Ethics in the Pastoral Epistles*, JSNTSup 34 (Sheffield: Sheffield Academic Press, 1989), 176. Mounce rejects this view, stating, "The two verses are to be seen as moving from a general statement about slaves (v. 1) to the more specific situation of a slave's relationship to a Christian master (v. 2)" (*Pastoral Epistles*, 326). Also Philip H. Towner, *The Letters to Timothy and Titus*, NICNT (Grand Rapids: Eerdmans, 2006), 380–81, although he still acknowledges the possibility of the other view (381n9).

40. There is an echo here of Isa. 52:5 (quoted in Rom. 2:24). See Towner, *Timothy and Titus*, 382; Mounce, *Pastoral Epistles*, 327; Marshall, *Pastoral Epistles*, 630.

41. Mounce, *Pastoral Epistles*, 327.

In this way we should not assume that instructions to slaves are an implicit endorsement of slavery itself. Paul was not primarily concerned to change the societal structures around him.[42] He was most certainly concerned to protect the reputation of the gospel.

In the next verse, Paul adds a comment to those slaves who were privileged to have Christian masters. In such a situation, it was tempting for a slave to take advantage of the equality in Christ he shared with his master. Paul must have been aware that this very thing was happening in the Ephesian church, hence these commands.[43] There are two imperatives addressed to these slaves. First, negatively, they are not to be disrespectful. This instruction is followed by a *hoti* clause, which either cites the reason for the slaves' disrespect or grounds the command.[44] These slaves were exploiting the fact that they and their masters were equal in Christ, but Paul says just the opposite should be true.

The second imperative contrasts with the first and puts forth the positive command. Rather than disrespecting one's master, slaves must serve all the more. This imperative, like the first, is followed by a *hoti* clause.[45] And, like the first *hoti* clause, there is ambiguity here as well.[46] On the one hand, the clause could refer to the benefit that Christian masters bestow on their slaves. This reading would accord with the use of *euergesia* (good service), which is something given by a superior to an inferior. This reading also fits with the more common meaning of *antilambanō*, which means "devote oneself to."[47] Thus, the masters are seen as those who are devoted

42. I will discuss this further at the end of this chapter, in the section, "Why Does the New Testament Not Condemn the Institution of Slavery?"

43. See Mounce, *Pastoral Epistles*, 325, 328; Towner, *Timothy and Titus*, 383.

44. The phrase "that they are brothers" is ambiguous. Marshall, *Pastoral Epistles*, 631, demonstrates the alternative ways it could be read. On the one hand, it could mean "slaves should not show less respect to their masters on the grounds that they are [merely] brothers [and so not superior to them]." Or it could mean "the reason why slaves should respect their masters is because they are brothers [and therefore to be treated with love]." Marshall then states, "On the whole, the former interpretation seems more probable, but even when taken this way the sentence may well imply the corollary that if the masters are brothers (with all that this description implies), this should rather be a basis for even better service."

45. Knight, *Pastoral Epistles*, 246: "Both halves of the verse follow the same pattern: imperative with slaves as subject, followed by *hoti* clause with masters as the subject."

46. Donald Guthrie, *The Pastoral Epistles: An Introduction and Commentary*, TNTC, rev. ed. (Grand Rapids: Eerdmans, 1990), 122: "*Those who benefit from their service* may refer to the masters or to the slaves. . . . Perhaps the ambiguity was intentional to remind both master and slaves that the *benefit* which would accrue if both were 'faithful and beloved' was mutual" (italics original).

47. BDAG, s.v. "*antilambanō*," 2; BDF, 170 (3).

to the well-being of their slaves.[48] It is difficult, though, to discern how the clause is functioning in the context if taken this way.[49]

On the other hand, the clause could refer to the benefit that the masters receive from their slaves. Another possible meaning of *antilambanō* is "to benefit by."[50] This meaning seems to fit better with the logic of the verse, for the benefit can be seen as a further comment on the command to serve all the more.[51] If taken this way, Paul is making a surprising statement about the status and worth of slaves. He makes the slave the benefactor, rather than the master, and thus turns a common perception on its head.[52]

Regardless of which reading one chooses, it should be noted that Paul views Christian slaves and Christian masters as brothers. Thus, he brings together individuals whose social status would have set them worlds apart. He does not tell slaves to forsake their status as slaves. Rather, he tells them to regard their masters as worthy of all honor, and he instructs those with believing masters to serve all the more. He does not attack the institution of slavery. But something even deeper and more radical is happening here. In Christ, slaves and masters become brothers.

In Titus 2, Paul gives instructions for various groups of individuals. He addresses older men in verse 2, older women in verse 3 (and their ministry to the younger women, vv. 4–5), and younger men in verse 6. He then instructs Titus personally in verses 7–8, and lastly addresses slaves in verses 9–10. Three times in this passage, Paul states the purposes for which Christians must adhere to these commands. The first is connected to the instructions for younger women. Paul bestows on the older women the responsibility of teaching and training the younger women to be godly wives and moth-

48. Reggie M. Kidd, *Wealth and Beneficence in the Pastoral Epistles: A "Bourgeois" Form of Early Christianity?* SBLDS 122 (Atlanta: Scholars Press, 1990), 140–56, offers a detailed discussion of the "slaves-as-benefactors" reading versus the "masters-as-benefactors" reading, siding with the latter.

49. David C. Verner, *The Household of God: The Social World of the Pastoral Epistles* (Chico, CA: Scholars Press, 1981), 144. Verner still opts for this view, but says, "The author would be arguing that masters should be served diligently, 'because they are "faithful" and "beloved," (people) who devote themselves to works of beneficence.' However, that all Christian masters are devoted to beneficent works is a questionable assumption that surely would not have strengthened the author's case from the slave's perspective."

50. BDAG, s.v. "*antilambanō*," 4.

51. Marshall, *Pastoral Epistles*, 633; Towner, *Timothy and Titus*, 387; Knight, *Pastoral Epistles*, 247; Gordon D. Fee, *1 and 2 Timothy, Titus*, NIBC (Peabody, MA: Hendrickson, 1984), 139.

52. Towner, *Timothy and Titus*, 390: "Paul has turned the tables. The slaves serve, but in God's surprising *oikonomia* they do so from a position of power; nobility and honor, the rewards of benefaction, are accorded here implicitly to the slaves."

ers. The first purpose is stated, in verse 5: "that the word of God may not be reviled." Second, in verses 7–8, Paul states that Titus's behavior must be exemplary "so that an opponent may be put to shame, having nothing evil to say about us." Third, in verse 10, Paul undergirds his instructions to slaves with another purpose clause, this time stated positively: "so that in everything they may adorn the doctrine of God our Savior."[53]

Everything that the slave does has the potential of communicating something about Christian teaching. If the slave who claims to be a Christian is rebellious and disrespectful, this will reflect negatively on the gospel. But if the slave is submissive and pleasing and honest, these characteristics will "adorn the doctrine of God our Savior." It is noteworthy that these individuals who are lowest in society have great potential to display the transforming power of the Christian faith. Indeed, it may be their low position that increases this potential, since their predicament would naturally incline one toward resentment and rebellion rather than respectful submission.[54]

These passages fall under the umbrella of Webb's fourth criterion: "Purpose/Intent Statements." In determining whether a text applies today, we must ask ourselves whether the original intent can still be fulfilled.[55] He says of the slavery issue, "In our context the continued practice of slavery-type submission no longer achieves the stated purpose of winning others to Christ."[56] Webb's further comments on how we must apply the abiding principles found in these instructions are helpful. "Clearly the underlying principle of showing deference/respect in order to win people (employers) continues to have transcultural relevance."[57]

However, when Webb argues that wifely submission, like slavery, no longer fulfills its New Testament purpose (1 Peter 3:1; Titus 2:5),[58]

53. Towner, *Timothy and Titus*, 738: "Logically, any of the *hina* clauses could apply to all of the instructions. In the case of the closing purpose, what is most noticeable, in comparison with the previous two, is the climactic effect achieved by its placement at the end, by its language, and by its missiological thrust."

54. Thomas D. Lea and Hayne P. Griffin Jr., *1, 2 Timothy, Titus*, NAC, vol. 34 (Nashville: Broadman Press, 1992), 308: "Surely the gospel's transforming power in the lives of those who had every reason to be bitter would stand out clearer and brighter than in those who lived in freedom and dignity unknown to slaves."

55. Webb, *Slaves, Women, and Homosexuals*, 105.

56. Ibid., 106.

57. Ibid.

58. Ibid., 107–8. Also see Willard M. Swartley, *Slavery, Sabbath, War and Women: Case Issues in Biblical Interpretation* (Scottdale, PA: Herald Press, 1983), 202. I will discuss the issue of purpose/

he has presented a subjective argument. It then falls to each of us to determine whether a husband will find his wife's submission attractive or repulsive. Webb assumes that "unilateral-type submission and obedience of a wife toward her unbelieving husband, adorned by her addressing him as 'master/lord,' generally fails to fulfill the mission statements within the biblical text."[59] Put this way, it is hard to disagree with him, for we are all uncomfortable with the prospect of demanding that wives speak to their husbands as "master/lord." But the mention of Sarah's obedience to Abraham, "calling him lord," is simply part of the Old Testament illustration from which Peter is drawing. He does not explicitly command women to call their husbands "lord." Even if he did, it would be reasonable to view it as a cultural component of the passage. The fact that there is a component of the text that we would not apply in the same way today does not allow us to disregard the clear principles taught here. And when we look at the principles of wifely submission, respectful and pure conduct, and the imperishable beauty of a gentle and quiet spirit, it is not at all clear that these things would repulse an unbelieving husband. For this reason, I conclude that the purpose/intent criterion is not determinative for our view of slavery or the submission of wives. The debate must center on other aspects of the relevant passages.[60]

Other Relevant Passages

We have seen from these passages that the New Testament does not leave the institution of slavery untouched. The commands to slaves and masters do not reinforce the *status quo*, but rather undermine it in significant ways. While it is true that the New Testament does not condemn slavery, it must be acknowledged that it does not endorse it either. It simply assumes the reality of slavery, and speaks to individuals in whatever situation they find themselves. The instructions to these individuals would

intent statements briefly again in the next chapter, and then in more detail in chapter 5.

59. Webb, *Slaves, Women, and Homosexuals*, 107.

60. Webb acknowledges that a command may have more than one purpose. "Perhaps unilateral, patriarchy-type submission should be viewed as transcultural based on other purposes. Such a possibility clearly exists." But he maintains that, based on the explicit evangelistic purpose given for a wife's submission, "we must take the underlying transcultural principle—showing deference and respect tends to win people to a cause—and utilize an alternative form of that principle in our setting" (*Slaves, Women, and Homosexuals*, 108).

have challenged the cultural norms of the day,[61] and if heeded, would radically transform the master-slave relationship.[62]

In addition to the passages discussed above, we find other texts that might have had a transforming effect on the Christian's perception of slavery. The following passages are hotly debated, and they might or might not indicate an antislavery sentiment in the New Testament. However, the point remains that the New Testament does not endorse or command slavery. As in the previous passages, we find that slavery is an assumed reality, and one that is being transformed by the power of the gospel.

Philemon

In this personal letter, Paul appeals to Philemon on behalf of the runaway slave Onesimus. Apparently, Onesimus had fled from his master Philemon[63] (v. 15) and had even stolen from Philemon (vv. 18–19). Onesimus escaped to Rome (or Ephesus),[64] where he somehow crossed paths with the great apostle, who was in prison, and Onesimus was converted under his ministry. Now Paul sends him back to his master, pleading with Philemon to forgive the offenses and receive his slave back graciously.

61. Lincoln, *Ephesians*, 426: "What strikes most modern readers about this part of the code is its reinforcement of the subordination of slaves within the household. But perhaps most striking to contemporary readers in a setting where there was no questioning of such social structures was the writer's address to slaves as full members of the Christian community who are seen as equally responsible with their masters to their common Lord." There were, in fact, those who promoted the humane treatment of slaves, but the New Testament is distinct in the way it instructs both masters and slaves to fulfill their respective roles as moral agents responsible before God. See Harris, *Slave of Christ*, 54. Seneca is an example of one who encouraged civility in the relationship between slaves and masters. See, for example, *Epistles* 47:18–19 (LCL 75 [1917]: 311–13), quoted in part by Harris, *Slave of Christ*, 41.

62. F. F. Bruce, *The Epistle to the Ephesians: A Verse-by-Verse Exposition* (Westwood, NJ: Revell, 1961), 125: "The slave was legally a member of the master's household or family, and *if a Christian master took seriously Paul's injunction to masters, his slaves would be members of his family in more than a merely legal sense, and have more real protection than they might have if manumitted*. But slavery under the best conditions is slavery none the less, and it could not survive where the gospel had free course" (emphasis added).

63. John Knox, *Philemon among the Letters of Paul: A New View of Its Place and Importance*, rev. ed. (Chicago: University of Chicago Press, 1935; New York and Nashville: Abingdon Press, 1959), proposes that Archippus, not Philemon, was the master of Onesimus, and thus the recipient of this letter. For a critique of this position, see Eduard Lohse, *Colossians and Philemon*, Hermeneia, trans. William R. Poehlmann and Robert J. Karris (Philadelphia: Fortress Press, 1971), 186–87; C. F. D. Moule, *The Epistles of Paul the Apostle to the Colossians and to Philemon*, CGTC (Cambridge: University Press, 1957), 14–18.

64. For discussion, see F. F. Bruce, *The Epistles to the Colossians, to Philemon, and to the Ephesians*, NICNT (Grand Rapids: Eerdmans, 1984), 193–96, who finds the arguments for Rome to outweigh those for Ephesus.

What Paul intends to communicate *between the lines* is debated. Possibly, Paul has in mind Onesimus's release in order to continue serving him in his imprisonment.[65] Or maybe his desire was simply that Philemon would manumit Onesimus for the purpose of Christian ministry in general.[66] It is also possible that Paul just wanted Philemon to spare Onesimus any punishment that could have been inflicted on him because of his offenses.[67] What is clear is that Paul desires Onesimus to be received back by Philemon with graciousness and forgiveness. He beseeches Philemon to "receive him as you would receive me" (v. 17). Then he leaves the details to Philemon's discretion. "Confident of your obedience, I write to you, knowing that you will do even more than I say" (v. 21). In this way, he allows Philemon to maintain his honor[68] and to extend grace and mercy of his "own accord" (v. 14).

Paul's letter to Philemon is not a treatise on slavery, much less a plea for its abolition.[69] As seen above, it is not even clear that Paul wanted Philemon to free Onesimus. J. B. Lightfoot writes, "It is a remarkable fact that St. Paul in this epistle stops short of any positive injunction. The word 'emancipation' seems to be trembling on his lips, and yet he does not once utter it."[70] Lightfoot goes on to say that Paul "tells [Philemon] to do very much more than emancipate his slave, but this one thing he does not directly enjoin."[71]

65. F. F. Bruce, *Paul: Apostle of the Heart Set Free* (Grand Rapids: Eerdmans, 1977), 406, says that Paul "is asking Philemon of Colossae, one of his own converts, not only to pardon his slave Onesimus and give him a Christian welcome, but to send him back so that he can go on helping Paul as he had already begun to do."

66. David Garland, *Colossians and Philemon*, NIVAC (Grand Rapids: Zondervan, 1998), 304: "Paul wants Philemon to set Onesimus free for a greater service in the gospel whether he returns to Paul's side to serve him or not. This is the 'even more' (v. 21) and the 'good thing' (v. 14 Garland's translation; NIV 'favor') that Paul hopes for but does not dare ask."

67. The punishment awaiting a runaway slave would have been fierce. See B. M. Rapske, "The Prisoner Paul in the Eyes of Onesimus," *NTS* 37 (1991): 189–90. Bartchy, "Slavery," observes, "Although Roman law probably is not directly relevant to the relations among Paul, Philemon, and Onesimus, Roman practice suggests that Paul was pleading with Philemon at the least not to delay Onesimus's anticipated manumission because of the wrongs he had done."

68. See James D. G. Dunn, *The Epistles to the Colossians and to Philemon: A Commentary on the Greek Text*, NIGTC (Grand Rapids: Eerdmans, 1996), 306.

69. Bruce, *Paul*, 400–401: "The letter [of Philemon] throws little light on Paul's attitude to the institution of slavery. . . . What this letter does is to bring us into an atmosphere in which the institution could only wilt and die."

70. J. B. Lightfoot, *Saint Paul's Epistles to the Colossians and to Philemon: A Revised Text with Introductions, Notes and Dissertations*, Classic Commentary Library (1879; reprint, Grand Rapids: Zondervan, 1956), 323.

71. Ibid., 324.

For Webb, this letter represents a "seed idea," meaning it subtly challenges this social structure and points beyond it.[72]

In this letter, Paul speaks to the relationship of a particular slave and a particular master, and his entreaty to the master is one that erases the barrier of status between the two. Paul's desire is that Onesimus return to his master "no longer as a slave but more than a slave, as a beloved brother" (v. 16). In this way, without confronting the institution of slavery directly, he *does* undermine it by setting master and slave on equal footing.[73]

Galatians 3:28; 1 Corinthians 12:13; Colossians 3:11

These verses provide additional examples of the leveling effect of being in Christ.[74] Paul declares that these deeply entrenched social divisions are transcended by our unity in Christ. "There is neither Jew nor Greek, there is neither slave nor free, there is no male and female, for you are all one in Christ Jesus" (Gal. 3:28). Similarly, in 1 Corinthians 12:13, "For in one Spirit we were all baptized into one body—Jews or Greeks, slaves or free—and all were made to drink of one Spirit." And in Colossians 3:11, "Here there is not Greek and Jew, circumcised and uncircumcised, barbarian, Scythian, slave, free; but Christ is all, and in all." In these statements, Harris says, "The New Testament represents a direct challenge to the fundamental pillar on which slavery was built—the belief that the 'slave-free' division was natural and necessary in both principle and practice within any well-ordered society."[75] For Webb, these verses fall under the category of "seed ideas."[76]

1 Timothy 1:10

In this vice list, Paul condemns "enslavers" (ESV), "kidnappers" (NASB), or "slave traders" (NIV). He includes this category in a list of sinners for whom the law is still in effect. The word used here, *andrapodistēs*, is a New Testament *hapax legomenon*. It refers to "one who acquires

72. Webb, *Slaves, Women, and Homosexuals*, 84.

73. Harris, *Slave of Christ*, 59, after acknowledging that Paul voices no objection to slavery per se, says, "Yet he indirectly undermines the institution of slavery by setting the master-slave relation on a new footing when he highlights Onesimus's status as a dearly loved Christian brother."

74. The hermeneutical implications of Gal. 3:28 will be discussed in chapter 6.

75. Harris, *Slave of Christ*, 65.

76. Webb, *Slaves, Women, and Homosexuals*, 84.

[persons] for use by others, slave-dealer, kidnapper."[77] The vice list alludes to various commandments in the Decalogue, and this vice is connected to the prohibition against stealing (the eighth commandment).[78] Exodus 21:16 and Deuteronomy 24:7 both condemn stealing and selling persons. Murray Harris concludes, "While both Testaments assume the practice of slavery, both repudiate kidnapping and dealing in slaves."[79] Webb apparently agrees with this assessment, for he cites Exodus 21:16, Deuteronomy 24:7, and 1 Timothy 1:10 as examples of his first criterion: "preliminary movement."[80]

J. Albert Harrill argues that the use of *andrapodistēs* in 1 Timothy 1:10 is a stereotype used to criticize the opponents. It does not, in his view, undermine slavery in the slightest. It simply exploits a commonly held prejudice against slave traders, who had the reputation of being dishonest and immoral. Harrill uses the following analogy to illustrate his point:

> Ancient slave dealers enjoyed a reputation similar to that of used-car sellers today: although the used-car seller functions as a standard example of an untrustworthy and unsavory person, users of the example do not mean to condemn the selling of used cars in general or even to suggest that *all* used-car sellers are bad.[81]

He bases his conclusion on a thorough study of ancient literature, detailing the vices of those involved in trading slaves and the derogatory way in which *andrapodistēs* was used.[82] Therefore, rather than seeing this verse as undermining the institution of slavery, Harrill states that it "reinforces cultural stereotypes present in the ideology of ancient slavery and in the ancient Christian congregation that received this letter."[83]

Therefore, it might not be legitimate to use this verse as evidence that the New Testament opposes slavery. On the other hand, it certainly says nothing *in support* of slavery.

77. BDAG, s. v. "*andrapodistēs.*"

78. Towner, *Timothy and Titus*, 128, states, "According to the pattern of presenting worst cases of Decalogue violations, this activity would correspond to the commandment that condemns stealing (Exod. 20:15)."

79. Harris, *Slave of Christ*, 54.

80. Webb, *Slaves, Women, and Homosexuals*, 75n8.

81. J. Albert Harrill, *Slaves in the New Testament: Literary, Social, and Moral Dimensions* (Minneapolis: Fortress Press, 2006), 126.

82. The chapter is titled, "The Vice of the Slave Trader," 119–44.

83. Ibid., 141–42.

1 Corinthians 7:21

This verse has been the fodder for much exegetical debate. The discussion centers on the question of what object is to be understood in the case of ellipsis at the end of the verse. Paul writes, "Were you a slave when called? Do not be concerned about it. (But if you can gain your freedom, avail yourself of the opportunity.)" The phrase, "avail yourself of the opportunity," translates only two Greek words, *mallon chrēsai.* Three interpretations of this verse are defended by scholars, and each supplies a different object for *chrēsai.* On one reading, the verse is seen as an encouragement to slaves to gain their freedom if it is offered to them. Thus the ESV, as quoted above. On this interpretation, "freedom" is the understood object, which is found in the protasis of the conditional sentence. The ESV "avail yourself of the opportunity" is referring to the opportunity of being manumitted.

In support of the "freedom" reading, it is argued that this would be the naturally understood object, since it is found in the preceding clause.[84] The aorist imperative (*chrēsai*) is also used in support of this reading, for the present tense would be expected if the verse was instructing slaves to remain in their current condition.[85] On this interpretation "but" has its usual adversative sense,[86] "if" (*ei kai*) is emphatic,[87] and *mallon* is elative/intensive.[88] Thus, "*But* (*alla*) *if indeed* (*ei kai*) you can gain your freedom, *by*

84. See the discussion of ellipsis in S. R. Llewelyn, "'If you can gain your freedom': Manumission and 1 Cor. 7:21," in *New Documents Illustrating Early Christianity*, vol. 6, *A Review of the Greek Inscriptions and Papyri Published in 1980–81* (North Ryde, New South Wales: Macquarie University Press, 1992), 63–70. He states, "An analysis of ellipsis in conditional sentences in the NT shows that what is omitted should be inferred from the immediately preceding clause" (68). His rendering of the verse is, "But if ever you are able to become free, avail yourself of it all the more" (70).

85. David Garland, *1 Corinthians*, BECNT (Grand Rapids: Baker Academic, 2003), 310. Also Archibald Robertson and Alfred Plummer, *A Critical and Exegetical Commentary on the First Epistle of St. Paul to the Corinthians*, ICC (Edinburgh: T & T Clark, 1911), 147–48: "Still more decidedly does the aorist (*chrēsai*, not *chrō*') imply a new condition."

86. Gordon D. Fee, *The First Epistle to the Corinthians*, NICNT (Grand Rapids: Eerdmans, 1987), 317; Garland, *1 Corinthians*, 310; C. F. D. Moule, *An Idiom Book of New Testament Greek* (Cambridge: Cambridge University Press, 1953), 21.

87. Garland, *1 Corinthians*, 310; J. Albert Harrill, *The Manumission of Slaves in Early Christianity*, Hermeneutische Untersuchungen. zur Theologie, 32 (Tübingen: J. C. B. Mohr, 1995), 119–20; Moule, *An Idiom Book of New Testament Greek*, 167n3.

88. Fee, *The First Epistle to the Corinthians*, 317. Harrill, *The Manumission of Slaves*, 108–9, 118–19, conducts a philological study of *mallon* with *chraomai* in ancient Greek literature and concludes that *mallon* is adversative when used with *chraomai*. However, he argues that in 1 Cor. 7:21 it is not adversative with respect to becoming free, but rather it is adversative with respect to

all means (*mallon*) use [your freedom]." Arguments from context include the observation that this clause obviously deviates from the pattern of the other instructions in the passage, and therefore it should be read as a genuine exception.[89] This view is persuasive, but it is not critical to my argument. Webb also interprets the verse in this way, listing it as a "seed idea."[90]

The second interpretation finds the opposite to be the case. Paul is not encouraging manumission, but is rather encouraging slaves to remain in their position, *even if* freedom is offered. So the NAB (New American Bible), "Were you a slave when your call came? Give it no thought. Even supposing you could go free, you would be better off making the most of your slavery." On this reading, "slavery" (found in the question at the beginning of v. 21) is supplied as the object of *chrēsai*. Here, *alla ei kai* is concessive,[91] and *mallon* is adversative with respect to becoming free.[92] Thus, "Even if (*alla ei kai*) you can gain your freedom, instead (*mallon*) use [your slavery]."

This view places the verse in the context of the passage, not as an exception but as a reinforcement of the theme, namely, "Each one should remain in the condition in which he was called" (v. 20, also v. 24).[93] Also, the *gar* of the following verse is used in support of this reading. "For he who was called in the Lord as a slave is a freedman of the Lord" (v. 22).

---

the statement: "Do not be concerned about it." He bases this conclusion on a parallel between 1 Cor. 7:21 and a quote from Vettius Valens, in which a "different situation calls for a different course of action." Therefore, the different situation of being able to gain freedom then prompts the slave *to be concerned about it*, and go free.

89. Garland, *1 Corinthians*, 310; Fee, *The First Epistle to the Corinthians*, 318.

90. Webb, *Slaves, Women, and Homosexuals*, 84.

91. Jean Héring, *The First Epistle of Saint Paul to the Corinthians*, trans. A. W. Heathcote and P. J. Allcock (London: Epworth Press, 1962), 55. Margaret E. Thrall, *Greek Particles in the New Testament: Linguistic and Exegetical Studies* (Grand Rapids: Eerdmans, 1962), 79, cites 2 Cor. 7:8a, Col. 2:5, and 2 Cor. 4:16 as places where *ei kai* means "although." She does not think it is concessive here, however. "An examination of the whole chapter in which the advice to slaves occurs shows that it contains no examples of *ei kai* meaning 'although' or 'even if,' but has two instances of an emphatic *kai* in a conditional protasis (1 Cor. 7:11, 28), one before and one after the verse under consideration. It is therefore probable that this verse contains a third example of the idiom" (81).

92. J. N. Sevenster, *Paul and Seneca*, Supplement to Novum Testamentum, vol. 4 (Leiden: E. J. Brill, 1961), 189: "*mallon* would be virtually meaningless if Paul were advising: then make use of that opportunity to become free; but it fits in very well if he is advising those who are slaves to do instead the unexpected, namely to remain in bondage despite the fact that there is an opportunity of their gaining their freedom."

93. Ibid., 190: "By [remaining in one's position], even when there is the possibility of changing his social status, a Christian has all the more chance of proving that, since being called, he no longer need be concerned about the external situation in which he was called."

This verse is seen as the ground for remaining in slavery. The slave can remain in physical slavery, because he has been set free spiritually.[94]

Finally, a third alternative has been offered. Scott Bartchy translates the verse in this way: "Were you a slave when you were called? Don't worry about it. But if, indeed, you become manumitted, by all means [as a freedman] live according to [God's calling.]"[95] He supplies the object, "God's calling," which is referred to in verses 17, 20, and 24,[96] and he finds in Josephus an alternative use of the verb *chraomai* ("to live according to").[97]

Why Does the New Testament Not Condemn the Institution of Slavery?

The question of why the New Testament does not explicitly condemn the institution of slavery is a difficult one, and it may not find a fully satisfying answer. One wishes for a clear statement condemning slavery, but it cannot be found. Kevin Giles and others would answer this question with the assertion that the NT, in fact, *endorses* slavery. There is no condemnation of slavery because the NT writers substantially agreed with the cultural practices around them.

But, as I have argued, the New Testament does not endorse slavery. There is no clear *condemnation* of the institution, but neither is there any clear *commendation* of it. There are also details of the cultural situation and the nature of the early church that are suggestive of why we do not find any explicit denunciation of slavery. For instance, as mentioned above, there was already a system for the manumission of slaves. Slaves would work for several years and would eventually earn their freedom. Therefore, the total abolition of slavery was not an urgent burden on the hearts of the first-century Christians, partly, it seems, because of the way the system worked.

There is also the fact that slavery was such a predominant feature of their society. It was hard to imagine life without it. Slavery was a significant component of how the economy worked. Even if some envisaged a society

94. C. K. Barrett, *A Commentary on the First Epistle to the Corinthians*, HNTC (New York: Harper & Row, 1968), 171. But cf. Garland's response to this point, *1 Corinthians*, 310.

95. S. Scott Bartchy, *MALLON CHRESAI: First Century Slavery and the Interpretation of 1 Corinthians 7:21* (Missoula, MT: Scholars Press, 1973), 183.

96. Ibid., 155.

97. Ibid., 155–59.

without slavery, the fledgling church was in no place to abolish it. Such a movement by the church would have been soundly rejected, and the early Christians would have been seen merely as a rebellious group that undermined the structures of society.[98] Thus, any attempt to abolish slavery would have been counterproductive to the main mission of the church.[99]

This point leads to a more fundamental reason for the New Testament's absence of a direct assault on slavery, namely, that Christianity is not a religion of social revolution. The direct impact of the gospel is on the individual human heart. That is where the transformation begins, not in social institutions. Murray Harris writes,

> If Christianity is viewed as basically a movement of social reform, then this silence regarding slavery is indeed surprising, if not culpable. But Christianity in its essence is concerned with the transformation of character and conduct rather than with the reformation of societal structures. . . . The principal change sought is in the individual, and the secondary in society, through transformed individuals.[100]

These various reasons (some pragmatic, some based on conviction) give us hints as to why we do not find in the New Testament a direct attack on the institution of slavery.

It is also helpful to compare slavery with other evils that the Bible accommodated but never endorsed. Divorce is one example. Deuteronomy 24:1–4 gives instructions on how a man should go about divorcing his wife if "she finds no favor in his eyes because he has found some indecency in her." These instructions do not condemn divorce, but neither is there an endorsement of the practice. Jesus' words to the Pharisees in Matthew 19 make it clear that divorce is an accommodation to the hardness of the human heart: "Because of your hardness of heart Moses allowed you to

98. Harris, *Slave of Christ*, 67: "Any public attack on slavery would have laid the early Christians open to the charge that their religious teaching was merely a front for social revolution. Their evangelistic mission would have been seriously compromised."

99. Lightfoot, *Saint Paul's Epistles to the Colossians and to Philemon*, 323: "Slavery was inwoven into the texture of society; and to prohibit slavery was to tear society to shreds. Nothing less than a servile war with its certain horrors and its doubtful issues must have been the consequence. Such a mode of operation was altogether alien to the spirit of the Gospel."

100. Harris, *Slave of Christ*, 67–68. Similarly, Schreiner, *1, 2 Peter, Jude*, 136: "[New Testament writers] did not believe that overhauling social structures would transform culture. Their concern was the relationship of individuals to God, and they focused on the sin and rebellion of individuals against their Creator." See also Garland, *Colossians and Philemon*, 356.

divorce your wives, but from the beginning it was not so" (Matt. 19:8). Divorce is permitted, but not endorsed.[101]

A related issue is polygamy, a practice that was permitted and yet never endorsed. We find many instances of polygamy in the Bible, even among individuals who are praiseworthy in other respects (i.e., Abraham and David). But the fact that these men had more than one wife does not constitute an endorsement of polygamy.[102] Like divorce, it was permitted even though it was contrary to God's design for marriage. The issues of divorce and polygamy are not identical to the issue of slavery, but they at least indicate there are practices that the Bible accommodates without endorsing.

The question of why the New Testament does not condemn the institution of slavery is not an easy one, and it has no simple answers. However, the question is not made easier by the assertion that patriarchy is an additional evil that the biblical writers failed to condemn. This position does not resolve the dilemma, but rather complicates it further. The question expands to, "Why does the NT fail to condemn the institution of slavery, *and* why does the NT also fail to condemn patriarchy?" Of course, the writers who hold to this view have thoughtful responses to these questions, but my point is simply to show that the question confronts all of us, to varying degrees. The discussion of these questions will continue in greater detail in the chapters dealing with hermeneutics.[103]

Conclusion

This survey of the NT statements concerning slavery has examined the grounds and purposes that undergird the biblical instructions to slaves. I have also commented on other relevant passages and addressed the question of why we do not find in the NT a clear condemnation of slavery. While the New Testament does not condemn slavery, it also seems evident that it does not commend it. The instructions to slaves and to masters, and the other passages that deal with slavery, do not enshrine the

101. Giles rejects the use of this example in comparison with the slavery question. See *The Trinity and Subordinationism*, 240n20.

102. Norman L. Geisler, *Baker Encyclopedia of Christian Apologetics* (Grand Rapids: Baker, 1999), s.v. "Polygamy."

103. Chaps. 5–6.

institution of slavery as something that is ordained by God. Rather, the New Testament writers assume the reality of slavery and speak to masters and slaves alike in their specific roles. Kevin Giles incorrectly asserts that there is a strong "biblical" case for slavery. The issue is much more complex than that. An additional complex question, which Giles and others address, is how the NT statements concerning slavery are similar and/or dissimilar to the NT statements concerning women. In the next chapter I will conduct a similar study of the women's passages, and in chapter 4 compare and contrast the two.

3

NEW TESTAMENT STATEMENTS CONCERNING WOMEN

This chapter examines the women's passages in the same way the previous chapter examined the slavery passages, interacting here with seven passages in which exhortations are addressed to women/wives. The discussion is organized by looking at the exhortations that are supported by a ground clause (Eph. 5:22–33; Col. 3:18–19; 1 Tim. 2:9–15; 1 Cor. 11:2–16; 1 Cor. 14:33b-35), and then briefly looking at those exhortations that are followed by a purpose clause (1 Peter 3:1–7; Titus 2:3–5).[1] In this way, the present chapter will mirror the previous one.

Since a basic assumption of the trajectory hermeneutic is the parallel between the women's passages and the slavery passages, it is important to closely examine the flow of thought in each set of texts. The fruit of this exegesis will be seen in the next chapter, which will compare and contrast the women's passages and the slavery passages. If it can be shown that the two sets of texts are significantly different, then a basic assumption of the redemptive-movement hermeneutic will be undermined.

1. I have chosen these passages because of the way they parallel the slavery commands. In contrast, 1 Corinthians 7 contains instructions to wives, but does not provide a sufficient parallel to the slavery passages to be helpful in this study. Also, 1 Timothy 3:11 briefly exhorts deaconesses (or the wives of deacons; the meaning of *gunaikas* is debated), and 1 Timothy 5:9–16 provides qualifications for widows to be helped by the church. I will not include these passages in the discussion.

New Testament Commands to Women

In six of the seven texts, *gunē* (in either singular or plural form) is used for the person(s) addressed. In certain contexts the term refers to wives, and in others it refers to women in general. Titus 2:3–5 does not use the term *gunē*, but instructs older women (*presbutidas*) to train younger women (*tas neas*) in various aspects of their lives.

A form of the verb *hupotassō* (submit) is found in five of the passages. First Timothy 2:9–15 lacks the verb form, but contains the noun form *hupotagē* (submission) in verse 11. First Corinthians 11:2–16 contains neither the verb nor the noun, but rather the instruction is to cover one's head. Still, the passage has to do with the differing roles of men and women, the covering (or uncovering) of one's head being an outward symbol of those differences.

The relevant instructions are found either as an imperative (Col. 3:18; 1 Cor. 11:6; 1 Cor. 14:33–35 [contains 3 imperatives]; 1 Tim. 2:11), or in the form of a participle (Eph. 5:21; 1 Peter 3:1; Titus 2:5), or as an indicative with infinitives (1 Tim. 2:12). Women are exhorted to submit to their own husbands (Eph. 5:22; Col. 3:18; Titus 2:4) or to be submissive in the context of the church (1 Tim. 2:11; 1 Cor. 11:6 [by covering their heads]; 1 Cor. 14:34).

Ground for Obedience

Accompanying each of the relevant instructions is either a ground clause or a purpose clause. I understand five of them to be ground clauses. Two are introduced by *gar* (1 Cor. 11:8; 1 Tim. 2:13), one is introduced by *hoti* (Eph. 5:23), and two are introduced by comparative conjunctions (*hōs* in Col. 3:18; *kathōs* in 1 Cor. 14:34).[2]

References to Creation: 1 Timothy 2:9–15

First Timothy 2:13–14 and 1 Corinthians 11:8–9 each make references to creation in connection with the instructions given to women.[3] In

2. I understand the comparative conjunctions to be functioning causally. See Daniel B. Wallace, *Greek Grammar beyond the Basics* (Grand Rapids: Zondervan, 1996), 674, where he lists *hōs* and *kathōs* as conjunctions that are used causally.

3. Eph. 5:31 also refers to creation by quoting Gen. 2:24 (see discussion later in this chapter). Andreas J. Köstenberger, "Women in the Church: A Response to Kevin Giles," *EQ* 73 (2001): 218,

1 Timothy 2 the instruction is given in verses 11–12. Paul uses an imperative in verse 11, "Let a woman learn quietly with all submissiveness." Verse 12, then, uses an indicative with two infinitives, "I do not permit a woman to teach or to exercise authority over a man." The verse concludes with another infinitive, "rather, she is to remain quiet," which reiterates the statement of verse 11.

These instructions have been debated at much length.[4] For the purposes of this study I will not fully discuss the various interpretations of verses 11–12. This is unnecessary because the burden of the trajectory hermeneutic is not to contest the meaning of verses 11–12, but rather to argue that Paul's instruction was limited to first-century Ephesus.[5] Therefore, the focus of this section will be to examine how verses 13–14 are related to the instructions of verses 11–12.

The conjunction *gar* introduces verses 13–14 and connects them to verses 11–12.[6] Some argue that *gar* functions in an explanatory sense

---

makes a distinction between "order of creation" and "creation order." He understands 1 Timothy 2:13 and 1 Corinthians 11:8 to be citing the order of creation, and he views 1 Timothy 2:14 and 1 Corinthians 11:2–16 as references to creation order. William J. Webb, *Slaves, Women, and Homosexuals: Exploring the Hermeneutics of Cultural Analysis* (Downers Grove, IL: IVP, 2001), 123–45, discusses 1 Timothy 2:13 under the heading, "Basis in Original Creation," and he refers to "creation order" in terms of "man created first; woman second" (130). I will simply categorize these passages as "references to creation" and work inductively to understand how each reference is functioning.

4. Thomas R. Schreiner, "An Interpretation of 1 Timothy 2:9–15: A Dialogue with Scholarship," in *Women in the Church: An Analysis and Application of 1 Timothy 2:9–15*, ed. Andreas Köstenberger and Thomas R. Schreiner, 2nd ed. (Grand Rapids: Baker Academic, 2005), 97: "Almost every word in verses 11–12 is disputed."

5. William Webb, *Slaves, Women, and Homosexuals*, 225, speaks very favorably of *Women in the Church*, ed. by Köstenberger, Schreiner, and Scott Baldwin. Webb refers to the book as "one of the finest *exegetical* treatments of 1 Timothy 2 available today" (italics original), and says that the authors "develop the text in its lexical and grammatical aspects in much the same way as I would be inclined." Because of Webb's general agreement with the complementarian exegesis of 1 Timothy 2:9–15, most of the debated issues in the text become superfluous to this study.

6. Max Küchler, *Schweigen, Schmuck und Schleier: Drei neutestamentliche Vorschriften zur Verdrängung der Frauen auf dem Hintergrund einer frauenfeindlichen Exegese des Alten Testaments im antiken Judentum*, Novum Testamentum Et Orbis Antiquus, vol. 1 (Freiburg: Universitätsverlag, 1986), 12, argues that vv. 13–14 ground all of vv. 9–12. "Der erste Teil (Verse 9–12) ist exhortativ-paränetisch gehalten und bringt konkrete Bestimmungen. zum Verhalten der Frauen. Der zweite Teil (Verse 13f) ist indikativisch-thetisch formuliert und enthält die exegetischen Begründungen. zu den Bestimmungen. des ersten Teils (10)." He sees a chiasm in vv. 9–14 (13). Gordon D. Fee, *1 and 2 Timothy, Titus*, NIBC (Peabody, MA: Hendrickson, 1984), 73, also understands vv. 13–14 "to support what has been said in verses 9–12 (not simply vv. 11–12)." I. Howard Marshall and Philip H. Towner, *A Critical and Exegetical Commentary on the Pastoral Epistles*, ICC (Edinburgh: T & T Clark, 1999), 461, objects: "The issue of adornment seems to conclude with the positive alternative in v. 10. Küchler's argument that vv. 9–10 need an exegetical grounding is weak (none is provided for v. 8), since the case is self-evident."

here.[7] The causal meaning, however, is much more common,[8] and the sequence of imperative followed by a reason (introduced by *gar*) is well attested in the Pastorals.[9] It is also difficult to understand how verse 13 might function as an example.[10]

William Webb apparently assumes the causal sense of *gar* in verse 13, for he discusses it under the heading "Basis in Original Creation." He defines his seventh criterion in this way: "A component of a text may be transcultural, if it is rooted in the original-creation material and, more specifically, its creative order."[11] Of 1 Timothy 2:13, he writes, "On the grounds of this creative order he grants men, not women, the prominent/authoritative teaching positions in the church."[12] It is important to note Webb's assumption that verse 13 is a ground for verses 11–12, because most egalitarians argue that it is explanatory.[13]

7. See Philip B. Payne, "Libertarian Women in Ephesus: A Response to Douglas J. Moo's Article, '1 Timothy 2:11–15: Meaning and Significance,'" *TrinJ* 2 NS (1981): 175–77. See also David M. Scholer, "1 Timothy 2:9–15 and the Place of Women in the Church's Ministry," in *Women, Authority and the Bible*," ed. Alvera Mickelsen (Downers Grove, IL: IVP, 1986), 208; Alvera Mickelsen, "An Egalitarian View: There is Neither Male nor Female in Christ," in *Women in Ministry: Four Views*, ed. Bonnidell Clouse and Robert G. Clouse (Downers Grove, IL: IVP, 1989), 203. R. T. France, *Women in the Church's Ministry: A Test Case for Biblical Interpretation* (Grand Rapids: Eerdmans, 1995), 67–68, seems to adopt this view. He writes, "[Eve] thus illustrates the way some of the Ephesian women were behaving, asserting their independence and open to be deceived by false teaching." Also, Ben Witherington, *Women in the Earliest Churches*, SNTSMS 59 (Cambridge: Cambridge University Press, 1988), 122.

8. Payne, "Libertarian Women," 176, cites A. T. Robertson as one who takes the explanatory meaning of *gar* to be primary, in *A Grammar of the Greek New Testament in the Light of Historical Research*, 2nd ed. (New York: Hodder & Stoughton, George H. Doran, 1915), 1189–91, 433. In response, Douglas J. Moo, "The Interpretation of 1 Timothy 2:11–15: A Rejoinder," *TrinJ* 2 NS (1981): 202–3, demonstrates that Robertson "stands virtually alone in this opinion." The most common use of *gar* is illative/causal (giving a reason).

9. Moo, "Rejoinder," 203n9, lists the following examples: 1 Tim. 3:13; 4:5, 8, 16; 5:4, 11, 15; 2 Tim. 1:7; 2:7, 16; 3:6; 4:3, 6, 10, 11, 15; Titus 1:10; 2:11; 3:3, 9, 12.

10. Ibid. Moo asserts that Payne's interpretation does not, in fact, take the *gar* as explanatory. "[Payne] views vv. 13–14 as illustrative of 'how serious the consequences can be when a woman deceived by false teaching conveys it to others.' Now this interpretation appears to imply a *causal* function for *gar*: the disastrous consequences which stemmed from *one* woman's false teaching constitutes the *reason* why Paul prohibits women in Ephesus from spreading false teaching" (emphasis original). Schreiner, "An Interpretation of 1 Timothy 2:9–15," 105, critiques Alan Padgett's view that v. 13 is a typological illustration of the preceding verses. Alan Padgett, "Wealthy Women at Ephesus: 1 Timothy 2:8–15 in Social Context," *Interpretation* 41 (1987): 25–27. The causal meaning of *gar* seems to be the simplest and most straightforward reading.

11. Webb, *Slaves, Women, and Homosexuals*, 134.

12. Ibid.

13. See note 7 above for references. Webb focuses on the primogeniture logic in these verses, which I will discuss in chapter 6.

Verses 13–14 make two complementary points. First, in verse 13, Paul points to the fact that Adam was formed before Eve. His reference is to the account in Genesis 2, where the man was formed (*eplasthē*). The word is used four times in Genesis (LXX), all in chapter 2.[14] Paul uses the passive form in 1 Timothy 2:13.[15] Thus, Paul cites the order of creation to ground his instruction in verse 12. God formed Adam first, and he subsequently formed the woman from Adam's rib as a "helper fit for him" (Gen. 2:18, 20). These aspects of the creation order indicate the differing roles of men and women.

Verse 14, then, refers to the events of Genesis 3. The sentence is structured in a manner similar to verse 13, with Adam mentioned in the first part of the verse and the woman mentioned in the second part. The connection to Genesis 3 is found in the reference to deception. Adam was *not* deceived, but the woman was deceived and became a transgressor. In Genesis 3:13 (LXX), the only place in Genesis where this same word for "deceived" is found, it appears in the words of Eve. When the Lord God questioned her, she responded, "The serpent deceived me, and I ate." In both verse 13 and verse 14 it seems Paul is drawing our attention not merely to a couple words, but to the whole context of Genesis 2–3.[16] In those chapters we see the order of creation (Adam formed first) and the order of the fall (woman deceived first).

We cannot take Paul's statement that "Adam was not deceived" in an absolute sense. In Romans 5:12, responsibility for the fall is placed squarely on Adam (also 1 Cor. 15:21–22). This, along with the "first, then" order of verse 13, makes it likely that the same order is implied in verse 14. It is not that Adam was not deceived, but that he was not deceived *first*.[17] The serpent, cunning as he is, approached the helpmate rather than the God-ordained leader in the relationship.

14. God is the subject of the verb in each case. The man is the object in 2:7, 8, 15. In v. 19 the objects are the beasts and the birds.

15. Paul uses *plassō* elsewhere only in Rom. 9:20, where he is quoting from Isa. 29:16. This observation seems to demonstrate the dependence of 1 Tim. 2:13 on Gen. 2. See William D. Mounce, *Pastoral Epistles*, WBC, vol. 46 (Nashville: Thomas Nelson, 2000), 131.

16. Ann L. Bowman, "Women in Ministry: An Exegetical Study of 1 Timothy 2:11–15," *Bibliotheca Sacra* 149 (1992): 203–4.

17. Paul W. Barnett, "Wives and Women's Ministry (1 Timothy 2:11–15)," *EQ* 61 (1989): 234. Others interpret the statement that "Adam was not deceived" to mean that Adam sinned knowingly, whereas Eve was thoroughly deceived. See George W. Knight III, *The Pastoral Epistles: A Commentary on the Greek Text*, NIGTC (Grand Rapids: Eerdmans, 1992), 143–44; Moo, "Rejoinder," 204. However, this would seem to be a reason for restricting *men* from teaching (Schreiner, "An Interpretation of 1 Timothy 2:9–15," 113–14).

Traditionally, verse 14 has been taken to mean that women are more easily deceived than men.[18] Daniel Doriani follows this traditional understanding, that women are in some sense more easily deceived. However, he does not attribute this to a deficient intellectual capacity for women, but rather to the different proclivities of men and women.[19] Thomas Schreiner, in the first edition of *Women in the Church*, agreed.[20] But in the second edition Schreiner states in an endnote, "I accepted Doriani's view in the first edition of this book. But it seems that this view also strays from the text, even if one agrees that such differences exist between men and women. If Paul argued that women were deceived because of innate dispositions, the goodness of God's creative work is called into question."[21]

Webb discusses the view of Doriani and Schreiner as presented in the first edition of *Women in the Church*. He commends them for their fine exegesis and agrees that "the traditional rendering is the most supportable reading of the text."[22] But he goes on to criticize Doriani and Schreiner for their modification of the traditional view. Webb concludes by saying that he agrees "both with the historic and the (new) revised-historic view of 1 Timothy 2:14 that Paul is saying that 'women are more easily deceived than men,'" but that the situation is different today.[23] It was true in the past that women were more easily deceived than men, but the social factors that produced such a reality have changed. "So the text was suitable and accurate in its day due to cultural factors of an associative nature. Applying 1 Timothy 2:14 today, however, requires that we move up the ladder of abstraction and work with the underlying transcultural principle: *seek teachers and leaders who are not easily deceived*"[24] (emphasis original).

Elsewhere, Webb develops this point further from 1 Timothy 4:7, where Paul warns of "old wives' tales" (NIV), "fables fit only for old women"

18. For a historical survey of the interpretation of 1 Tim. 2, see Daniel Doriani, "A History of Interpretation of 1 Timothy 2," in *Women in the Church: A Fresh Analysis of 1 Timothy 2:9–15*, ed. Andreas Köstenberger, Thomas R. Schreiner, and H. Scott Baldwin (Grand Rapids: Baker, 1995), 213–67. Webb also provides a historical summary, demonstrating that the traditional interpretation of 1 Tim. 2:14 is that women are deceived more easily than men (*Slaves, Women, and Homosexuals*, 263–68).

19. Doriani, "A History of Interpretation of 1 Timothy 2," 266.

20. Köstenberger, Schreiner, and Baldwin, *Women in the Church*, 145–46.

21. Köstenberger and Schreiner, *Women in the Church*, 2nd ed., 225n210.

22. Webb, *Slaves, Women, and Homosexuals*, 225.

23. Ibid., 230.

24. Ibid.

(NASB).[25] Webb sees this as additional evidence that "ancient women were far more vulnerable to myths and fables than was the case with men."[26] It certainly seems that women were afforded far fewer opportunities than men in the first century, including formal education. Webb states, "Many women in ancient cultures lived in a 'small world' of social exposure that often ranged not much further beyond the home than to the well and the marketplace. The world of older women was even smaller."[27] However, while this was generally the case, there was also much variety in the social

25. William Webb, "The Limits of a Redemptive-Movement Hermeneutic: A Focused Response to T. R. Schreiner," *EQ* 75 (2003): 238–39.

26. Ibid., 339. See also R. F. Collins, *1 & 2 Timothy and Titus: A Commentary*, The New Testament Library (Louisville: Westminster John Knox, 2002), 121: "By deriding them as the tales of 'old hags' (*graōdēs*, a term used by Strabo in his *Geography*), the Pastor reflects a patriarchal, cultural bias in which women are considered to be silly little people led astray by their passions, whose ability to learn is such that they should not be allowed to teach 'real men' (2:11–12; see 2 Tim. 3:6). The colloquial expression 'old wives' tale' is a faint echo of that cultural prejudice." For a different argument, see Dennis Ronald MacDonald, *The Legend and the Apostle: The Battle for Paul in Story and Canon* (Philadelphia: Westminster Press, 1983), 14: "In this book I shall argue that the author of the Pastoral Epistles wrote in Paul's name in order to counteract the image of Paul as given in stories told by women." Speaking of the stories found in the *Acts of Paul*, MacDonald makes a case that "those who told the stories probably were celibate women in Asia Minor who expected Christ soon to destroy the world and to rescue the righteous. This apocalypticism was attended by contempt for Asia Minor social institutions, especially the household. In Chapter III, I shall suggest that the author of the Pastoral Epistles, knowing these 'old wives' tales' and incensed by their use of Paul's memory to sanction socially radical sectarianism, put his hand to the quill in order to depict a more domestic, quiescent, and respectable Paul," 34 (see also 77). Steven L. Davies, *The Revolt of the Widows: The Social World of the Apocryphal Acts* (Carbondale and Edwardsville, IL: Southern Illinois University Press, 1980), 95–129, goes a step further than MacDonald, contending that the authors (not just the storytellers) of many of the Apocryphal Acts were women. He makes the point that the emphasis on women's liberation in the Apocryphal Acts was eventually trumped by the male hierarchy of the day (114, 128–29). Davies' view is cited and rejected by Luke Timothy Johnson, *The First and Second Letters to Timothy: A New Translation with Introduction and Commentary*, AB, vol. 35A (New York: Doubleday, 2001), 243–44; Philip H. Towner, *The Letters to Timothy and Titus*, NICNT (Grand Rapids: Eerdmans, 2006), 305n12. Davies' view is also summarized by Frances Young, *The Theology of the Pastoral Letters* (Cambridge: Cambridge University Press, 1994), 119. Earlier in the book, Young makes the following observation: "It is not altogether clear whether there is any connection between such old wives' tales and the gossiping of younger unmarried widows mentioned in 5:11–13, though some connection may be hinted at in the fact that [in 5:11–13] the young widows are unmarried and [in 4:1–7] the condemnation of marriage is forbidden" (6).

27. Webb, "The Limits of a Redemptive-Movement Hermeneutic," 339. For further details, see Valerie Abrahamsen, "Women: Early Christianity," in *The Oxford Companion to the Bible*, ed. Bruce M. Metzger and Michael D. Coogan (New York: Oxford University Press, 1993), 815: "While there is considerable evidence for independent and wealthy women, most women lived in slavery, near poverty, or middle-class stability; therefore, most worked for wages for their own economic survival and that of their families, even if they were married to a merchant or freedman. In some cases, women may have been secluded in their homes, but for the most part they moved freely in many spheres of the Greco-Roman world—the agora, baths, businesses, and religious associations."

opportunities of women.[28] Many women enjoyed the benefits of literacy and various levels of either formal or less-formal education.[29]

Acknowledging the general gap in education between men and women, it is certainly possible that Paul's reference to "old wives' tales" reflects a cultural reality that many older women were given to telling fables. Paul uses two adjectives to describe the "myths," the second (*graōdeis*) being a *hapax legomenon* in the New Testament. Ceslas Spicq says, "At root, these are tales or twaddle that grandmothers or nurses tell to small children: monster stories or Aesop's fables . . . the expression then became a rhetorical characterization and a polemical insult: that which flies in the face of reason and presupposes an incredulity unworthy of an honest person."[30] For example, Strabo tells Eratosthenes that he is wrong for saying that "poetry is a fable-prating old wife (*graōdē*)."[31] The stereotype must have been rooted in some aspect of reality, and therefore we must conclude that some of the elderly women were prone to passing along fables.

However, while conceding this point, Webb's conclusion still rests on a thin foundation. First, it is not at all clear that Paul is intending to make a statement about the lack of education among women or their susceptibility to being deceived. We must remember that the comment refers specifically to *older* women, so it cannot be taken as a blanket statement about women. We must also consider the fact that the term was commonly used

28. For some examples of the diversity of situations, see Ben Witherington III, "Women (New Testament)," in *ABD*, 958. For instance, "In Athens married citizen-women seem to have been confined to domestic activities, whereas women in Asia Minor, Macedonia, and Egypt engaged in their own private businesses, served in public offices, and had prominent roles in various religious cults." He also says, "It is notable that in Roman society, unlike some parts of Greece, the education of women was considered important and desirable. Even among poorer families both daughters and sons received at least a rudimentary education, while in wealthier families all children regularly had tutors."

29. Catherine C. Kroeger, "Women in Greco-Roman World and Judaism," in *Dictionary of New Testament Background*, ed. Craig A. Evans and Stanley E. Porter (Downers Grove, IL: IVP, 2000), 1279: "The ancient novel appears to have been developed to suit the tastes of literate, Greek-reading women, especially in Asia Minor." Also see the examples of female philosophers given by Craig S. Keener, *Paul, Women, and Wives: Marriage and Women's Ministry in the Letters of Paul* (Peabody, MA: Hendrickson, 1992), 97n66. And see the helpful discussion of "Women and Education" by S. M. Baugh, "A Foreign World: Ephesus in the First Century," in *Women in the Church: An Analysis and Application of 1 Timothy 2:9–15*, ed. Andreas J. Köstenberger and Thomas R. Schreiner, 2nd ed. (Grand Rapids: Baker Academic, 2005), 33–35.

30. Ceslas Spicq, *TLNT*, trans. and ed. James D. Ernest (Peabody, MA: Hendrickson, 1994), 1:285n5.

31. Strabo, *Geography* 1.2.3 (LCL 49 [1917]: 59). For additional quotations, see Spicq, *TLNT*, 1:285n5. Also see Marshall, *Pastoral Epistles*, 550n71; Mounce, *Pastoral Epistles*, 251.

to speak of foolish prattle. Paul might or might not have been thinking of the gender aspect of the term at all. Thus, Webb's suggestion may be an etymological fallacy, for the gender component of the verb has become less clear.[32] The phrase "old wives' tales" is still used today, and it would be incorrect to assume that it implies the ignorance of elderly women. It has taken on a more general connotation of superstitious beliefs. It seems that this shift was already happening somewhat in Paul's day. Philip Towner says, "Whatever the term's origin, it had ossified into a common saying that conveyed no intentional chauvinism."[33] George Knight comments that *graōdeis* carries no "negative overtones about either age or sex," citing 1 Timothy 5:1 "for Paul's own insistence that there be no negative attitudes relating to these matters."[34] Therefore, the thesis is untenable that Paul's reference to "old wives' tales" implies that women are more easily deceived than men.

On the one hand, Paul recognized that some women were weak, as he refers in 2 Timothy 3:6 to the false teachers "who creep into households and capture weak women." But he also recognized the capabilities of women to provide solid instruction for their children, as Lois and Eunice did for Timothy (2 Tim. 1:5; 3:15).

This observation is related to the larger point that makes Webb's view problematic, namely, that women are not absolutely restricted from teaching or leading. They are only restricted from teaching or exercising authority *over men*. If women are more easily deceived, then the logical conclusion would be to restrict them from all teaching. It is also significant that Paul's other mention of Eve's deception (2 Cor. 11:3) is applied to the congregation as a whole. It is not used to make a statement about women's susceptibility to deception.[35] And finally, it must be noted that Paul does not cite lack of education, or any other social factor, as the reason women should not teach or have authority over men.[36]

32. I am not denying that other writers might have continued using the term with the gender aspect in the forefront of their minds, but this is not clearly the case with Paul. For examples of word-study fallacies, see D. A. Carson, *Exegetical Fallacies*, 2nd ed. (Grand Rapids: Baker, 1996), 27–64.

33. Philip H. Towner, *1–2 Timothy & Titus* (Downers Grove, IL: IVP, 1994), 106–7.

34. Knight, *The Pastoral Epistles*, 195.

35. Ronald Y. K. Fung, "Ministry in the New Testament," in *The Church in the Bible and the World*, ed. D. A. Carson (Grand Rapids: Baker, 1987), 202.

36. Schreiner states, "Webb strays from what Paul actually says and, to explain the meaning of v. 14, resorts to a multitude of explanations that are not mentioned or implied by Paul" ("An Interpretation of 1 Timothy 2:9–15," 225n204).

To summarize, 1 Timothy 2:13–14 grounds the instruction of verses 11–12 in the order of creation. Adam was formed first, indicating his headship in marriage. Eve, the helpmate, was the first to be deceived, for the serpent undermined God's design by approaching the helper rather than the head.

References to Creation: 1 Corinthians 11:2–16

In 1 Corinthians 11:2–16, as in 1 Timothy 2:13–14, Paul grounds his instruction with references to creation.[37] This passage begins by drawing an analogy for Christ's headship over every man, man's headship over woman,[38] and God's headship over Christ. William Webb's fourteenth criterion is "Basis in Theological Analogy," which he deems inconclusive. Based on theological analogies connected to slavery,[39] monarchy, primogeniture, and right-handedness, he asserts that theological analogy does not necessarily mean that the related biblical instruction is transcultural.[40]

While I do not contest the statement that theological analogy is inconclusive in determining whether a text is transcultural, I also believe that there are important differences among the theological analogies that Webb cites. In the slavery passages where a theological analogy is used (Eph. 6:5–9; Col. 3:22–4:1; 1 Peter 2:18–25), the example given is not intended as a basis for the institution of slavery.[41] Rather, examples are offered as illustrations for appropriate behavior. In contrast, the analogy found in 1 Corinthians 11:3 reveals something profound about the nature of these relationships. More than an illustration concerning behavior, this verse is a statement about reality. Of course, it has

37. This passage presents many interpretive difficulties, many of which I will not discuss. My focus will remain on the explicit instruction to women and the ground for that instruction. The discussion, therefore, will mainly deal with vv. 7–12. Also, it will not be necessary to rehearse many of the egalitarian interpretations of this passage, because those who utilize the redemptive-movement hermeneutic do not deny the emphasis on male headship in this passage. Rather, as we will see, they focus on the emphasis Paul gives to mutuality in vv. 11–12.

38. *Gunē* could refer specifically to wives (ESV, RSV) or to women in general (most other translations). Bruce Winter, *After Paul Left Corinth: The Influence of Secular Ethics and Social Change* (Grand Rapids: Eerdmans, 2001), 127, argues that the mention of the veil indicates that married women are spoken of here. Many others, however, maintain that marriage is absent from the discussion in 1 Cor. 11, and therefore the reference is to women in general. See Hans Conzelmann, *1 Corinthians*, Hermeneia, trans. James W. Leitch (Philadelphia: Fortress Press, 1975), 184. Also Leon Morris, *1 Corinthians*, TNTC (Grand Rapids: Eerdmans, 1985), 149–50.

39. Keeping with the theme of this study, I will focus on comparing 1 Cor. 11 (and later Eph. 5) with the theological analogies used in slavery passages.

40. Webb, *Slaves, Women, and Homosexuals*, 186–87.

41. See discussion in previous chapter.

clear implications for behavior, as the passage goes on to explain, but they are built on the statement in verse 3 which provides a glimpse into the structures of the universe. I am not attempting to argue that the theological analogy, on its own, establishes the abiding application of male headship in this text,[42] but I am hoping to caution against treating the various theological analogies all in the same way. There are significant differences between the analogies used in the slavery passages and the analogies given in 1 Corinthians 11 and Ephesians 5, and we need to be attentive to those differences.

Verse 4 begins the discussion of head coverings in the context of corporate worship. Men should not cover their heads when they pray or prophecy (v. 4). Women, on the other hand, *should* cover their heads when they pray or prophecy (v. 5). First, Paul states the dishonor associated with a man *covering* his head, and a woman *uncovering* her head (vv. 4–5). Two imperatives are given in verse 6, contained in the two apodoses of the contrasting conditional statements. The emphasis is clearly on the imperative that concludes the verse, "let her cover her head."

Verse 7, then, gives a ground for this imperative by pointing to the order of glory, in a way related to verse 3 and its order of headship.[43] The construction in the verse suggests it is the last phrase of verse 7 that functions as the ground for verse 6.[44] Thus, the argument is that the woman should cover her head because she is the glory of man.[45]

42. I do not believe that the culture-specific instruction concerning head coverings applies in the same way in all cultures, but the underlying principle of male headship transcends culture. See Thomas R. Schreiner, "Head Coverings, Prophecies and the Trinity," in *Recovering Biblical Manhood and Womanhood: A Response to Evangelical Feminism*, ed. John Piper and Wayne Grudem (Wheaton, IL: Crossway, 1991), 129: "Today, except in certain religious groups, if a woman fails to wear a head covering while praying or prophesying, no one thinks she is in rebellion. Lack of head coverings sends no message at all in our culture. Nevertheless, that does not mean that this text does not apply to our culture. The principle still stands that women should pray and prophesy in a manner that makes it clear that they submit to male leadership."

43. The statements are not parallel, but they make related points. Christ's headship over man (v. 3) is related to the statement that man is the image and glory of God (v. 7), while the man's headship over woman (v. 3) is related to the statement that she is the glory of man (v. 7).

44. See Judith M. Gundry-Volf, "Gender and Creation in 1 Corinthians 11:2–16: A Study in Paul's Theological Method," in *Evangelium, Schriftauslegung, Kirche: Festschrift für Peter Stuhlmacher zum 65. Geburtstag*, ed. Jostein Ådna, Scott Hafemann, and Otfried Hofius (Göttingen: Vandenhoeck & Ruprecht, 1997), 152–53. The earlier part of the verse supports the statement in v. 4. Thus, "the 'for' with which the argument begins [in verse 7] indicates that Paul intends to reinforce the point of vv. 4–6, that men ought *not* to be covered, while women should be" (Gordon D. Fee, *The First Epistle to the Corinthians*, NICNT [Grand Rapids: Eerdmans, 1987], 513).

45. The fact that v. 7 describes the man as "the image and glory of God" and the woman as "the glory of man" should not be taken to contradict the fact that woman is also created equal in the image of God (Gen. 1:27). Rather, we see here that *how* she bears the image of God is connected to

Webb points out that "in 1 Cor. 11:8–9 the 'from' and 'for' arguments are not related to a prohibition against women teaching men. Rather, they support the proposition that 'woman is the glory of man' (1 Cor. 11:7)."[46] This statement concurs with what I have just stated, and I acknowledge that, unlike 1 Timothy 2, this passage does not contain an explicit prohibition against women teaching men. Webb goes on, "This proposition relates to the question of how much of a woman's beauty/glory should be visible in a worship setting—an issue of modesty."[47] Webb seems to be missing the force of verse 7, for the issue at stake is more than just modesty, as shown by the references to the distinctions between men and women throughout the passage. More than relating to the question of modesty, these verses strongly assert, and provide a basis for, male headship. Webb concedes this point, "for the sake of discussion," and therefore the argument turns to whether Paul's rationale transcends culture.[48]

The reference to the man as the image (*eikōn*) and glory (*doxa*) of God alludes to the creation of mankind in Genesis 1. The LXX uses the term *eikōna* twice in Genesis 1:26–27: "Then God said, 'Let us make man in our image (*eikōna*), after our likeness. . . . in the image (*eikōna*) of God he created him; male and female he created them."[49] Paul's use of *eikōn* in 1 Corinthians 11:7 serves as a prelude to the more significant term, *doxa*. It is *doxa*, not *eikōn*, that he repeats in the next phrase, "but woman is the *glory* of man."[50]

---

the fact that she is the glory of man and was made from man. See Bruce Ware, "Male and Female Complementarity and the Image of God," in *Biblical Foundations for Manhood and Womanhood*, ed. Wayne Grudem (Wheaton, IL: Crossway, 2002), 84–87. Ware has a helpful discussion of these theological questions in which he asserts that the implication of 1 Corinthians 11:7–9 seems to be that "in being created as the glory of the man, the woman likewise, in being formed through the man, is thereby created in the image and glory of God," 86.

46. Webb, *Slaves, Women, and Homosexuals*, 274.

47. Ibid.

48. Ibid., 275: "Since some advocates of patriarchy argue against positions of authority for women using material from 1 Cor. 11, and since the broader discussion relates to hierarchical ideas, let us say—for the sake of discussion—that Paul is arguing for male headship (and not just addressing the glory issue). Even if the 'from' and 'for' arguments support male headship, one still has to establish whether these arguments are culturally or transculturally valid."

49. The term is used three other times, in Gen. 5:1, "When God created man, he made him in the likeness (*eikona*) of God"; 5:3, "When Adam had lived 130 years, he fathered a son in his own likeness, after his image (*eikona*), and named him Seth"; 9:6, "for God made man in his own image (*eikoni*)."

50. C. K. Barrett says, "In this context Paul values the term image only as leading to the term glory" (*A Commentary on the First Epistle to the Corinthians*, HNTC [New York: Harper & Row, 1968], 252). Concerning the absence of a statement that the woman also bears the image of God,

Here the OT background shifts from Genesis 1 to Genesis 2.[51] Paul states that "woman is the glory of man," and then in verses 8–9 he gives an explanation of this assertion, which, in turn, supports the command that the woman cover her head (v. 6). Paul highlights two important components of the creation account in Genesis 2. First of all, "For man is not from woman, but woman from man." Paul makes the same point in 1 Timothy 2:13: "Adam was formed first, then Eve."[52]

In the Genesis 2 account, verse 7 records the creation of the man. Then in verse 18 God declares, "It is not good that the man should be alone," and he announces his intent to "make him a helper fit for him." He proceeds, however, to make the animals and bring them before the man to be named. At the end of this process it is clear that the man is still alone, despite being surrounded by animals. As verse 20 bluntly states, "But for Adam there was not found a helper fit for him." At this point God caused the man to sleep, took one of his ribs, and made the woman. The man states in response, "She shall be called Woman, because she was taken out of Man" (v. 23). In this way, the woman is clearly "from" the man. She was created after him, and also literally from his side. Paul uses these important details from the creation account to give a basis for his point concerning male headship. And he emphasizes the point not only with a positive statement, but also with a negative one. He does not simply state that woman is from man, but begins by denying the contrary, "man is not from woman."[53]

Paul's second statement, "For indeed man was not created for woman, but woman for man" (v. 9), is also derived directly from the details of Genesis 2. The woman was made to be "a helper fit for [the man]" (Gen. 2:18, 20). Then in Genesis 2:22, God "brought her to the man." Again, this observation from creation is first stated negatively, and then positively. Thus, verses 8–9 demonstrate clearly and boldly from Genesis 2 God's design for male headship.

Verses 8–9 are counterbalanced by verses 11–12.[54] An adversative conjunction begins verse 11. However we interpret verse 10, the point

---

Gundry-Volf states, "It is best understood as an intentional omission for the sake of stressing that woman is the glory of man" ("Gender and Creation," 156). See also David E. Garland, *1 Corinthians*, BECNT (Grand Rapids: Baker Academic, 2003), 522–23.

51. Gundry-Volf, "Gender and Creation," 156.

52. Garland, *1 Corinthians*, 522.

53. The structure of these statements also creates a double chiasm in vv. 8–9 that will be mirrored in vv. 11–12. See Fee, *1 Corinthians*, 523.

54. Verse 10 is complicated but is not germane to the present discussion.

to be observed is that Paul qualifies in some sense the emphasis he has given to male headship. It is also interesting to note the reversal of the chiastic pattern. Verses 8–9 followed the pattern—man, woman, woman, man. Verses 11–12 both follow the pattern—woman, man, man, woman.[55] The point of verses 11–12 is not pivotal to the argument of the section,[56] but Paul inserts this statement of equality lest his previous statements be misunderstood or abused.[57] Here he provides a glimpse into the beautiful complexity of God's design for men and women. While there is a certain priority in the role assigned to men, which is rooted in creation (vv. 8–9), there is also a profound interdependence that God has established between men and women (vv. 11–12). Verse 11 describes this interdependence in terms of woman not being apart from man, or man apart from woman. Then Paul adds the phrase "in the Lord." This mutuality between man and woman is "in the Lord."

Thus, the passage asserts not only the differences between men and women, but also their equality. But does the assertion of mutuality cancel out the differences in role? Krister Stendahl writes, "Paul's parenthesis in the argument concerning subordination in 1 Corinthians 11 is best understood as an incidental reference to the insight expressed more fully in Galatians 3:28."[58] He goes on to say, "If we are right in describing the statements of 1 Corinthians 11:11–12 and Galatians 3:28 as *pointing beyond* what is actually implemented in the New Testament church, then they must be allowed their freedom; and the tension which they constitute must not be absorbed or neutralized in a comprehensive and hence harmonized 'biblical view'" (emphasis mine).[59]

55. Fee, *1 Corinthians*, 522.

56. Garland, *1 Corinthians*, 529.

57. Joël Delobel, "1 Cor. 11:2–16: Towards a Coherent Interpretation," in *L'Apôtre Paul: Personnalité, style et conception du ministère*, ed. Albert Vanhoye, Bibliotheca ephemeridum theologicarum lovaniensium 73 (Leuven: Leuven University Press / Peeters, 1986), 384: "The one-sidedness of Paul's presentation of creation in vv. 3.7–9 is felt by every reader. Paul seems to need such a presentation in his search for a strong argument to counter the behaviour of women in Corinth. However, it is not a lack of coherence if within the same pericope, the other aspect of creation order, namely the equal value of man and woman, is also briefly mentioned."

58. Krister Stendahl, *The Bible and the Role of Women*, trans. Emilie T. Sander (Philadelphia: Fortress Press, 1966), 35.

59. Ibid. Similarly, Richard N. Longenecker, *New Testament Social Ethics for Today* (Grand Rapids: Eerdmans, 1984), 80; Paul K. Jewett, *Man as Male and Female: A Study in Sexual Relationships from a Theological Point of View* (Grand Rapids: Eerdmans, 1975), 113. See also F. F. Bruce, "'All Things to All Men': Diversity in Unity and Other Pauline Tensions," in *Unity and Diversity in New Testament Theology: Essays in Honor of George E. Ladd*, ed. Robert A. Guelich (Grand Rapids:

This idea is a key component of the redemptive-movement hermeneutic. Webb cites 1 Corinthians 11:11–12 as an example of a "seed idea," one of Webb's eighteen criteria for evaluating whether a component of a text is cultural. He acknowledges that "egalitarians should probably concede that Paul is not intending to overturn completely all of his previous discussion, at least not in this particular situation within the setting of Corinth and within his generation."[60] Then he says,

> [T]he phrase "in the Lord" (much like "in Christ") suggests that Paul may have in mind not simply the Christian community as a redeemed people, but as a redeemed people *quite apart from the social realities of the old world* that they still lived in and that in some measure they still reflected in their midst. If so, 1 Corinthians 11:11–12 provides another seed idea whose potential could only be realized as the larger social climate permits (italics original).[61]

Thus, for both Stendahl and Webb verses 11–12 do not merely provide a counterbalance to the comments on male headship, but rather they point beyond male headship to an equality "in the Lord" that will become possible as the cultural trappings of patriarchy are removed.

In an appendix and then in more detail in a later article, Webb seeks to bolster this argument by appealing to the two prepositions used in 1 Corinthians 11:12.[62] He points out that Paul describes woman as coming "from" (*ek*) man, while man is "through" (*dia*) woman. Based on a study of ancient embryology, Webb avers that Paul's use of these prepositions reflects the view of his day that women were "reproductive gardens." The common understanding was that the male provided the seed, while the woman provided the garden in which the seed grew.[63] Modern embryology, however, demonstrates that the woman's role in the formation of a child

---

Eerdmans, 1978), 95: "'In Christ'—within the community of faith—any such idea of feminine inferiority has been obliterated."

60. Webb, *Slaves, Women, and Homosexuals*, 87.

61. Ibid.

62. William Webb, "Woman Created *From* Man and *For* Man: An Assessment of 1 Corinthians 11:8–9," Appendix D in *Slaves, Women, and Homosexuals*, 274–78. He also mentions 1 Cor. 11:12 in relation to his eighteenth criterion, "Scientific and Social-Scientific Evidence," where he discusses, among other things, the ancient view that women are "reproductive gardens," 223n11. He develops these ideas in the article, "Balancing Paul's Original-Creation and Pro-Creation Arguments: 1 Corinthians 11:11–12 in Light of Modern Embryology," *WTJ* 66 (2004): 275–89.

63. Webb discusses three views found among ancient writers, "Balancing," 276–79.

is much more significant, and therefore it is not enough to speak of man simply coming "through" woman. Webb states, "if Paul were alive today, he would update his procreation point to argue that 'man comes through (*dia*) woman *and* man comes from (*ek*) woman.'"[64] In the conclusion of this essay, Webb summarizes how he thinks these observations should impact our understanding of gender relationships:

> The thesis of this essay is that Paul's counterbalancing procreation argument must be given *much greater weight* in forging our contemporary application of gender relationships than was ever possible in Paul's day. Contemporary application of Paul's counterbalance argument brings an entirely new sense to creation theology—one that celebrates an *ek* and *dia* contribution for the female to the male (not simply *dia*) and thus adds far more weight to the female status within male-female relationships.[65] (emphasis original)

Because Paul's understanding of embryology was limited by his cultural context, it must also be assumed that his understanding of gender relationships was similarly limited. Therefore, our advances in embryology ought to shed new light on 1 Corinthians 11 and point us farther beyond the particulars of what is instructed there. This is Webb's argument concerning verse 12, which fits into his broader program of finding cultural clues that limit the application of certain texts and thus prompt us to move beyond them.

But are these assumptions justified in the text? Is it reasonable to assume that Paul's prepositions reflect a particular understanding of embryology? It seems that the verse makes the simple point that while woman is "from" man (Gen. 2:21–22), it is also true that man is born "through" woman. In this way Paul balances what he has said about male headship with the reminder that men are also dependent on women. There is a beautiful and mysterious interdependence between the sexes.

When we ask why Paul used two different prepositions in verse 12 rather than repeating *ek*, we find an answer that is much simpler and more straightforward than Webb's. Judith Gundry-Volf warns against making too much of these prepositions, and points out that the switch to

64. Ibid., 282.
65. Ibid., 288.

dia is somewhat surprising because *ek* is more likely to carry the meaning of "birth *from, of, by*."[66] She concludes that the switch from *ek* to *dia* "maintains the difference between man and woman and avoids a flat contradiction with 11:8, which says 'man is *not* from (*ek*) woman.'"[67] This seems to be a clear and simple explanation for these prepositions which does not impose unnecessary assumptions onto the passage. Paul very well could have stated that man is "from" woman. Indeed, he uses *ek* in this way elsewhere (cf. Gal. 4:4, 22–23).[68] But he switched to *dia* so as not to contradict the point he stressed just a few verses earlier.

The hermeneutical questions concerning "seed ideas" will be dealt with in chapter 5. For the purpose of this chapter, I conclude based on the above exegesis that there is not sufficient evidence within this passage to detect a "tension"[69] between verses 8–9 and verses 11–12. The priority of male headship grounded in the creation account need not be canceled out or relegated to obsolescence because of the statements in verses 11–12. Neither, of course, should we understand male headship to mean that women are in any way less important than men. We cannot ignore how God designed men and women to be dependent on one another.

The Law

Moving from 1 Corinthians 11 to 1 Corinthians 14, we find another admonition to women which includes a ground clause. Here Paul states that "the women should keep silent in the churches," and he cites "the Law" as support. While some have attempted to discard these verses, this is not a convincing option.[70] Admittedly, it is a difficult passage, and at first reading

66. Gundry-Volf, "Gender and Creation," 162. See BDAG, s.v. "*ek*, 3a."

67. Ibid., 162–63.

68. BDAG, s.v. "*ek*, 3a."

69. See Stendahl's quote above.

70. Some have argued that these verses are an interpolation (e.g., Fee, *1 Corinthians*, 699–708; Conzelmann, *1 Corinthians*, 246). Others have argued that the verses are a quotation which Paul is denouncing (e.g., Walter C. Kaiser Jr., *Toward an Exegetical Theology: Biblical Exegesis for Preaching and Teaching* [Grand Rapids: Baker, 1981], 76–77, 119). For a thorough interaction with these possibilities, and a rejection of them, see Anthony C. Thiselton, *The First Epistle to the Corinthians: A Commentary on the Greek Text*, NIGTC (Grand Rapids: Eerdmans, 2000), 1147–52. For further discussion on the textual question, see Curt Niccum, "The Voice of the Manuscripts on the Silence of Women: The External Evidence for 1 Cor. 14:34–5," *NTS* 43 (1997): 242–55; David W. Bryce, "'As in All the Churches of the Saints': A Text-Critical Study of 1 Corinthians 14:34–35," *Lutheran Theological Journal* 31 (1997): 31–39; Philip B. Payne, "Fuldensis, Sigla for Variants in Vaticanus, and 1 Cor. 14:34–5," *NTS* 41 (1995): 240–62; J. M. Ross, "Floating Words: Their Significance for

it seems to contradict what is assumed in 1 Corinthians 11. Therefore we must look carefully into the immediate context of 1 Corinthians 14, and also the broader context of 1 Corinthians 11 (as well as 1 Tim. 2), in order to properly understand Paul's point.

Following the initial statement concerning silence, Paul explains with a positive and negative statement.[71] The women are *not* permitted to speak, *but* should be in submission. Then the instruction is undergirded by a reference to the Law. Verse 35 gives further explanation, instructing the women to learn from their husbands at home. The verse ends by reiterating the main point of these verses, while adding the dimension of shame: "For it is shameful for a woman to speak in church."

Two significant questions arise at this point. First, in what capacity is Paul mandating the women to be silent in the churches? Is he commanding absolute silence, or is the application of the command limited in some way? In 1 Corinthians 11:5 Paul assumes and condones the practice of women praying and prophesying in church gatherings. Therefore, assuming that he would not flatly contradict himself later in the same letter, we must assume that 14:33–35 is not calling for absolute silence. The context of chapter 14 provides an important clue, for the previous verses give instructions for prophesying and weighing prophecies. Twice (prior to v. 34) we find a command to be silent. In verse 28 it pertains to speaking in tongues without an interpreter, and in verse 30 it has to do with prophesying in an orderly fashion.[72] It seems that these observations suggest a plausible solution, namely, that the call for silence is in reference to the weighing of prophecies (v. 29).[73]

The second question is more pertinent to this study, and it has to do with Paul's mention of the Law. What is Paul referring to when he cites the

---

Textual Criticism," *NTS* 38 (1992): 153–56; D. A. Carson, "'Silent in the Churches': On the Role of Women in 1 Corinthians 14:33b-36," in *Recovering Biblical Manhood and Womanhood: A Response to Evangelical Feminism*, ed. John Piper and Wayne Grudem (Wheaton, IL: Crossway, 2006), 133–37; E. Earle Ellis, "The Silenced Wives of Corinth (1 Cor. 14:34–5)," in *New Testament Textual Criticism: Its Significance for Exegesis: Essays in Honour of Bruce M. Metzger*, ed. Eldon Jay Epp and Gordon D. Fee (Oxford: Clarendon Press, 1981), 213–20.

71. Raymond F. Collins, *First Corinthians*, Sacra Pagina Series, vol. 7 (Collegeville, MN: The Liturgical Press, 1999), 521, notes how the antithetical statement (negative then positive) puts the emphasis on the latter, as in v. 33a.

72. Earle Ellis and Ben Witherington have both pointed to the use of "keep silent" in vv. 28, 30, and 34 as an indication that the interpolation theory is "unjustified." E. Earle Ellis, *Prophecy and Hermeneutic in Early Christianity: New Testament Essays*, Wissenschaftliche Untersuchungen. Zum Neuen Testament 18 (Tübingen: Mohr / Siebeck, 1978), 27n25; Witherington, *Women in the Earliest Churches*, 91.

73. See Carson, "Silent in the Churches," 142–44.

Law as a reason why women should not speak but be in submission? Various answers have been given. Some suggest that it could be Roman law,[74] others see this as rabbinic tradition,[75] or a reference to Paul's own "ruling."[76] However, Paul's quotation from the Law in verse 21 (Isa. 28:11–12) makes these suggestions unlikely. It is better to understand Paul's reference to the Law in verse 34 similarly, although it does not include a quotation.

The problem, of course, is that there is not a specific Old Testament passage that commands women to be silent.[77] But when we understand Paul's point in these verses, we can begin to see how his reference to the Law might be functioning. For his main concern is not that women be absolutely silent. Rather, his aim is to uphold God's ordained roles for men and women. In the context of weighing prophecies in a church setting, this would require women to be respectful of the church's male leadership. Especially for those wives who might wish to publicly critique their own husbands, they should respectfully reserve those comments and questions for home.[78] Thus, it is likely that Paul has in mind something from the Old Testament that relates to this issue.

Various conclusions have been drawn as to what passage(s) Paul is alluding. Leifeld suggests that Numbers 12:1–15 might be in view, for there Miriam is punished for criticizing Moses.[79] Many have pointed to Genesis 3:16, the punishment given to the woman after the fall.[80] But this conclusion is problematic, as F. F. Bruce points out.

> This is unlikely, since in MT and LXX Gen. 3:16 speaks of the woman's instinctive inclination or passionate desire . . . towards her husband, of which he takes advantage so as to dominate her. The reference is more

74. Linda L. Belleville, "Women in Ministry," in *Two Views on Women in Ministry*, ed. James R. Beck, 2nd ed. (Grand Rapids: Zondervan, 2005), 77.

75. Jewett, *Man as Male and Female*, 114; Kaiser, *Toward an Exegetical Theology*, 76–77, 119.

76. Ralph P. Martin, *The Spirit and the Congregation: Studies in 1 Corinthians 12–15* (Grand Rapids: Eerdmans, 1984), 87.

77. Garland, *1 Corinthians*, 672.

78. Simon J. Kistemaker, *Exposition of the First Epistle to the Corinthians*, New Testament Commentary (Grand Rapids: Baker, 1993), 513.

79. Walter L. Liefeld, "Women, Submission and Ministry in 1 Corinthians," in *Women, Authority and the Bible*, ed. Alvera Mickelsen (Downers Grove, IL: IVP, 1986), 149–50.

80. F. W. Grosheide, *Commentary on the First Epistle to the Corinthians*, NICNT (Grand Rapids: Eerdmans, 1953), 343; Archibald Robertson and Alfred Plummer, *A Critical and Exegetical Commentary on the First Epistle of St. Paul to the Corinthians*, ICC (Edinburgh: T & T Clark, 1911), 325; Stendahl, *The Bible and the Role of Women*, 29–30, who mentions Gen. 3:16 specifically and also Gen. 1–3 as a whole.

> probably to the creation narratives of Gen. 1:26ff; 2:21ff, on which Paul has based the argument of 11:3ff. (a different argument than the present one).[81]

In other words, Genesis 3:16 is descriptive, not prescriptive, and therefore would not serve as a basis for Paul's instruction.[82]

The more natural reference, as Bruce noted, would be the creation narratives of Genesis 1–2. Simon Kistemaker notes the other references to creation in 1 Corinthians (6:16 quotes Gen. 2:24; 11:8–9 alludes to Gen. 2:18, 21–23), then states, "And, last, in the current passage he refers to the role the wife must fulfill with respect to her husband, namely, to be his helper."[83] If the issue at stake in this context is that of the proper roles of men and women in the worship service, a reference to God's creation order would be apropos. And the fact that Paul referred to creation in chapter 11 would explain why he can abbreviate his remark here, simply stating, "as the Law also says."

The parallels among 1 Corinthians 11, 1 Corinthians 14, and 1 Timothy 2 are noteworthy. Each passage addresses the role of women. First Corinthians 11 and 1 Corinthians 14 each include references to shame (*aischron* in 11:6; 14:35, found elsewhere only in Ephesians 5:12; Titus 1:11. Also, *kataischunei* is used in 11:4–5). First Corinthians 14 and 1 Timothy 2 are linked in the following ways: *epitrepō* (1 Cor. 14:34; 1 Tim. 2:12), *manthanō* (1 Cor. 14:35; 1 Tim. 2:11), *hyupotassomai/hypotagē* (1 Cor. 14:34; 1 Tim. 2:11). The structure of these two passages is also similar. First Corinthians 14:34–35 begins with a call for silence and ends with the statement that it is shameful for a woman to speak in church. In 1 Timothy 2:11–12 the mention of quietness forms an inclusio. I do not want to make too much of these connections, but they do seem to suggest a similar line of reasoning in the three passages.[84] If this is the case, then Paul's reference to the Law in 1 Corinthians 14:34 would be roughly equivalent to the ground given in 1 Timothy 2:13–14 and in 1 Corinthians 11:8–9.

81. F. F. Bruce, *1 and 2 Corinthians*, New Century Bible (Greenwood, SC: Attic Press, 1971), 136.

82. Jewett, *Man as Male and Female*, 114, makes this same point against taking Gen. 3:16 as the background, although he concludes that the reference is to rabbinic authority.

83. Kistemaker, *First Epistle to the Corinthians*, 512–13.

84. Carson, "Silent in the Churches," 142–43: "Paul is probably not referring to Genesis 3:16, as many suggest, but to the creation order in Genesis 2:20b-24, for it is to that Scripture that Paul explicitly turns on two other occasions when he discusses female roles" (1 Cor. 11:8–9; 1 Tim. 2:13).

Thus these three passages, each of them dealing with the role of women, ground this instruction in the order of creation[85] (although I say this with less certainty in the case of 1 Cor. 14).

Male Headship/Christ's Headship

In Ephesians 5:22, Paul instructs wives to submit (*hypotassomenoi* implied from v. 21) to their own husbands. Then the ground is given, "for the husband is the head of the wife even as Christ is the head of the church."

As I discussed in relation to 1 Corinthians 11, Webb classifies theological analogy as an inconclusive criterion by which to determine whether a command is transcultural. With respect to Ephesians 5:22–33, he says that Paul could have used the same Christological analogy in an egalitarian sense, and he cites Philippians 2:1–11 as an example.[86] I agree that theological analogy does not deem a particular instruction transcultural. However, there are some unique features to Ephesians 5 that may set it apart from the other theological analogies cited by Webb.[87]

Indeed, the beginning of the passage bears similarities to other theological analogies found in the New Testament. Wives are instructed to submit to their own husbands "as to the Lord." Just a few verses later, in Ephesians 6:5–8, slaves are instructed to obey their earthly masters

85. Contra Kevin Giles, *The Trinity and Subordinationism: The Doctrine of God and the Contemporary Gender Debate* (Downers Grove, IL: IVP, 2002), 256: "The evidence is compelling: there is no common appeal to the creation order, however understood, in the Household Codes. At best there is *one example* of an appeal to the *chronological* ordering of the sexes in creation, matched by an appeal to the responsibility of the woman for the Fall (1 Tim. 2:13–14). This means that the appeal to creation is *the exception to the rule*, not the pattern. Where there is a second example of an appeal to the creation narratives to ground an apostolic ruling on head coverings (1 Cor. 11:3–16), no one thinks the ruling is universally binding" (emphasis original).

86. Webb, *Slaves, Women, and Homosexuals*, 188–89. In note 9 he says, "Paul can just as easily apply the same Christological-submission theology along egalitarian lines when he calls for mutual, not unilateral, submission (Phil. 2:1–11)." Webb proceeds to discuss how Hosea's relationship to Gomer is an analogy of Yahweh's relationship to Israel, and if we were to take this as transcultural it would mean that a husband can publicly strip his wife if she is unfaithful (Hos. 2). "We cannot use the theological analogy in Ephesians 5 to endorse that material as completely transcultural without doing the same in Hosea 2" (*Slaves, Women, and Homosexuals*, 190). My response is to agree that a theological analogy is not enough to establish that a particular instruction is completely transcultural. However, I believe that what we find in Eph. 5 is much more than a theological analogy.

87. Wayne Grudem, "Should We Move Beyond the New Testament to a Better Ethic? An Analysis of William J. Webb, *Slaves, Women, and Homosexuals: Exploring the Hermeneutics of Cultural Analysis*," *JETS* 47 (2004): 340, says that Webb "has produced no examples that are actually parallel to Ephesians 5 or 1 Cor. 11:3."

"as you would Christ," "as servants of Christ," serving "as to the Lord." Colossians 3:22–24, likewise, instructs slaves to obey their masters and work "as for the Lord."[88]

However, the way the theological analogy develops in Ephesians 5 distinguishes it from the slavery passages. First, the analogy is drawn with striking detail. Verse 22 is only the beginning of the analogy. The exhortation is then grounded in a statement of male headship,[89] which is then amplified in connection to the overarching parallels in the passage. The husband's headship over his wife is parallel to Christ's headship over the church. Verse 24 states the same reality from the opposite point of view: the church's submission to Christ is parallel to the wife's submission to her husband. In verse 25 the instruction is no longer directed toward wives, but husbands, and the focus of the analogy shifts from headship and submission to sacrificial love. The same parallels remain, though, between husbands and Christ and between wives and the church, for husbands are to love their wives "as Christ loved the church and gave himself up for her." These observations are not conclusive, but they should at least help us see some of the unique features of Ephesians 5. We cannot too quickly draw a parallel between this passage and the theological analogies connected with slavery.

Second, we find in verse 31 a quotation from the creation account. Here is another feature of this passage that sets it apart from the others. Paul quotes Genesis 2:24 in a way that applies both to the union of Christ and the church and also to the union of husband and wife.[90] The quotation seems to be closely connected to the previous verse. It has no

88. The analogy in 1 Peter 2:18–25 seems more general. Christ is given as an example of suffering unjustly, which applies not only to slaves, but to anyone who suffers for doing good. Lauri Thurén, *Argument and Theology in 1 Peter: The Origins of Christian Paraenesis*, JSNTSup 114 (Sheffield: Academic Press, 1995), 140: "Formally the unit is aimed at slaves, but the slaves simultaneously function rhetorically as an example of every addressee's situation in the society or most of the addressees' position in the congregation."

89. It is important to note that Webb does not follow other egalitarians in arguing that *kephalē* means source. He states in a footnote, "I tend to agree with patriarchalists on the lexical study" (*Slaves, Women, and Homosexuals*, 188n8), and then cites Schreiner's article as "a good review of the evidence for understanding 'head' to have an authoritative component to its meaning in 1 Cor. 11:3–5 (and Eph. 5:23–24)." See Schreiner, "Head Coverings," 127–28.

90. Ernest Best, *A Critical and Exegetical Commentary on Ephesians* (Edinburgh: T & T Clark, 1998), 553: "The whole verse applies to the latter relationship [human marriage] but it is its second half which is particularly relevant to the former [Christ and the church]."

introductory formula, but it fits nicely into the flow of thought.[91] Thus, Paul again (as in 1 Tim. 2, 1 Cor. 11, and possibly 1 Cor. 14) refers to God's creation ordinances in the context of providing instruction for the roles of men and women. Third, verse 32 indicates that this passage is revealing something of immense importance. The quotation from Genesis 2:24 is referring not only to human marriage, but also to the mystery of Christ's union with the church, as the following statement makes clear.[92]

In these ways we must acknowledge the unique nature of this passage. Paul is doing much more than presenting a theological analogy. He is revealing a profound feature of God's design for marriage and its connection to His plan of redemption. From the beginning, God established male headship and wifely submission to be a picture of Christ's relationship to the church.

As Is Fitting in the Lord

In Colossians 3:18, Paul instructs wives to submit to their own husbands, and then he grounds the command in the fact that it "is fitting in the Lord." This statement is slightly different than the analogies discussed above, in which slaves are instructed to obey their earthly masters "as you would Christ," or wives are instructed to submit to their own husbands "as to the Lord." What we see in Colossians 3:18 is not an analogy, but a ground for submission. Paul is not illustrating the nature of the submission, but giving a basis for it. The prepositional phrase "in the Lord" modifies what immediately precedes it, "as is fitting," rather than modifying the imperative, "submit." This connection becomes clear when we examine the similar structure two verses later, where Paul instructs children to obey their parents, and gives as a ground: "for this pleases the Lord."[93]

91. For discussion, see Harold W. Hoehner, *Ephesians: An Exegetical Commentary* (Grand Rapids: Baker Academic, 2002), 772.

92. For the various views of how *mustērion* is being used, see Peter O'Brien, *The Letter to the Ephesians*, Pelican New Testament Commentaries (Grand Rapids: Eerdmans, 1999), 430–35; Andreas J. Köstenberger, "The Mystery of Christ and the Church: Head and Body, 'One Flesh,'" *TrinJ* 12NS (1991): 86–92. Whether *mustērion* is referring to Christ and the church or to the typological relationship between human marriage and Christ's union with the church, my point stands, which is simply to show that this is much more than a theological analogy.

93. Peter T. O'Brien, *Colossians, Philemon*, WBC, vol. 44 (Waco, TX: Word Books, 1982), 222; T. K. Abbott, *A Critical and Exegetical Commentary on the Epistles to the Ephesians and to the*

It is true that "it is fitting" is an idea that was common in Stoic writings.[94] However, Paul adapts it thoroughly into a Christian mindset by attaching to it those revolutionary words: "in the Lord." F. F. Bruce writes, "The phrase 'as is fitting' has a thoroughly Stoic ring about it; but it ceases to be Stoic when baptized into Christ by the added words: 'in the Lord.' "[95] Thus, Paul establishes the exhortation for wifely submission, not simply as a cultural norm to uphold, but as an integral component of the Christian life.

It is significant to observe that Paul uses the phrase "in the Lord" in verses 18 and 20, in connection with the instruction for wives to submit to their husbands and the instruction for children to obey their parents. But the phrase is absent in verse 22 where slaves are told to obey their earthly masters.[96] Ernest Best writes, "It is very noticeable that while Paul uses the formula 'in Christ' of the mutual duties of husband wife, parent and child, he does not use it of the mutual duties of masters and servants."[97] Best attributes this to the nature of marriage and family as opposed to the nature of the master-slave relationship. He says, "The family is a unit, and if one part of it is in Christ it is all in him (cf. 1 Cor. 7:12–16), so that the duties of one member towards another can be said to be 'in Christ.' "[98] This is not the case in the master-slave relationship.

Observing this distinction adds concurring evidence to the thesis that the New Testament instructions for women are significantly different from the instructions for slaves. From Colossians 3:18 we simply observe that Paul provides a basis for wifely submission that is rooted "in the Lord," and there is a noticeable difference between this and his instructions to slaves in the same context.

Colossians, ICC (Edinburgh: T & T Clark, 1897), 293.

94. See Eduard Schweizer, *The Letter to the Colossians: A Commentary* (Minneapolis: Augsburg, 1976), 221–22.

95. F. F. Bruce, *The Epistles to the Colossians, to Philemon, and to the Ephesians*, NICNT (Grand Rapids: Eerdmans, 1984), 164.

96. The participial phrase, "fearing the Lord," is found at the end of the verse, but the formula "in the Lord" is absent.

97. Ernest Best, *One Body in Christ: A Study in the Relationship of the Church to Christ in the Epistles of the Apostle Paul* (London: Society for Promoting Christian Knowledge, 1955), 27n1. See also C. F. D. Moule, *The Epistles of Paul the Apostle to the Colossians and to Philemon*, CGTC (Cambridge: University Press, 1957), 128n1.

98. Best, *One Body in Christ*, 27n1.

Purpose of Obedience

In two passages we find exhortations to women that are followed by a purpose clause. First Peter 3:1 instructs wives to be subject to their own husbands. Then the purpose is given, "so that even if some do not obey the word, they may be won without a word by the conduct of their wives." Titus 2:5 contains a similar purpose clause. The older women are to train the younger women in various ways, one being submission to their husbands. The purpose is then given, "that the word of God may not be reviled." In 1 Peter 3:1 the purpose is evangelism, and in Titus 2:5 the purpose is not to tarnish the reputation of God's Word.

These are significant for the redemptive-movement hermeneutic, because the purpose statements are taken as indications that a passage may be culturally bound. Webb states the criterion this way: "A component of a text may be culturally bound, if by practicing the text one no longer fulfills the text's original intent or purpose."[99] Looking specifically at 1 Peter 3, the question for us today is whether the evangelistic purpose can still be fulfilled through wifely submission. Peter H. Davids, with the same reasoning as Webb, suggests not: "We may find that a direct application of Peter's teaching in modern and postmodern societies would subvert his original intentions."[100] Davids says that those who apply the exhortation of this passage to all cultures are actually moving in the opposite direction of Peter's intent. "Rather than promoting harmony with culture, they set Christian marriage partners at odds with culture and thus heighten the tension, and Christianity is perceived as undermining culture in a retrogressive way. This is precisely what 1 Peter is seeking to minimize."[101]

I will take up this hermeneutical discussion in chapter 5, but for the present discussion it is sufficient to state my agreement that these purpose statements do not argue in favor of interpreting these commands in a transcultural way. On the other hand, I do not believe they show that the commands are necessarily cultural. They are not definitive one way or the other on the issue.[102]

99. Webb, *Slaves, Women, and Homosexuals*, 105.

100. Peter H. Davids, "A Silent Witness in Marriage: 1 Peter 3:1–7," in *Discovering Biblical Equality: Complementarity without Hierarchy*, ed. Ronald W. Pierce and Rebecca Merrill Groothuis (Downers Grove, IL: IVP, 2004), 235.

101. Ibid., 236.

102. Webb says, "Granted, there may be more than one purpose involved in giving a biblical command. Perhaps unilateral, patriarchy-type submission should be viewed as transcultural

Conclusion

This chapter has surveyed the New Testament commands to women, giving the most attention to ground clauses that distinguish these commands from those given to slaves. In 1 Timothy 2, 1 Corinthians 11, and possibly 1 Corinthians 14, the commands to women are grounded by references to creation. The next chapter will show more clearly how this distinguishes the women's passages from the slavery passages.

based on other purposes. Such a possibility clearly exists" (*Slaves, Women, and Homosexuals*, 108).

4

Comparing the Data

The purpose of this chapter will be to summarize and compare the points made in the previous two chapters. We will observe similarities between the two sets of passages, but the focus will be on the key differences. Finally, this chapter will address the issue of the Household Codes and whether it is legitimate to draw distinctions within them.

Similarities: Purpose of Obedience

Kevin Giles makes a case for understanding the exhortations to women and slaves in the same way. The Bible endorses slavery, he maintains, just as it does male headship, and his conclusion is that "Scripture can endorse social structures no longer acceptable."[1] In seeking to establish the fundamental connection between the exhortations to women and to slaves, Giles rightly observes that they are usually found in the same contexts.[2] The instructions to women in Ephesians 5:22, Colossians 3:18, and 1 Peter 3:1 are closely connected to the instructions given to slaves in Ephesians 6:5, Colossians 3:22, and 1 Peter 2:18. Giles asserts, "This in itself would suggest that the exhortations are of the same nature and

1. Kevin Giles, "The Biblical Argument for Slavery: Can the Bible Mislead? A Case Study in Hermeneutics," *EQ* 66 (1994): 4.

2. Kevin Giles, *The Trinity and Subordinationism: The Doctrine of God and the Contemporary Gender Debate* (Downers Grove, IL: IVP, 2002), 256.

force."[3] His assumption is plausible. A clear similarity between the two sets of commands is that they are found together within the Household Codes.

What Giles points to as the most significant similarity is the common appeal to the example of Christ. "The most common ground for *all* the exhortations, whether to women or slaves, is the example of Christ, who willingly subordinated himself in the incarnation and taught that the great in his kingdom would be those who assumed the ministry of servants (Mark 10:45; Luke 22:25–26)."[4] Speaking very generally, we can cite this as a similarity. In 1 Peter 2 we find an extensive and direct appeal to Christ's example, which is preceded by an exhortation to slaves and followed by an exhortation to wives. In other places there are references to the Lord, although not a specific appeal to Christ's example. For instance, in Colossians 3:18 Paul tells wives to submit to their husbands "as is fitting in the Lord," and in verse 24 he encourages slaves with the truth that "you are serving the Lord Christ" (see also Eph. 6:6, "as servants of Christ").

However, when all of the passages under discussion are closely examined, Giles's statement must be significantly modified. For 1 Peter 2 is the only passage among the Household Codes where we find a specific appeal to Christ's example related to submission. In Ephesians 5 there is a connection to Christ's example, but it is directed to husbands, that they should sacrificially love their wives "as Christ loved the church and gave himself up for her." Nowhere do we find Christ's example given as the ground for a command to women, and in the slavery passages the connection with Christ's suffering appears only in 1 Peter 2.

If we were to observe any similarities between the exhortations to women and to slaves, it would not be the example of Christ, but the purpose statements that are attached to some of the commands. In each passage where a purpose statement is given it is related to the reputation of Christianity. In 1 Timothy 6:1, Paul expands on his instructions to slaves with the following purpose: "so that the name of God and the teaching may not be reviled." Similarly, in Titus 2, slaves are told to be submissive to their own masters, and verse 10 gives the purpose: "so that in everything they may adorn the doctrine of God our Savior." In that same context,

3. Ibid.
4. Ibid., 257.

just a few verses earlier, the instruction for women to be submissive to their own husbands is followed by the purpose statement, "that the word of God may not be reviled" (v. 5). Between the exhortation to women and the exhortation to slaves is an exhortation to Titus. Paul tells Titus that his behavior and teaching must be exemplary, "so that an opponent may be put to shame, having nothing evil to say about us" (v. 8).

Finally, we also find a purpose clause in 1 Peter 3, where wives are told to be submissive to their own husbands, "so that even if some do not obey the word, they may be won without a word by the conduct of their wives." Here it is an evangelistic purpose, closely related to the statements in the other three passages. The intention in each passage is to see people attracted to the gospel rather than repelled by it, and one way that can happen is by Christians living submissive and upright lives in whatever societal position they find themselves.

While it is interesting to observe these similarities, they do not justify treating the two sets of exhortations in the same way. Giles's assessment is misleading, for his general statement about the example of Christ being the most common ground for all the exhortations can only be clearly substantiated in one text (1 Peter 2–3). The more common similarity is found in the purpose statements.[5]

Differences: Ground for Obedience

When we examine the ground clauses connected to the exhortations, we see a significant divergence between the two groups of passages. Again, Giles's portrayal is misleading, for he limits his comparison to the Household Codes and quickly dismisses the other important texts. Thus he concludes,

> The evidence is compelling: there is no common appeal to the creation order, however understood, in the Household Codes. At best there is *one example* of an appeal to the *chronological* ordering of the sexes in creation, matched by an appeal to the responsibility of the woman for the Fall (1 Tim. 2:13–14). This means that the appeal to creation is *the exception to the rule*, not the pattern. Where there is a second example of an appeal to the creation narratives to ground an apostolic ruling on

5. The next chapter will address the issue of purpose statements further. Also see the discussion in the "Purpose of Obedience" sections in both chapters 2 and 3.

> head coverings (1 Cor. 11:3–16), no one thinks the ruling is universally binding.[6] (italics original)

He dismisses 1 Corinthians 14:34 by citing three interpretations of the passage and then asserting, without defense, "whatever is concluded on any of these questions, one thing is clear: this exhortation is not grounded on an appeal to a creation order established before the Fall; the appeal is to 'the law.'"[7] One of the interpretations he cites is that of D. A. Carson, which Giles does not portray accurately. He writes, "Others have suggested that the issue in this text is not the subordination of wives to husbands but of women to the prophets."[8] But this draws a false dichotomy that is not present in Carson's chapter. Carson concludes that the command in 1 Corinthians 14:34 applies to the oral weighing of prophecies,[9] and it is from this point that I assume Giles makes his statement about this interpretation. But the suggestion that the silence called for is in reference to the weighing of prophecies does not mean that "the issue in this text is not the subordination of wives to husbands," as Giles says. It is both/and, not either/or. The reason women are restricted from weighing prophecies is that it would undermine the pattern of male headship that God has ordained for His creation.

Also, Giles overlooks the important point made by Carson that "the law" is likely referring to Genesis 2:20b–24. Carson observes that Paul appealed to "the law" earlier in the chapter (14:21), and goes on to write, "Paul is probably not referring to Genesis 3:16, as many suggest, but to the creation order in Genesis 2:20b–24, for it is to that Scripture that Paul explicitly turns on two other occasions when he discusses female roles (1 Cor. 11:8–9; 1 Tim. 2:13)."[10] If the reference is to Genesis 2, then the exhortation *is* grounded on an appeal to the creation order established before the fall.[11] Giles does not interact with this possibility, but rejects it without providing any basis for doing so.

6. Giles, *The Trinity and Subordinationism*, 256. Concerning 1 Cor. 11, the instruction about head coverings is not universally binding, but that does not mean the principle of male headship that is stressed in the passage also lacks universal application.

7. Ibid., 255.

8. Ibid., citing Carson's article, "Silent in the Churches," in *Recovering Biblical Manhood and Womanhood: A Response to Evangelical Feminism*, ed. John Piper and Wayne Grudem (Wheaton, IL: Crossway, 1991), 133–47.

9. Carson, "Silent in the Churches," 142. Also see my discussion of 1 Cor. 14 in the previous chapter.

10. Ibid., 142–43.

11. Again, see my discussion in the previous chapter.

Concerning Ephesians 5, Giles maintains that "Paul seeks to transform the patriarchal understanding of marriage without attacking it directly. . . . The ground for the appeal is Christological and the paradigm ecclesiological. The only time the creation narratives are mentioned is in Ephesians 5:31, where the making one of man and woman in marriage is the issue."[12] But it is significant that Paul quotes Genesis 2:24 in this passage. These verses reveal something profound about the design of the universe—that husbands are to demonstrate sacrificial love as they lead their wives, and wives are to submit to their husbands as the church submits to Christ. Paul cites the creation narrative, to highlight not only the one-flesh union of marriage, but also the union of Christ and his church. God's intention for marriage (i.e., the distinct roles of husband and wife) was established at creation to serve as a living parable of Christ's relationship with the church.[13] Therefore, Giles incorrectly minimizes the reference to Genesis 2:24, and more importantly, misses the weight of the theological grounding. He refers to the fact that the passage is "the most theologically grounded of all the material in the Household Codes," but he does not recognize the significance of the theological grounding.[14]

I will now summarize the exegetical conclusions from the previous chapter concerning the exhortations to women, and then contrast them with the exhortations to slaves. Contrary to Giles, there *is* a repeated appeal to the creation narrative in the women's passages. In those passages where a purpose clause is given (Titus 2:4–5; 1 Peter 3:1), the creation narrative is not cited, thus making these passages similar to the slavery exhortations in which a purpose clause is given (1 Tim. 6:1; Titus 2:9–10). But of the five other passages that contain an exhortation to women, there is a clear reference to creation in three of them (1 Tim. 2:12–14; 1 Cor. 11:2–16; Eph. 5:22–33), and arguably in four (1 Cor. 14:34). Colossians 3:18–19, being a very concise exhortation to wives and husbands, does not provide a deep theological or scriptural basis for the instruction. Admittedly, in Ephesians 5:22–33 the reference to creation is not the fundamental ground for the

12. Giles, *The Trinity and Subordinationism*, 255–56.

13. See my discussion of Eph. 5 in the previous chapter, and the fuller evaluation of "theological analogy" in chapter 5.

14. In another book, Giles discusses Ephesians 5:22–33 in more depth. He says this of the theological analogy, "The basic point of Paul's analogy between the husband-wife relationship and the Christ-church relationship seems to be simply the oneness that is characteristic of both," *Women and Their Ministry: A Case for Equal Ministries in the Church Today* (East Malvern, Australia: Dove Communications, 1977), 90n15.

commands. However, it is still significant that Genesis 2:24 is cited, and there is also the weighty theological connection between the husband-wife relationship and Christ's relationship to the church, which must be considered. I do not want to make too much of the quotation from Genesis 2:24 here, but I do want to show that there is a repeated appeal to the creation narrative in the women's passages, contrary to Giles's assessment of the passages.

In 1 Timothy 2, Paul grounds his prohibition of women teaching or exercising authority over men in the order of creation. "For Adam was formed first, then Eve" (v. 13), which points to Adam's headship in the marriage. "And Adam was not deceived, but the woman was deceived and became a transgressor" (v. 14), which refers to the fact that Eve was *the first* to be deceived, for the serpent undermined God's design by approaching the helper rather than the head. Thus, a clear and detailed reference to the order of creation, and the order of the fall, is given as the rationale for the instruction in verses 11–12.

In 1 Corinthians 11:8–9 there is also a clear and detailed reference to the order of creation. Verse 3 establishes the principle of male headship by drawing an analogy between Christ's headship over every man, man's headship over woman, and God's headship over Christ. In verse 6 the imperative is given for the wife to cover her head, and she is to do so because "woman is the glory of man" (v. 7). Then verses 8–9, like 1 Timothy 2, ground this in the way that God created man and woman. First of all, the woman was made "from" the man (v. 8). And secondly, she was made "for" the man (v. 9). In this way, Paul uses the Genesis 2 account to demonstrate God's design for male headship, while he goes on to remind us of God's design for the interdependence of man and woman (vv. 11–12).

The statements concerning husbands and wives in Ephesians 5 also contain a reference to the creation narrative (Gen. 2:24 in Eph. 5:31, as mentioned above in response to Giles). Also, in the previous chapter, I argued that the "theological analogy" of the Ephesians 5 passage is much more than an analogy. It is, rather, a statement of God's design for marriage. God created it to portray the spiritual reality of Christ's relationship to the church, which includes the important dynamic of headship and submission.

Finally, it is likely that 1 Corinthians 14 also contains a reference to creation. The call for women to be silent in the churches is best understood as referring to weighing prophecies. Paul prohibited women from participating in this way because it would essentially involve a woman teaching or exercising authority over a man (1 Tim. 2:12). Even if the weighing of prophecies is not in view, it is clear that Paul's prohibition is related to the appropriate roles of men and women in the church. His intention is to uphold God's design for manhood and womanhood in the context of the church's corporate worship. And once we recognize the similarities among 1 Timothy 2, 1 Corinthians 11, and 1 Corinthians 14, the reference to "the Law" in 1 Corinthians 14:34 is best read as a reference to the creation account.

In stark contrast with this, the slavery passages lack any references to creation. The commands to slaves are grounded in a fundamentally different way. In the slavery passages, the common ground for the instruction is the reminder of God's reward for well-doing. In Ephesians 6, Paul commands slaves to obey their earthly masters, and to serve them well, as they would Christ, "knowing that whatever good anyone does, this he will receive back from the Lord, whether he is a slave or free" (v. 8). Colossians 3:24–25 provides a similar ground, although here the threat of punishment is included: "knowing that from the Lord you will receive the inheritance as your reward. You are serving the Lord Christ. For the wrongdoer will be paid back for the wrong he has done, and there is no partiality." In 1 Peter 2:19, suffering unjustly is portrayed as "a gracious thing." And in verse 20, "if when you do good and suffer for it you endure, this is a gracious thing in the sight of God." In other words, such conduct will find favor in God's eyes.

The common appeal to reward in these ground clauses reinforces the observation that the commands to slaves, and the theological analogies used in those contexts, are designed to encourage and motivate individuals who are oppressed in various ways. The intent is *not* to establish slavery as a God-ordained institution.

Household Codes

The remaining question has to do with the Household Codes and whether it is legitimate to apply the wife/husband exhortations differently than the slave/master exhortations.[15] Giles argues strongly that the parallel

15. The discussion involves mainly Eph. 5:22–6:9; Col. 3:18–4:1; 1 Peter 2:18–3:7. But also in the Pastorals, household instructions appear in 1 Tim. 2:8–15; 6:1–2; Titus 2:1–10. Giles, *The Trinity*

instructions must be read in the same way. This argument, of course, seems reasonable. Indeed, in Ephesians 5–6 and in Colossians 3 the three relationships are addressed one right after the other (wives/husbands; children/fathers; slaves/masters).[16] In light of this, it would seem counterintuitive to say that two of these remain applicable today, while the third does not.

Giles asserts, "Most commentators, both past and present, have argued that these paired exhortations are of the same nature, and the nineteenth-century American evangelicals who argued in support of slavery emphasized this."[17] It is true that advocates of slavery maintained the parallel between the slavery texts and the women texts. What is interesting to note, however, is the fact that some abolitionists differentiated the two. Apparently unaware of this, Giles goes on to say, "The assertion by contemporary hierarchical-complementarians that these parallel exhortations to women and slaves to be subordinate are to be contrasted is an entirely novel idea, never heard before the 1970s and rejected universally by critical scholarly studies of the Household Codes or Rules."[18] Some abolitionists in the nineteenth century, though, clearly distinguished the two sets of commands in their opposition of slavery.[19] Albert Barnes, for example, cites several differences between slavery and the relationship of husband and wife, and maintains that the apostles did not present the two as parallel.[20] Therefore, contrary to Giles, it is not a novel idea to sharply

and Subordinationism, 253; James D. G. Dunn, "The Household Rules in the New Testament," in *The Family in Theological Perspective*, ed. Stephen C. Barton (Edinburgh, T & T Clark, 1996), 43.

16. George W. Knight III, "Husbands and Wives as Analogues of Christ and the Church: Ephesians 5:21–33 and Colossians 3:18–19," in *Recovering Biblical Manhood and Womanhood: A Response to Evangelical Feminism*, ed. John Piper and Wayne Grudem (Wheaton, IL: Crossway Books, 1991), 170, summarizes the logical flow in these passages, referring particularly to Eph. 5:22–6:9: "It is true that these three relationships (husbands and wives, parents and children, masters and slaves) are dealt with here as a kind of unit. They are treated one after another as different relationships within the larger household moving from the most central (husbands and wives) to the next most crucial (parents and children) to the extended relationship that might exist in some households (masters and slaves)."

17. Giles, *The Trinity and Subordinationism*, 252–53. He goes on to quote from Charles Hodge, *A Commentary on the Epistle to the Ephesians* (London: Banner of Truth, 1964), 366.

18. Giles, *The Trinity and Subordinationism*, 253. He cites two scholarly articles as "good summary articles on the state of research at this time." However, neither article clearly makes Giles's point: Dunn, "The Household Rules," and D. L. Balch, "Household Codes," in *Greco-Roman Literature and the New Testament*, ed. D. E. Aune (Atlanta: Scholars Press, 1988): 25–50. Giles makes the same assertions in "Women in the Church: A Rejoinder to Andreas Köstenberger," *EQ* 73 (2001): 242.

19. See my section in chapter 1, "Emancipation of Slaves and Women."

20. Albert Barnes, *An Inquiry into the Scriptural Views of Slavery* (Philadelphia: Perkins and Purves, 1846), 276–77.

distinguish the slave-master relationship from the wife-husband relationship. The question of novelty, although important, is not the main issue, however. We must determine from the texts themselves whether there is warrant for viewing these exhortations differently.

The comparison of these relationships is complicated by the fact that sandwiched between them are exhortations concerning children and parents. In both Ephesians 5:22–6:9 and Colossians 3:18–4:1 the instructions follow the same pattern, with the instructions to children and fathers appearing in the middle. This pair of exhortations—that children obey their parents and fathers not provoke their children—is the least debated in these passages. For virtually no one would argue that children no longer need to obey their parents. Thomas Schreiner cites this as a weakness in the egalitarian argument, which insists on the parallel between the commands given to wives and husbands and the commands given to slaves and masters. "Those who say that the admonition to wives is culturally bounded by appealing to the matter of slavery must also (to be consistent) say that the admonition for children to obey their parents no longer applies today."[21] In the same way, George Knight points to the middle set of instructions as a reason why it would be wrong to deny the first and third. "But if the argument advanced above is true, then it cuts all the way across the board. Not only would the teaching about husbands and wives cease to be normative and fall away with slavery, but so would the teaching about parents and children, which is positioned between the other two relationships!"[22]

At the very least, this point levels the playing field concerning the Household Codes. Giles accuses complementarians of illegitimately distinguishing between the first and third pair of commands, but by declaring those commands to be obsolete he is faced with the question of how to evaluate the middle pair of instructions.[23]

I. Howard Marshall seeks to deal with this issue by suggesting that the command to children is not applicable today in the same way it was in the first century. He acknowledges that the "instructions to parents and children appear to be commonsensical and Christian," but then he

21. Thomas R. Schreiner, "Women in Ministry," in *Two Views on Women in Ministry*, 2nd ed., ed. James R. Beck and Craig L. Blomberg (Grand Rapids: Zondervan, 2005), 216.

22. Knight, "Husbands and Wives," 176.

23. I was unable to find any discussion by Giles of the middle pair of instructions.

raises the question of "the age at which children cease to be under the strict authority of their parents."[24] He draws a distinction between then and now: "in the ancient world this subordination continued to a more advanced age than would be natural for us."[25] Also, "the father as patriarch had a much greater authority over sons and daughters than is the case today."[26] Thus, the argument is made that all three sets of instructions in these Household Codes must be applied differently today.

But Marshall does not claim that the fundamental command given to children is no longer applicable. Even if the original command included adult children in its scope, the main thrust of the instruction is certainly relevant today, as Marshall recognizes.[27] So the question is not whether there exist cultural features in these texts. I readily agree that there are (e.g., slavery, and possibly some aspect of the parent-child relationship; and in another place, head coverings, 1 Cor. 11). But the ultimate question at the center of this debate is whether male headship and wifely submission are among those cultural components. Giles maintains that they are, just as slavery is a cultural feature of the texts. The specific question is whether there is justification for distinguishing between the wife-husband commands and the slave-master commands.

I believe there is justification for this distinction, but let me clarify the nature of the distinction. I am not arguing that certain commands are abiding (instructions to wives) while others have become obsolete

24. I. Howard Marshall, "Mutual Love and Submission in Marriage: Colossians 3:18–19 and Ephesians 5:21–33," in *Discovering Biblical Equality: Complementarity without Hierarchy*, eds. Ronald W. Pierce and Rebecca Merrill Groothuis (Downers Grove, IL: IVP, 2004): 187–88.

25. Ibid., 188. He cites Peter T. O'Brien, *Colossians, Philemon*, WBC, vol. 44 (Waco, TX: Word Books, 1982), 224; idem, *Letter to the Ephesians*, PNTC (Grand Rapids: Eerdmans, 1999), 440–41. Marshall criticizes O'Brien for not giving any evidence for assuming that the reference to "children" is probably young children rather than grown children. In the latter citation, O'Brien writes, "The term 'children' primarily denotes relationship rather than age, and could on occasion include adult sons and daughters, who were expected to honour their parents, especially fathers, who could maintain authority in the family even until death. Here the text has in view children who are in the process of learning and growing up (cf. v. 4)." I believe the reference to Eph. 6:4 ("bring them up") is sufficient evidence to suggest that adult children are not in view here. See also Eduard Lohse, *Colossians and Philemon*, Hermeneia, trans. William R. Poehlmann and Robert J. Karris (Philadelphia: Fortress Press, 1971), 158–59n33. He gives evidence that *teknon* can refer to a grown child, but then says, "The reference here, however, is surely to children who are growing up and still subject to their parents; cf. Eph. 6:4."

26. Marshall, "Mutual Love," 188.

27. We should not overlook the fact that in Eph. 6:2–3, Paul grounds the command to children by quoting the fifth commandment from Ex. 20:12. Paul was not merely accommodating a cultural custom, but was upholding God's intention for family relationships.

(instructions to slaves). The wife-husband section and the slave-master section are *both* still applicable. In the commands to slaves and masters we can find principles that apply to employees and employers.[28] Thus, I would say that these injunctions still have application for our lives, but they cannot be read as a basis for the institution of slavery. And this is the difference between the two sets of commands. We find a weighty basis for the institution of marriage as God designed it, but there is no support for the institution of slavery. In this way the abiding relevance of the entirety of the Household Codes is affirmed. While there are surely elements that reflect first-century Greco-Roman culture, there are also principles that are to be upheld and obeyed by God's people regardless of time or place.

The debate, then, is not centered on whether or not the Household Codes must be taken as a unit. We must examine each relationship that is addressed and determine the nature of the commands. My aim in the previous chapters, and in this chapter's summary, has been to show that there are fundamental differences between the ground clauses related to gender roles and the ground clauses related to slaves. In the next chapters I will address several pertinent hermeneutical questions.

28. This is a debated point. Francis Foulkes, *Ephesians*, TNTC (Grand Rapids: Eerdmans, 1989), 173: "But although the numerous slaves who had come into the Christian fold were in the apostle's mind as he wrote these words, the principles of the whole section apply to employees and employers in every age, whether in the home, in business, or in the state." On the other end of the spectrum, Dunn writes, "But such rules can no more directly be transferred to the different circumstances of today than can the rules, say, of Susannah Wesley (mother of John and Charles Wesley) for bringing up children. No more can we read Paul's counsel to Christian slaves as a manual for shopfloor ethics" ("The Household Rules," 62). I agree with the balanced assessment of Harold W. Hoehner, *Ephesians: An Exegetical Commentary* (Grand Rapids: Baker Academic, 2002), 816: "The application of this passage to contemporary times must be done with caution. Paul was writing specifically for a society where slavery was a legal institution. However, there are certainly some principles from the passage that can be applied to employee/employer relationships in the present time."

5

Hermeneutical Considerations: Part 1

This chapter and the next will deal with several hermeneutical questions related to slavery and the issue of women's roles. The focus will be on William Webb's criteria that he presents in *Slaves, Women, and Homosexuals.*[1] The first section of this chapter will address more fully the issue of theological analogy. The second section will discuss two of Webb's criteria that are closely related: preliminary movement and seed ideas. The last section will deal with purpose/intent statements. The next chapter will include a study of four additional issues that are even more pivotal in the discussion: basis in original creation, primogeniture, specific instructions versus general principles, and the relationship between creation and redemption.

Theological Analogy

Webb writes, "A component of a text may be transcultural if its basis is rooted in the character of God or Christ through theological analogy."[2] He considers this criterion inconclusive, and seeks to demonstrate this by providing examples of theological analogy, only some

1. William J. Webb, *Slaves, Women, and Homosexuals: Exploring the Hermeneutics of Cultural Analysis* (Downers Grove, IL: IVP, 2001).
2. Ibid., 185.

of which support transcultural commands. He first cites verses that command love, holiness, and forgiveness, and relate those commands to God's love, holiness, and forgiveness.[3] Webb then states, "Assuming that the call for Christian love, holiness and forgiveness is transcultural in nature (although I have not made the case here), these examples show that theological analogy often accompanies instructions with a transcultural status."[4]

The next four examples are intended to show that this is not always the case. He deals with slavery, citing Ephesians 6:5–9, Colossians 3:22–4:1, and 1 Peter 2:18–25, discussing the fact that slavery proponents appealed to theological and Christological analogies as evidence that slavery should be an abiding practice. Webb concludes, "However, if slavery should be assessed as cultural within Scripture (a position developed above), then obviously theological analogy at times accompanies biblical instructions with a dominant cultural component."[5] Similarly, proponents of monarchy have pointed to theological analogies to support their position, says Webb. "After all, God and Christ are frequently presented as ruling kings (e.g., 1 Tim. 6:15; Rev. 17:14; 19:16). Along with the biblical instructions to submit to the king, it was argued that only a monarchy properly represented God's sovereign reign over the earth."[6]

Next, Webb cites primogeniture as another cultural component of the Bible that is connected to theological analogies. "For instance, the exalted status of Christ is frequently patterned around the special status given to the firstborn."[7] Webb's last example is right-handedness, which he examined briefly earlier in the book in his section on "breakouts."[8] There he observes several texts that reflect the ancient Near Eastern assumption that right-handedness is superior to left-handedness (Gen. 48:18; 1 Chron. 6:39; Ex. 15:6, 12; Ps. 110:1; cf. Matt. 22:44). Then he cites

3. Ibid., 185–86. He quotes or references the following verses: "Beloved, if God so loved us, we also ought to love one another" (1 John 4:11; cf. John 15:12). "You shall be holy, for I am holy" (1 Peter 1:16; cf. Lev. 11:44–45; 19:2; 20:7). "Be kind to one another, tenderhearted, forgiving one another, as God in Christ forgave you" (Eph. 4:32).

4. Ibid., 186.

5. Ibid.

6. Ibid. He refers to the debates over monarchy in several places (107, 153, 186–87, 203), but he does not document any sources.

7. Ibid., 187. He cites Col. 1:15–18; Rom. 8:29; Heb. 1:6; cf. Ps. 89:27; Ex. 13:1–16. I will discuss primogeniture fully in the next chapter.

8. Ibid., 92–93.

Judges 3:12–30 (cf. 20:16) in which left-handedness breaks out of the cultural right-handed paradigm.

In his summary of these examples of theological analogy, Webb develops a "double-sided guiding principle":

> To the extent that the theological analogy is direct and in a sense "literal" in its overlap of the human and divine, it is more likely to endorse transcultural concepts. In a (more) "literal" sense God *is* a lover, a forgiver and one who is holy. On the other hand, to the extent that the theological analogy is less direct and less literal, it is more prone to reflect cultural concepts. God is *not* literally a slave, a monarch, a firstborn or a right-handed individual (italics original).[9]

So Webb's inference from these examples is that the degree of overlap will determine whether the theological analogy is supporting something that is transcultural. He then makes a statement that is very important for this discussion, and it contains a significant and valid point: "When the biblical text addresses human sociological structures, there is a significant possibility that the theological analogy is intended to motivate behavior within existing structures without necessarily endorsing the structures themselves as transcultural."[10]

This is helpful, because it is exactly what we see happening in the slavery passages. The theological analogies are used to motivate the behavior of those who are being persecuted or afflicted in some way, but in no way is there an endorsement of the structures that are the means of affliction. This is seen clearly in 1 Peter, as I discussed in chapter 2.[11] In 1 Peter 3 there is a theological analogy related to how believers should respond to suffering and persecution. In a way similar to the instructions to slaves, suffering Christians are told, "But even if you should suffer for righteousness' sake, you will be blessed" (v. 14). Peter instructs, "in your hearts honor Christ the Lord as holy" and make your defense "with gentleness and respect, having a good conscience" (vv. 15–16). Also similar to the commands to slaves, he says, "For it is better to suffer for doing good, if that should be God's will, than for doing evil" (v. 17). In verse 18 Peter points to the example of Christ's suffering, "For Christ also suffered

9. Ibid., 187.
10. Ibid.
11. See section on "Ground for Obedience" in chapter 2.

once for sins." As I pointed out in chapter 2, we certainly would not use this theological analogy to argue that Peter is in any way endorsing the persecution or slandering of Christians. Similarly, the same analogy used in 1 Peter 2 should not be read as an endorsement of slavery. As Webb says, it is meant to motivate behavior, not support a structure of society.

The crucial question, then, is whether Webb's statement applies to the structure of male headship. Is it legitimate to conclude, as we have done with the slavery issue in 1 Peter, that the theological analogies in Ephesians 5 and 1 Corinthians 11 are used merely to motivate behavior without endorsing male headship?[12] Arguing against this conclusion are some important differences between what we have observed in 1 Peter and the theological analogies of Ephesians 5 and 1 Corinthians 11—differences that are overlooked by Webb. I have noted some of these differences in my exegesis of Ephesians 5 and 1 Corinthians 11 in chapter 3, namely that these two passages are more than analogies. They are not just making a comparison, but describing significant aspects of God's nature that are to serve as a pattern for male-female relationships. Below I will examine some additional key differences between the examples that Webb provides.

After providing the "neutral" examples of theological analogy, Webb turns to the women's passages that contain a theological analogy. The problem with his reasoning here is that he too quickly identifies Ephesians 5 and 1 Corinthians 11 with the examples he has given of slavery, monarchy, primogeniture, and right-handedness. There may be some general similarities in that a correlation is made between the human realm and the divine realm. But this generalized similarity is not strong enough to justify Webb's conclusions. This brings to light a difficulty in this discussion, which is the vagueness of what Webb is calling "theological analogy." Based on his examples, he is using this phrase to refer to a very broad category. It may still be legitimate to conclude that all of these passages are using some kind of theological analogy, generally speaking. What is illegitimate, though, is to draw a specific conclusion from such general comparisons. Here is Webb's conclusion:

12. Webb says, "While the head analogy may contain elements of authority and rightful ownership of glory, this does not mean that it has or should have transcultural implications for gender relationships. The theological analogy may simply have been applied to an existing cultural form in order to motivate behavior within that form," *Slaves, Women, and Homosexuals*, 188.

> The texts of Ephesians 5 and 1 Corinthians 11 fall into the second set of examples illustrated in the neutral section above. Surely, if we can learn anything from the slavery and monarchy debates of the past (not to mention the other examples cited above), it would be that theological analogy can just as easily append cultural-component injunctions in Scripture as it can transcultural instructions.[13]

Again, it is a valid point that "theological analogy [according to Webb's examples] can just as easily append cultural-component injunctions in Scripture as it can transcultural instructions." Webb has made some helpful observations in establishing this point. However, what he has not established is the conclusion that Ephesians 5 and 1 Corinthians 11 are, in fact, in the category of culturally bound instructions. This conclusion is a leap of logic that is not grounded in any compelling observations from the texts themselves.

Based on Webb's "double-sided guiding principle" that he developed from the various examples, we must infer that the general connection he is seeing between male headship, slavery, monarchy, primogeniture, and right-handedness is that they are all "less direct and less literal" than the analogies connected to love, holiness, and forgiveness.[14] But the vagueness of these assertions is seen in the fact that I could just as easily make a case for the opposite point. It could be argued that Christ's headship over the church is analogous to the husband's headship over his wife in a direct and literal way such that male headship is to emulate Christ's headship just as our love, holiness, and forgiveness is to emulate God's love, holiness, and forgiveness. The point is that determining whether an analogy is more or less literal is a subjective endeavor. We may all agree that in "a (more) 'literal' sense God *is* a lover, a forgiver and one who is holy," while he "is *not* literally a slave, a monarch, a firstborn or a right-handed individual."[15] But when it comes to the debated question of male headship, Webb fails to show us why this belongs in the latter category. He has not established his point from his examples.

An additional unfounded assertion is that Paul could have used the Christological analogy of Ephesians 5 in an egalitarian culture and

13. Ibid.
14. Ibid., 187.
15. Ibid.

"reapplied it to an egalitarian relationship between husband and wife."[16] In this case, Paul would have encouraged not only the husband, but also the wife, to sacrificially love and serve each other as Christ did for the church. Webb cites Philippians 2:1–11 as an example of Paul applying "the same servant Christology to mutual submission contexts that he does to unilateral submission situations."[17] This passage would certainly fit into Webb's category of theological analogy. It is very similar, in fact, to the examples of love, holiness, and forgiveness that Webb has cited. Here Christians are enjoined to be humble as Christ is humble. But it seems to be a stretch to call this a mutual submission text when the word "submission" is not used. The instruction concerns humility, not submission. Of course, there are similarities and overlap between the two, but they are not the same. Therefore, we cannot label Philippians 2:1–11 a mutual submission text, and Webb's assumption that Paul could have reapplied the Christological analogy of Ephesians 5 to an egalitarian relationship is left without any support or parallel.

Webb also discusses theological analogy in the book of Hosea. He quotes from Hosea 2:3 in this way: "I [Hosea] will strip her [Gomer] naked and make her as bare as on the day she was born."[18] Webb acknowledges that it would be easy to think of this analogy purely in terms of divine judgment. But he rightly observes that "the text is not really talking about a judge. The main actor is a husband, a husband who disciplines his wife for her promiscuity."[19] Then he concludes, "The dilemma with theological analogy should be apparent. We cannot use the theological analogy in Ephesians 5 to endorse that material as completely transcultural without doing the same in Hosea 2."[20]

Let us first examine the analogy in Hosea 2. Throughout chapters 1–3, the relationship between Hosea and Gomer provides a vivid illustration of Yahweh's relationship to Israel. At certain points Hosea and Gomer are primarily in view, for instance when personal details are given concerning their relationship and their children. But at other points the

16. Ibid., 188.

17. Ibid., 189. The Scripture reference is in the footnote.

18. Ibid.

19. Ibid., 190. See A. A. Macintosh, *A Critical and Exegetical Commentary on Hosea*, ICC (Edinburgh: T & T Clark, 1997), 41: "In these circumstances the scene which Hosea envisages is that of a family quarrel rather than that of a law court." For the idea that the law court is in view, see Hans Walter Wolff, *Hosea*, Hermeneia (Philadelphia: Fortress Press, 1974), 33.

20. Webb, *Slaves, Women, and Homosexuals*, 190.

husband-wife relationship is used mainly as a parable of Yahweh and Israel. Chapter 2 seems to fall into the latter category. A. A. Macintosh observes that "[chapter 2] contains material largely concerned with the relationship of Yahweh and Israel but explained by the ubiquitous parable of a man's love for his unfaithful wife. Here there is not explicit personal testimony; rather, appeal is made by the use of the parable to the feelings of those who receive the words."[21] So in the imagery of the marriage relationship, Israel is being warned by God to flee from her idolatrous ways.

The reference in verse 3 to stripping the wife naked is curious. As Webb points out, this is hard to grasp for the modern reader, for it seems to be an inappropriate and demeaning punishment. Scholars have suggested that this practice was commonly connected with divorce or as a punishment for unfaithfulness. But Duane Garrett does not find these interpretations compelling, and sees in this passage (along with similar statements in Jer. 13:22–27; Ezek. 16:37–39; Nah. 3:4–5) the threat of exile.[22] He observes that in Hosea 2:10 and Ezekiel 16:37–39 the husband strips his wife *in the presence of her lovers*. This is something that "no injured husband would do," Garrett says. "Clearly, the imagery has moved out of the realm of actual Israelite customs for dealing with an adulteress and into an artificial, parabolic world in which metaphors are molded to suit the prophet's message. The 'lovers' are the foreign nations and their gods, and the exposure of the woman is the abandonment of Israel to foreign domination."[23] He concludes, "We have no grounds for asserting that Hosea cast Gomer naked out of his house, much less that he called in her former clients and stripped her in their presence. . . . Unlike 1:2–3 or 1:8, 2:3 is not autobiographical; its real focus is the exile and devastation that is ahead for the nation."[24]

21. Macintosh, *Hosea*, 114. See also Gary V. Smith, *Hosea, Amos, Micah*, NIVAC (Grand Rapids: Zondervan, 2001), 58: "Chapter 2 centers on reflections concerning the problems described in chapter 1, though they focus more on the relationship between God and Israel rather than on Hosea and Gomer."

22. Duane A. Garrett, *Hosea, Joel*, NAC, 19A (Nashville: Broadman & Holman, 1997), 78: "Behind the metaphor of nakedness in the prophets is the threat that the people will go into exile, and ancient art work routinely portrays exiles naked. Thus the nakedness of the woman in these passages probably has more to do with the realities of conquest in the ancient world than with their divorce laws."

23. Ibid.

24. Ibid., 78–79.

These observations call into question the claim that Hosea 2 contains a theological analogy comparable to Ephesians 5. The statements in Hosea 2 are directed primarily toward the nation of Israel. The focus is not on Hosea and Gomer, and hence it should not be understood as conveying what Hosea literally did to Gomer. Rather, it describes a spiritual reality in human terms. The stripping of Gomer functions as a metaphor of Yahweh's disciplinary action against Israel.

There are two significant differences between Hosea 2 and Ephesians 5 that undermine the parallel Webb seeks to establish. First, it is crucial to recognize that the book of Hosea contains no commands for husbands to strip their wives if they commit adultery. The passage is descriptive (and metaphorical), not prescriptive. This is also the case in the examples of slavery, monarchy, primogeniture, and right-handedness, for the Bible does not contain explicit commands for any of these practices.[25] They are present as a piece of the culture in which the Bible was written, and they are used metaphorically to describe spiritual realities. But we do not encounter instructions to perpetuate these structures or customs. On the other hand, Ephesians 5 gives clear and specific commands to wives and husbands. This text *is* prescriptive, and thus establishes a significant difference from Hosea 2 and from many other analogies that describe rather than prescribe.[26]

Second, Hosea 2 describes God's relationship to Israel in terms of a human marriage, which is very different from Ephesians 5 where human marriage is described in terms of Christ's relationship to the church. In the first case, the analogy is working from the human realm to the divine realm, whereas in the second case the analogy works from the divine realm

25. As I have argued, agreeing with Webb, these analogies are used to "motivate behavior within existing structures without necessarily endorsing the structures themselves as transcultural" (*Slaves, Women, and Homosexuals*, 187). See also Wayne Grudem, "Should We Move Beyond the New Testament to a Better Ethic? An Analysis of William J. Webb, *Slaves, Women, and Homosexuals: Exploring the Hermeneutics of Cultural Analysis*," *JETS* 47 (2004): 331.

26. I am aware that commands are given to slaves, and the debated point, of course, is whether or not those commands are of the same nature as the commands to women. But I am thinking here mainly of the ways in which slavery, monarchy, primogeniture, and right-handedness are used to describe spiritual realities. Webb makes reference to the fact that "God is 'lord' or 'master' in heaven who directs the affairs of his people, like an earthly master would govern his slaves." Similarly with monarchy, "God and Christ are frequently presented as ruling kings." In terms of primogeniture, "the exalted status of Christ is frequently patterned around the special status given to the firstborn." And finally, "a right-handed analogy was used to depict the strength of God's actions and of Christ's enthronement" (Webb, *Slaves, Women, and Homosexuals*, 186–87).

to the human realm. Hence, Hosea 2 does not formally match Webb's description of a theological analogy. The statement of this criterion is, "A component of a text may be transcultural if its basis is rooted in the character of God or Christ through theological analogy."[27] But in Hosea 2:3 there is nothing rooted in the character of God or Christ. The analogy is working in the opposite direction, and would more properly be labeled an *anthropo*logical analogy. A human relationship is used as a metaphor to describe God's relationship with His people. This is an *anthropo*logical analogy, whereas Ephesians 5 is a *Christ*ological analogy—Christ's relationship to the church is given as the pattern to be emulated in human marriage. This point applies to the other examples as well. When metaphors of slavery, monarchy, primogeniture, or right-handedness are used to describe God or Christ, it is a human illustration that is used to describe a divine characteristic. An element from the culture is being used to describe God or Christ, whereas in Ephesians 5 and 1 Corinthians 11 the nature of God and Christ is used to demonstrate the pattern for male-female roles. The two sets of analogies are functioning in markedly different ways.

Therefore, we can deduce a clearer principle from these examples. In the case of anthropological analogies, we should not draw from them a necessary endorsement of the human institution or custom that is being used. The divine side of the analogy certainly remains true, but that does not mean the earthly illustration is necessarily intended to be transcultural. Especially since these earthly conditions are not prescribed, we have no good reason to interpret the analogies as such. So when we read that God is "King of kings and Lord of lords" (1 Tim. 6:15; see also Rev. 17:14; 19:16, speaking of Christ), we are given a helpful illustration of God's sovereign power and authority. But we would not be justified in using that illustration to argue in favor of a monarchical form of government. Similarly, the statement that Jesus Christ sits at the right hand of the Father (Ps. 110:1; Matt. 22:44; 26:64) tells us something about the honor bestowed on the Son, but that cannot be taken to mean right-handedness is better than left-handedness.[28] Again, a cultural notion has been used to make a theological point. Thus Webb's principle should be modified by observing this critical distinction. When the analogy is working from the human realm to the divine realm, it is quite possible that the human

27. Ibid., 185.

28. Being left-handed myself, I say this emphatically!

illustration is cultural. However, when a divine characteristic is given as a pattern to emulate, then the presence of an analogy gives no basis for concluding that it is cultural.

The last point I want to make about theological analogy is simply to reiterate the unique nature of Ephesians 5 and 1 Corinthians 11.[29] In the other examples given by Webb, some kind of comparison is made for the purpose of describing a spiritual reality or motivating behavior within a cultural structure. But in 1 Corinthians 11 and Ephesians 5, Paul is doing more than just making a comparison. In 1 Corinthians 11:3 he demonstrates the pattern of authority that exists in three important relationships—Christ's headship over man, a husband's headship over his wife, and God's headship over Christ. Thus, a connection is made between the authority structure within the Godhead and the authority structure within marriage. And in Ephesians 5 Paul quotes Genesis 2:24 not merely in reference to human marriage, but as the mystery of Christ's union with the church. In neither passage is he simply drawing on an abstract reality in order to illustrate how he thinks husbands and wives should relate to one another. He is not just saying that one thing is like another. It is deeper than that. These passages are telling us something about how God designed the universe. The other examples of theological analogy, whatever terminology we use, do not provide a sufficient parallel to these passages dealing with male-female roles.[30]

I still agree with the statement that theological analogy is an inconclusive criterion by which to determine whether a passage is transcultural. I appreciate Webb's conclusion that theological analogies may very well appear in texts that motivate behavior but do not endorse a cultural structure. We part ways, however, concerning the question of whether this is the case in Ephesians 5 and 1 Corinthians 11. Each text must be examined individually, and when this is done we discover some compelling reasons to differentiate these two texts from the others.

Preliminary Movement and Seed Ideas

This section will interact with the first two criteria Webb presents in his book. They are closely related, and they are both included in his

29. For my exegesis on these passages, see chapter 3.
30. See Grudem, "Should We Move Beyond the New Testament Ethic," 332, 340.

chapter titled, "Persuasive Criteria." Prior to this chapter, Webb explains that his categorization of persuasive, moderately persuasive, and inconclusive criteria is based on the outcome of each criterion as it relates to the issue of women's roles.[31] His persuasive criteria, then, are considered pivotal in this debate, and he begins with the two I am going to address here: preliminary movement and seed ideas.

Preliminary Movement

With this criterion Webb analyzes the commands given to slaves and to women[32] *as they compare to the norms of the culture in which they were given*. Where the biblical commands are different from the cultural norms, there is "movement." The important question, then, is whether this should be considered "absolute movement," meaning the biblical commands portray how things are supposed to be, or "preliminary movement," meaning "the biblical author pushed society as far as it could go at that time without creating more damage than good; however, it can and should ultimately go further."[33] Within the discussion of this criterion, Webb does not give a final answer as to how this question should be answered. It is not his intention to do so. Rather, he merely intends to *raise* this question of whether the cultural movement we see in Scripture should be viewed as absolute or preliminary.[34]

Regarding slavery, he mentions several ways in which the biblical commands are kinder and less restrictive than the surrounding culture. Among many Old Testament examples, he includes the New Testament instructions to masters, enjoining them to treat their slaves well (Col. 4:1; Eph. 6:9). He also mentions the Bible's condemnation of slave trading, and he cites 1 Timothy 1:10 in a footnote.[35]

Regarding women, he discusses several Old Testament instructions that are much more humane than the norms in the ancient Near East. Moving to the New Testament, he observes "canonical movement" on the issue of divorce. As opposed to the Old Testament, where only men initiate divorce, the New Testament "extends the right of initiating divorce to

31. Webb, *Slaves, Women, and Homosexuals*, 68–69.

32. The third issue he addresses, as the title indicates, is homosexuality. But I am limiting this project to the commands given to slaves and women.

33. Webb, *Slaves, Women, and Homosexuals*, 73.

34. Ibid., 83.

35. Ibid., 75. The verse condemns "enslavers." See chapter 2 for a brief discussion of the verse.

women," citing in the footnote Mark 10:12 and 1 Corinthians 7:10–16.[36] He also refers to the Household Codes and the "softening of the husband side" of these codes. While wives are commanded to submit, husbands are not commanded to "rule" or "lead," but rather to "love." "Paul assumes the status quo for women; however, he pushes the boundaries for men with the direction of his command."[37]

In his summary of this criterion, Webb says that "the women texts, like the slavery texts, are generally 'less restrictive' or 'softening' relative to the broader culture."[38] This is a valid observation. In both cases, there is a welcomed "softening" of these relationships as compared with the original culture. Webb does not try to make too much of this point, which is fitting. Therefore, the question remains as to whether this movement is absolute or preliminary, so the discussion continues on to seed ideas.

Seed Ideas

Webb describes seed ideas as texts that "suggest and encourage further movement on a particular subject."[39] The question is whether Webb can demonstrate that the texts he adduces, in fact, do so. A more specific question arises as well, namely, Webb's precise meaning of "further movement." Webb's idea of movement, as suggested by the quotations in the last section, presupposes that an ultimate ethic exists that is *beyond* what the New Testament presents. He writes of redemptive movement earlier in the book, saying, "The interpreter extrapolates the biblical movement toward a more just, more equitable and more loving form. If a better ethic than the one expressed in the isolated words of the text is possible, and the biblical and canonical spirit is headed in that direction, then that is where one ultimately wants to end up."[40]

The question, though, is whether one needs to *move beyond* the ethic of the New Testament. We need not (indeed, we must not) move beyond the final and authoritative instructions of God's Word. To use Webb's terminology, what we see in the New Testament represents "absolute movement" rather than "preliminary movement." First, as I tried to show in

36. Webb, *Slaves, Women, and Homosexuals*, 78.
37. Ibid., 80.
38. Ibid., 83.
39. Ibid.
40. Ibid., 36.

chapter 2, the NT does not endorse slavery. It is not as though we need to find a way to move beyond the NT endorsement of slavery, because that endorsement does not exist. And while we would like the NT to explicitly condemn slavery, there are some reasonable explanations for why we do not find this.[41]

Second, I agree with the words of F. F. Bruce, which Webb cites in his section on the seed ideas related to slavery, that Paul's letter to Philemon brings "us into an atmosphere in which the institution could only wilt and die."[42] This is the way the ethic of the NT has worked itself out over the centuries. It is certainly a great disappointment that it took such a long time before societies began to abolish slavery. But we must affirm that human depravity is the reason for this, not a failure to see beyond the ethic of the NT. There is nothing deficient in the Bible's ethic, but there are great deficiencies in the way we apply that ethic in our own lives. So it was not a matter of finding an ultimate social ethic, but rather the NT ethic had to pervade the consciousness of a society such that it finally dismantled the institution of slavery.

I also resonate with Webb's quotation of Craig Blomberg, commenting on 1 Corinthians 7:21, "But Paul *sowed the seeds* for a revolutionary alternative in Christ which in time could only but threaten social institutions of oppression" (emphasis added).[43] Thus, we can speak of "seed ideas" without implying that an ethic beyond that of the NT is needed. The statements about slavery to which Webb points (1 Cor. 7:21 and Philem. 15–16; also the statements of unity in 1 Cor. 12:13; Gal. 3:28; Col. 3:11) certainly point beyond slavery, but they do not point beyond the ethic of the NT. They *constitute* the ethic of the NT, and as that ethic has impacted individuals, and in turn cultures, there have been major changes regarding slavery.

But Webb sees in these verses a movement toward a superior *ethic*, and he compares the movement regarding slavery with the movement

41. See my discussion in chapter 2 under the heading, "Why Does the New Testament Not Condemn the Institution of Slavery?"

42. F. F. Bruce, *Paul: Apostle of the Heart Set Free* (Grand Rapids: Eerdmans, 1977), 401.

43. Craig Blomberg, *1 Corinthians*, NIVAC (Grand Rapids: Zondervan, 1994), 148. Blomberg goes on to make a statement that addresses the question of why the NT doesn't condemn slavery: "At the most fundamental level, however, Scripture's cautious approach stems from the fact that spiritual rather than physical freedom is what ultimately determines how a person will live in the age to come, a life that makes the circumstances of this age pale into insignificance by comparison (2 Cor. 4:17; Rom. 8:18)."

regarding patriarchy. In an earlier chapter, he exhorts complementarians to recognize that "as with slavery, the patriarchy found within the Bible does not offer us an ultimate social ethic."[44] In the section on seed ideas pertaining to the issue of women's roles, Webb first points to the much-debated verse, Galatians 3:28. Is this verse referring solely to spiritual equality (the complementarian position), or are there significant social ramifications as well (the egalitarian position)? This is essentially how Webb frames the question.[45]

Richard Hove, a complementarian, demonstrates that the question may not be this simple, for he sees some significant social implications in this verse, while denying that those social implications are at odds with other NT statements (e.g., 1 Tim. 2; 1 Cor. 11; 14; Eph. 5; 1 Peter 3). He draws points of application from three principles. "First, all God's people are in Christ. Second, all God's people, by virtue of being in Christ, are one. Third, the great mercies and blessing of God are given to all God's people, without distinction, regardless of one's sex, race, or social/financial background."[46] These profound truths portrayed in the statement of Galatians 3:28 will play themselves out in many practical ways in the Christian community. For instance, there should be no boasting or feelings of superiority over others. There ought to be a tangible sense of unity in the body of believers, and therefore self-centeredness, racism, and sexism must all be combated. Nobody should feel like an outcast in the church.[47] We must embrace the diversity and universality of God's mission, "that people from all nations and walks of life comprise God's people."[48] There are many ways in which Galatians 3:28 has social implications for the church, and complementarians do not deny this.[49] The precise difference in viewpoint, then, relates to the nature and extent of the social implications.

As Webb proceeds in his discussion of Galatians 3:28, he contrasts Paul's urgency regarding the Jew-Gentile component with the lack of urgency regarding the slave-master and male-female components of the

44. Webb, *Slaves, Women, and Homosexuals*, 48.

45. Ibid., 84–85.

46. Richard Hove, *Equality in Christ? Galatians 3:28 and the Gender Dispute* (Wheaton, IL: Crossway, 1999), 121.

47. Ibid., 122–23.

48. Ibid., 123.

49. Ibid., 103. Hove says, "Complementarians agree with egalitarians that there are social implications for Galatians 3:28, but they have a different conception of what these social changes might look like."

verse. He says, "If one compares the inertia within the early church for Gentile equality to the pressure for equality in the cases of slavery and females, it would be like placing Niagara Falls next to a dripping tap."[50] This is true, but we must question Webb's explanation of why this is. He suggests pragmatic reasons. On the one hand, "Without [ethnic equality], there would probably be no universal gospel today." On the other hand, "for Paul to press for social implications in the slave and the female categories might have been detrimental."[51] There may be some truth in these statements. However, there was something else that contributed to the urgency of the Jew-Gentile issue. For example, when Paul confronted Peter in Galatians 2:11–14, his concern was that "their conduct was not in step with the truth of the gospel" (v. 14). In other words, it was a *theological* issue, not just a matter of expediency.[52] The inclusion of the Gentiles was bound up with the gospel, and therefore it was not simply a matter of social ethics. On the other hand, the institution of slavery was a cultural reality that the NT transformed from the inside out rather than attempting a social revolution. And the statement concerning male and female is addressed clearly and more fully in other places, in ways that do not contradict the unity proclaimed here.

The differences between the three categories listed in Galatians 3:28 cannot be explained simply in pragmatic terms. There are differences, indeed, but not because Paul was hesitant to confront his culture. Part of the problem with Webb's construction, along with other egalitarians, is that he assumes Galatians 3:28 is about *equality in roles*, when it is better understood to be mainly a statement concerning *unity*. Webb says, "One must now ask if the 'in Christ' formula should carry social implications for the equality of women. It certainly did in Paul's day for Gentiles. And, it did over the course of church history for slaves. Why should it not today for females?"[53] This verse could very well have reference to the *equality* of these categories of individuals, and certainly we affirm that men and

50. Webb, *Slaves, Women, and Homosexuals*, 86.

51. Ibid.

52. Similarly, Paul's opposition to circumcision was theological rather than pragmatic. See Thomas R. Schreiner, *Paul, Apostle of God's Glory in Christ: A Pauline Theology* (Downers Grove, IL: IVP, 2001), 54: "Paul did not resist the imposition of circumcision on Gentiles first and foremost because it would have hindered his mission; he resisted it because it was contrary to 'the truth of the gospel' (Gal. 2:5). Nor did Paul think avoiding circumcision made life easier, for by rejecting circumcision he exposed himself to persecution (Gal. 5:11; 6:17)."

53. Webb, *Slaves, Women, and Homosexuals*, 87.

women are equals. However, as Hove argues, the main thrust of the context is *unity*. He demonstrates that the statement "you are all *one* in Christ Jesus" cannot be taken to mean "you are all *equal* in Christ Jesus."[54] He studies other places where the phrase occurs and finds that "in fact, 'you are all one' is used of *diverse* objects to denote one element they share in common; it is not used of similar objects to denote that they are the same (italics original)."[55] Hence, Galatians 3:28 cannot be taken as a statement that male and female are equal in an unqualified sense. But Webb's argument is not this bold. He rather sees Galatians 3:28 as one piece of the puzzle—one (significant) verse that points us in a certain direction as it is pieced together with other indicators of redemptive movement.

Still, the argument is suspect, for it assumes a fundamental similarity between slavery and male headship. Webb fails to see some important differences between the categories mentioned in the verse. The following quotation from Ronald Fung is helpful in this regard.

> It appears that the three categories differ in nature, and that accordingly the social implementations for them are not the same. Whereas slavery, as a social institution created by sinful men, can and should be abolished, and the Jew/Gentile distinction, which retains its validity as a purely ethnic reality, has been transcended through the reconciliation accomplished by Christ (Eph. 2:14–16), the male/female distinction, unlike the other two, has its roots in creation itself and continues to have significance in the realm of redemption.[56]

This supports Hove's point that the *oneness* of this verse cannot mean *equal in every respect*. Certainly men and women are "one in Christ Jesus," but we cannot use that statement to cancel out other instructions that are rooted in creation. The oneness we share in Christ is compatible with the

54. Hove, *Equality in Christ?*, 69–76, 107–9.

55. Ibid., 108. Cf. Mark 10:8; John 10:30; Rom. 12:5; 1 Cor. 3:8, among others, cited by Hove, *Equality in Christ?*, 73–74, 108.

56. Ronald Y. K. Fung, "Ministry in the New Testament," in *The Church in the Bible and the World: An International Study*, ed. D. A. Carson (Grand Rapids: Baker, 1987), 184. He also states elsewhere, "It seems precarious to appeal to this verse in support of any view of the role of women in the Church, for two reasons: (a) Paul's statement is not concerned with the role relationships of men and women within the Body of Christ but rather with their common initiation into it through (faith and) baptism; (b) the male/female distinction, unlike the other two, has its roots in creation, so that the parallelism between the male/female pair and the other pairs may not be unduly pressed" (Ronald Y. K. Fung, *The Epistle to the Galatians*, NICNT [Grand Rapids: Eerdmans, 1988], 176n44).

distinct roles God has assigned to men and women; it is not necessary to set *oneness* and *role distinctions* at odds with one another.

The amazing truth of this verse should be neither minimized nor overstated. Complementarians are accused of the former, and egalitarians of the latter. We should recognize the new age that has dawned by virtue of Christ's work. In him these earthly distinctions are no longer barriers. Hove summarizes, "Galatians 3:28 definitely describes a new, important, and exciting change. It is not difficult to imagine Paul's enthusiasm as he proclaimed the truths of Galatians 3:26–29: You are *all* sons of God, you have *all* put on Christ, you are *all* fully heirs, you *all* have God's Spirit and call out *Abba*, Father."[57] On the other hand, it is not legitimate to use this verse to erase gender role distinctions that are established in other texts and rooted in creation.

The other verses that Webb addresses in this section are 1 Corinthians 11:11–12, which he analyzes again in an appendix and at much greater length in his article, "Balancing Paul's Original-Creation and Pro-Creation Arguments: 1 Corinthians 11:11–12 in Light of Modern Embryology."[58] I dealt with these verses in chapter 3, but here I want to probe further into the hermeneutical questions that are involved. Specifically, we must consider Webb's suggestion that if Paul's embryology was limited by his culture, then his understanding of gender relationships must have been similarly limited.

Webb points out that in 1 Corinthians 11:11–12, Paul describes woman as coming "from" man, while man is "through" woman. In Webb's mind, the choice of prepositions here conveys an ancient understanding of embryology, that women were "reproductive gardens." The common understanding was that the male provided the seed, while the woman provided the garden in which the seed grew. I quoted in chapter 3 from Judith Gundry-Volf, who offers a simpler and more reasonable explanation for the prepositions we find in these verses.[59] But what if Paul's statement in 1 Corinthians 11:11–12 really reflects his understanding of embryology? It is possible that his wording is connected to the idea that women are "reproductive gardens." Man is not born "from" woman, in Paul's

57. Hove, *Equality in Christ?*, 107.

58. William Webb, "Balancing Paul's Original-Creation and Pro-Creation Arguments: 1 Corinthians 11:11–12 in Light of Modern Embryology," *WTJ* 66 (2004): 275–89.

59. See the section on "References to Creation: 1 Corinthians 11:2–16" in chapter 3.

perception of things, but only "through" woman. If this is the case, how does that affect the way we interpret this passage? We will come to this question in due course.

Webb states in Appendix D, "The idea of man coming 'through' woman appears to reflect the ancient view of women as reproductive gardens, contributing nothing more than a fertile environment to the birthing process. Surely his distinction of woman 'from' man and man 'through' woman is culture-bound: scientific developments since Paul's day have proven such."[60] In Webb's more detailed treatment of these matters in his journal article, he outlines three ancient views of embryology: the traditional one-seed theory, Aristotle's modified one-seed theory, and the two-seed theory.[61] The second and third views are increasingly "egalitarian," but Webb notes that they still include "minor aspects of distorted inequality and a deficient view of a mother's contribution to her offspring."[62]

He then goes on to discuss Paul's statement in 1 Corinthians 11:12, and he first admits, "The preposition *dia* by itself in 'man comes through (*dia*) woman' tells us nothing about what position Paul himself held."[63] But then he asserts, "However, it is reasonably certain that Paul was arguing from a 'minimalist' embryo contribution perspective in 1 Cor. 11:12."[64] It seems that Webb has not seriously considered any other explanations for these prepositions.[65] Nor does he cite anyone who has suggested that the *dia* in verse 12 is somehow portraying a particular view of embryology.[66]

Although it seems unlikely, it is possible that Webb is on to something here. Therefore, we come to the question of how this insight would affect our interpretation of the passage. Webb first posits a primary implication: "Paul, if he were alive today, would acknowledge the significance and weight of the female contribution within procreation."[67] This is based on the

60. Webb, *Slaves, Women, and Homosexuals*, 275.

61. Webb, "Balancing," 276–79.

62. Ibid., 279.

63. Ibid.

64. Ibid., 280.

65. He just says, "The prepositional change from *ek* to *dia* is probably not a mere stylistic variation" (ibid.).

66. Again, see my comments on "References to Creation: 1 Corinthians 11:2–16" in chapter 3, and especially the quotations from Judith M. Gundry-Volf, "Gender and Creation in 1 Corinthians 11:2–16: A Study in Paul's Theological Method," in *Evangelium, Schriftauslegung, Kirche: Festschrift für Peter Stuhlmacher zum 65. Geburtstag*, ed. Jostein Ådna, Scott Hafemann, and Otfried Hofius (Göttingen: Vandenhoeck & Ruprecht, 1997), 162–63.

67. Webb, "Balancing," 281.

Copernican revolution that has occurred in our understanding of human embryology.[68] He suggests, then, that the advances in our understanding of the woman's *ek* contribution, and not just her *dia* contribution, "begins to tip the scales toward a much greater sense of balance and equality in gender status than would ever have been realized in the first-century Corinthian context."[69] The verses (1 Cor. 11:11–12) already served to balance what Paul said previously (vv. 8–9), but even that was limited by first-century embryology. Now we understand that Paul, if writing today, could refer to man coming *ek* woman and not just *dia* woman. Hence we can see a greater significance in this verse as it modifies what the rest of the passage is communicating. This is the essence of Webb's argument.

Webb draws out some secondary implications. Three are stated. First, "one wonders if a mother's half-of-the-chromosome (*ek*) contribution to the whole child should count for something when compared to an only-the-rib (*ek*) contribution from Adam to Eve." Second, "one wonders if the repeated enactment of the 'creation pattern' in procreation should count for something when compared to the singular event of the garden." And third, "one wonders if the production of female offspring within procreation theology should count for something since Paul's ancient-world argument looks only at the production of males through females."[70] It is Webb's assertion that Paul's limited understanding of embryology, and the development to our modern understanding of embryology, should heighten the significance of the "seed idea" in 1 Corinthians 11:12. Indeed, it should dramatically soften the teaching of male headship in this passage and elsewhere.

In the conclusion of the article, Webb reiterates his thesis: "Paul's counterbalancing procreation argument must be given *much greater weight* in forging our contemporary application of gender relationships than was ever possible in Paul's day" (emphasis original).[71] If Webb is right that Paul's choice of prepositions in this verse represent his ancient view of embryology (I am not yet convinced of this), then it could be that the verse should be given *at least some extra weight* in the way we apply it today. Regardless of whether Paul's discussion here is tied to specific

68. Webb compares the advances in human embryology to the Copernican revolution ("Balancing," 275).

69. Ibid., 282.

70. Ibid.

71. Ibid., 288.

views of embryology, the fascinating insights that Webb includes in this article should certainly give us a greater appreciation for the beautiful interdependence of the sexes. Modern embryology has given us a much clearer picture of this, a picture unavailable in Paul's day.

However, I disagree with Webb's further statement, summarizing the corollary arguments. "Correspondingly, a set of corollary arguments suggest that the 'applicational' weight of Edenic creation theology must be given *far less weight* in shaping the extent of hierarchy within male-female relationships today than was ever possible in Paul's day" (emphasis original).[72] I do not see how this statement follows logically, or is grounded in, the previous point. It may be true that a better understanding of procreation gives us a greater appreciation for the equality between the sexes, but it does not follow that the reference to creation order in verses 8–9 is diminished in any way. There continues to be a counterbalance between creation and procreation. In effect, Webb is trying to cancel out the significance of verses 8–9 with the statement in verse 12, based on the development of embryology. But this argument, as creative and fascinating as it may be, does not accomplish its goal. There are some helpful insights to be gleaned, but it does not provide a compelling reason for using Paul's latter point (verse 12) to overshadow his former one (vv. 8–9). The two still fit together in a complementary manner.

Nothing in Webb's "seed ideas" provides a compelling reason to move beyond the ethic of the New Testament. He does not demonstrate that further movement is implied or needed, and therefore we must conclude that what we are seeing in these passages is absolute movement, not preliminary movement.

Purpose/Intent Statements

I have discussed this criterion both in chapter 2 and chapter 3. There are four passages in view. Regarding slavery, Paul writes in 1 Timothy 6:1, "Let all who are under a yoke as slaves regard their own masters as worthy of all honor, *so that the name of God and the teaching may not be reviled.*" Similarly, in Titus 2:9–10, "Slaves are to be submissive to their own masters in everything; they are to be well-pleasing, not argumentative, not pilfering, but showing all good faith, *so that in everything they may adorn the*

72. Ibid., 288–89.

doctrine of God our Savior." In the passages that instruct women, there are also two places where we find purpose clauses, one of them in the same context as the verses just cited. Just a few verses earlier in Titus 2, Paul writes, "and so train the young women to love their husbands and children, to be self-controlled, pure, working at home, kind, and submissive to their own husbands, *that the word of God may not be reviled*" (vv. 4–5). Last, Peter's statement to wives also contains a purpose clause. "Likewise, wives, be subject to your own husbands, *so that even if some do not obey the word, they may be won without a word by the conduct of their wives,* when they see your respectful and pure conduct" (1 Peter 3:1–2).

Webb's statement of this criterion is as follows: "A component of a text may be culturally bound, if by practicing the text one no longer fulfills the text's original intent or purpose. The other side of this criterion is that a text is more likely to be transcultural to the degree that its original purpose is fulfilled when practiced in a subsequent culture and time."[73] In a footnote, Webb cites two places where this point has been made previously. First, Willard Swartley refers to this as he compares the issues of women and slavery: "Paul's conservative stance on both issues appears motivated (at some places) by a concern that the gospel not be defamed." In the next paragraph, he states, "This raises an important point when we interpret these texts, especially if unbelievers are now more offended when Christians argue for slavery or for male headship."[74] Second, Mary Hayter lays down three principles for applying New Testament teaching today, and the first two are closely related to this discussion. "The *first principle* is that *Church order,* including specific directives on women's place within the worshipping community, *should always be designed to meet the interdependent objectives of glorifying God and edifying the whole congregation*" (italics original).[75] Her second principle adds that church order should also "be designed to promote the proclamation of the Gospel."[76] She asserts that in the early church there was variety when it came to church order. There were consistent objectives, but various means of accomplishing

73. Webb, *Slaves, Women, and Homosexuals,* 105.

74. Willard M. Swartley, *Slavery, Sabbath, War and Women: Case Issues in Biblical Interpretation* (Scottdale, PA: Herald Press, 1983), 202. The passages he mentions are 1 Tim. 6:1; Titus 2:5, 9–10; 1 Cor. 11. He also refers to 1 Cor. 14:23 and 1 Thess. 4:9–12.

75. Mary Hayter, *The New Eve in Christ: The Use and Abuse of the Bible in the Debate about Women in the Church* (Grand Rapids: Eerdmans, 1987), 149.

76. Ibid., 150.

those objectives. In the same way, churches today should consider how best to meet the objectives of glorifying God, edifying the congregation, and proclaiming the gospel. "Church order, then, must not be rigid and inflexible, but adaptable to local conditions."[77]

In Webb's discussion, he proceeds to mention some neutral examples of purpose/intent statements. First is the holy kiss.[78] This command does not contain an explicit purpose clause, but the obvious intent is to demonstrate Christian charity and fellowship. But in our culture we would fail to accomplish this purpose, and even undermine it, if we implemented the command just as it is stated.[79] This is a helpful way of thinking about the problem of applying the holy kiss to our culture. If we were to greet others in our culture with a holy kiss, we would not be expressing Christian love and fellowship, but would rather make people feel very awkward and uncomfortable. Therefore, we apply these commands by discerning the intent of the physical action and adjusting it to what is appropriate in our culture (e.g., smile, handshake, hug). In this way, Webb's point is helpful and illuminating. He concludes, "The underlying principle of Christian community and friendship remains transcultural, while the holy kiss itself is a culture-bound expression of these values."[80] This is precisely how we ought to think about several passages (most notably in this discussion, the issue of head coverings in 1 Cor. 11). Therefore, Webb is helpful in his assessment of the holy kiss and how we ought to think about its application to our lives today.

However, as we move on to the other examples of purpose/intent statements (all of which include some kind of purpose statement, unlike the holy kiss), it becomes less clear that the purpose statements necessarily imply a cultural component to the text. As Wayne Grudem has pointed out, a redemptive-movement hermeneutic is not needed to address things such as the holy kiss. It is a relatively simple point, and one that is easily understood, that in some cases like this we find a cultural component that can and should be adjusted, while the underlying principle is still binding.[81] Webb's statements concerning the holy kiss are right in line with this, but he stretches this observa-

77. Ibid.

78. Rom. 16:16; 1 Cor. 16:20; 2 Cor. 13:12; 1 Thess. 5:26; 1 Peter 5:14.

79. Webb, *Slaves, Women, and Homosexuals*, 105–6.

80. Ibid., 106.

81. Grudem, "Should We Move Beyond the New Testament?," 341–42.

tion too far when he tries to apply it in certain other places, as I will try to demonstrate.

The other passages that Webb discusses have to do with slavery, civil government, and women. I have already quoted the verses pertaining to slaves and women. Webb also quotes from 1 Peter 2:13–15, in this way: "submit . . . to the king . . . [*purpose*] for it is God's will that by doing good you should silence the ignorant talk of foolish men."[82] In their entirety, the verses read this way, "Be subject for the Lord's sake to every human institution, whether it be to the emperor as supreme, or to governors as sent by him to punish those who do evil and to praise those who do good. For this is the will of God, that by doing good you should put to silence the ignorance of foolish people." Webb argues that applying these verses in a democratic society would be detrimental to the gospel. Just as "slavery-form submission" no longer achieves the purpose stated in 1 Timothy 6:1 and Titus 2:9–10, so also "monarchy-type submission" does not achieve the purpose of silencing the ignorance of foolish people. Rather, Webb insists that we must move "to a more abstracted level of application" in order to fulfill the stated purpose of the biblical instruction.[83] In the case of slavery, this means "showing deference/respect in order to win people (employers)."[84] In terms of government, we should apply these verses by showing honor and respect toward our political leaders and submitting to the law, but not by *obeying* the president or other government leaders.[85]

Thus far, the basic point is valid that "slavery-form submission" and "monarchy-type submission" reveal cultural components of these texts. Neither the institution of slavery nor a monarchical form of government can be supported by these passages. However, is Webb making too much of 1 Peter 2:13–15? Certainly there are differences between Peter's culture and ours, and our application of the passage will be affected by those differences, but it seems that Webb's portrayal of the situation puts the two farther apart than is warranted. It seems to be implied by Webb that the verses call for personal obedience to any commands that an emperor might

82. Webb, *Slaves, Women, and Homosexuals*, 106. The other four passages all contain a *hina* clause. The verses in 1 Peter 2 do not have an explicit purpose statement, but the ground/explanatory clause could be taken as an indication of the purpose for the command.

83. Ibid., 107.

84. Ibid., 106.

85. Ibid., 107.

give to a citizen.[86] But does this capture the thrust of Peter's admonition? Would it not be better to see the principle as something like this: "Be a submissive citizen, abiding by the rules of the land"? In Peter's culture, he could articulate this in terms of the emperor. In our democratic society, we think of it more in terms of our nation's laws. But the principle remains. We are to be submissive, law-abiding citizens.[87]

Thus, it is wrong to conclude that this command no longer fulfills its stated purpose. That would be true only if the instruction was at the same time an endorsement of monarchy. But if we recognize appropriately the principle that is conveyed, there is no reason to think that the purpose can no longer be fulfilled. As we conduct ourselves in our society as law-abiding citizens who are submissive to the governing authorities, we will be a positive witness for Christ and will silence those who want to ridicule Christianity. Similarly, in the case of slavery, the stated purpose of the instructions to slaves fails only if those instructions constitute an endorsement of the institution of slavery. I do not believe this is the case, as I argued in chapter 2.

Therefore, when we apply Titus 2:9–10 in the workplace, it does not mean we are supporting slavery. It simply means that employees should be submissive toward their employers, "well-pleasing, not argumentative, not pilfering, but showing all good faith." As this submissive, good-natured attitude is fostered by Christian employees, they will "adorn the doctrine of God our Savior." Thus, the case that Webb is trying to make in terms of purpose/intent statements is weakened considerably. It is not clear that by practicing these texts we are no longer fulfilling the text's original intent or purpose.[88]

This is related to a later criterion that Webb examines, which he considers to be a persuasive extrascriptural criterion. It is criterion 17: "Pragmatic Basis Between Two Cultures." There we find a diagram of Webb's ladder of abstraction. On the lower end of the ladder is the pragmatic basis for a command (e.g., leave the corners of your fields unhar-

86. He writes, "In a democratic society a Christian admonition to 'submit to' and 'obey' the president or prime minister is strikingly foolish" (ibid.).

87. To understand this instruction appropriately, we must keep in mind (1) that we are free people, servants of *God*, as Peter goes on to say in v. 16, and (2) that our obligation to submit to the governing authorities does not extend to situations where sin is involved (e.g., Acts 5:29).

88. To use Webb's words from his definition of this criterion (*Slaves, Women, and Homosexuals*, 105).

vested, Lev. 19:10).[89] Moving up the ladder brings us to the transcultural principle that we should help/feed the poor. At the top of the ladder, an even more abstracted principle is derived, namely, love your neighbor. The next example he uses is washing one another's feet. Again there are significant differences between the pragmatic concerns of our culture and the culture in which this command was given (John 13:14). Since we no longer deal with the factors that made foot-washing necessary in the first century, we must move up the ladder of abstraction to apply this command generally in terms of serving others.[90]

The ladder of abstraction is helpful, and so is Webb's assessment of the foot-washing command. The ladder of abstraction is also helpful in discussing issues such as the holy kiss and head coverings. But Webb is less persuasive in the way he "moves up the ladder" with respect to the issues of civil government and wifely submission. With respect to civil government, he derives the abstracted principle of *honoring leaders*, based on the pragmatic differences between cultures. But the clearer abstracted principle is to be *a submissive, law-abiding citizen*. In one way Webb agrees, for he refers to obeying the law.[91] Neither do I disagree with Webb that we should honor our leaders (1 Peter 2:17). However, the way in which we move up the ladder is crucial, and it seems that Webb's desire is to soften the submission command rather than preserve it and reapply it in a new setting. The principle of being a submissive, law-abiding citizen does more to preserve the essence of the command, while applying it to a democratic rather than a monarchical society.

Similarly with the submission commands to slaves, Webb draws the principle of "showing deference/respect in order to win people (employers)."[92] Again, it is true that we should show deference and respect toward employers, and that is certainly part of applying those passages. But we should derive a more specific principle, namely, submit to those in authority over you in the workplace. As Webb moves up the ladder the submission commands turn into deference, respect, and honor. But the principles of authority and submission should not be diminished just because of certain differences between cultures. Thus, Webb's abstracted

89. This is Webb's opening illustration of this criterion (ibid., 210).

90. Ibid., 211.

91. Ibid., 107, 212.

92. Ibid., 106.

principles assume the egalitarianism that he is seeking to prove. He uses the ladder of abstraction to subtly minimize the authority-submission structure that is present in these passages.

In society, in the workplace, in the local church,[93] and in the home, God has ordained a certain structure and order. Therefore, while we must reapply the biblical commands in a different setting, we must be careful to preserve the principle that is contained in the command. We should be cautioned against some of the ways Webb abstracts principles from specific commands, for his process of abstraction often fails to maintain enough of a link with the biblical instruction. For instance, from 1 Timothy 2:12 he derives the following principle: "choose teachers/leaders who are worthy of high honor within the congregation."[94]

To summarize, it is not clear that the purpose/intent statements necessarily imply a cultural component to the text. As Webb builds his case, it may appear to be persuasive. But two things should encourage caution. First, Webb's method of deriving principles does not clearly capture the heart of the original commands. Second, and related to the first, is the assumption that we can no longer fulfill the purpose statements in our culture. Both of these points are examples of Webb's tendency to portray certain hermeneutical questions as more complex than they are. The holy kiss, washing one another's feet, and commands concerning civil government are explained relatively easily (and Webb offers some helpful ways of doing this). But it becomes a stretch—and overly complex and subjective—when those explanations are imposed on the texts regarding women.

There is one more important point in the discussion of purpose statements, and that is the assertion that wives submitting to husbands in our culture would contradict the intention for which those commands were given in the New Testament. Webb says of 1 Peter 3, "For today's unbelieving husband who values his wife as a completely equal partner and who happily functions within a mutual-deference and mutual-honor framework, this kind of unilateral, patriarchy-type submission may actually repulse him and prevent him from being won to Christ."[95]

93. See Webb's brief discussion of elders in which he provides pragmatic reasons for the continuance of congregational submission to elders (ibid., 213). I would suggest that this structure relies on something much deeper than pragmatic concerns. It is, rather, part of God's ordained authority structure for the church.

94. Ibid., 145. I will interact with this further in the next chapter, in the section on primogeniture.

95. Ibid., 107–8.

There are two problems with this statement. First, it casts biblical submission in a negative light, assuming that the principles of these verses would be offensive in our society. But when we think about wifely submission as presented here, accompanied by respectful and pure conduct, and the imperishable beauty of a gentle and quiet spirit, it is not at all clear that these things would repulse an unbelieving husband.

Second, Webb's statement assumes that Peter gave these instructions primarily as a means to appease the culture of his day. In other words, Peter did not hold a deep-seated conviction that wifely submission was part of God's plan for marriage, but rather he saw it as a pragmatic means of furthering the Christian mission in that setting. Peter Davids states the point more boldly:

> Ironically, interpretations that focus on the unilateral obedience or submission of wives to husbands, regardless of cultural context, achieve the opposite of Peter's intention. Rather than promoting harmony with culture, they set Christian marriage partners at odds with culture and thus heighten the tension, and Christianity is perceived as undermining culture in a retrogressive way. This is precisely what 1 Peter is seeking to minimize.[96]

This is in line with the view presented by David Balch, who maintains that Peter's domestic code is mainly serving an apologetic function. Outsiders were ridiculing the Christian faith because of slaves and wives who had converted, and therefore "the author of 1 Peter encouraged the slaves and wives to play the social roles which Aristotle had outlined; this, he hoped, would shame those who were reviling their good behavior (3:16; 2:12)."[97]

We must question, though, whether Peter's main intent was to appease the culture. Not all agree with this assessment. John Elliott takes issue with Balch's proposal, stating that the exhortations given in 1 Peter cannot have as their goal conformity to the culture, for the Christian community was to have a "*distinctive* identity" (emphasis original).[98] He also says that Balch's

96. Peter H. Davids, "A Silent Witness in Marriage: 1 Peter 3:1–7," in *Discovering Biblical Equality: Complementarity without Hierarchy*, ed. Ronald W. Pierce and Rebecca Merrill Groothuis (Downers Grove, IL: IVP, 2004), 236.

97. David L. Balch, *Let Wives Be Submissive: The Domestic Code in 1 Peter*, SBLMS 26 (Chico, CA: Scholars Press, 1981), 109.

98. John H. Elliott, *A Home for the Homeless: A Sociological Exegesis of 1 Peter, Its Situation and Strategy* (Philadelphia: Fortress Press, 1981), 111.

interpretation "fails to account for the letter's repeated call for Christian separation from the world and it understates its missionary interests as well."[99] J. W. Pryor responds to both Balch and Elliott and asserts, "slaves and wives are called to behave in a certain way not because it will promote peace and may avoid conflict, nor out of conformity to society's expectations, but because the pattern of submission is the will of God to whom they are bound as his people (2:13)."[100]

These are significant points. On the one hand, it is plain that Peter desired that Christians live in harmony with the surrounding culture. On the other hand, this must not be viewed as the *main* goal. There was an evangelistic motive, as Webb and Davids observe. But we also see the goal of maintaining a distinctive identity, and ultimately of doing the will of God. Therefore, it is unwarranted to conclude that Peter would give certain instructions to the church simply for the purpose of conforming to the culture. He would not present a less-than-ultimate ethic for the pragmatic purpose of living in harmony with one's neighbors or even for the purpose of winning others to Christ. If Peter intended by this command that wives be submissive merely as a means to an end, surely there would be some clear indication of this. But no such indication can be found.[101]

In addition to this, we must recognize how Peter moves decisively *against* the cultural expectations of his day in this passage. Of course, he is moving against the culture by promoting the Christian gospel, and by advocating that Christian women continue in the faith even when that means rejecting the religion of a pagan husband. Davids provides a helpful portrait of the first-century landscape, showing what a radical idea this was in that setting, for it was expected that wives would follow the religion of their husbands.[102] But even in the marriage relationship, Peter instructs husbands in a way that would have been very different from the prevail-

99. Ibid.

100. J. W. Pryor, "First Peter and the New Covenant (II)," *Reformed Theological Review* 45 (1986): 47. Also see the comments on these views in Thomas R. Schreiner, *1, 2 Peter, Jude*, NAC, vol. 37 (Nashville: Broadman & Holman, 2003), 125–26.

101. Schreiner, *1, 2 Peter, Jude*, 151: "It must also be said that Peter gave no indication that the submission of wives is a temporary accommodation to the culture of his day. He firmly rejects, as we have seen, the notion that women are unequal to men. Nor is there any indication that he equates submission with inequality."

102. Davids, "A Silent Witness," 226–27. Davids argues that the cultural accommodation imposed on slaves and wives was for the purpose of advancing one very countercultural idea—the Christian gospel in a pagan society. "[Peter] wants to make Jesus the issue, not unnecessarily divisive behaviors" (234).

ing assumptions of his culture (1 Peter 3:7). Specifically, he commands husbands to show honor to their wives. Steven Bechtler says, "The expression 'bestowing honor' (*aponemō timēn*) is common in the literature of antiquity, but, so far as I can determine, 1 Peter's demand that the *husband* bestow honor on his *wife* is unique."[103] We also read the amazing statement of equality that Christian husbands and wives are co-heirs of the grace of life. So while Peter upholds the distinction in the roles of husbands and wives, he also emphasizes the fundamental equality between them.[104] This latter point would not have been a popular one.[105] Hence, we must doubt the thesis that Peter desired conformity with the culture. Therefore, it is not convincing (1) that the submission of wives in 1 Peter 3 was merely for the purpose of conforming to the culture, nor (2) that the principles of 1 Peter 3 can no longer fulfill the stated purpose today.

CONCLUSION

In each section of this chapter, certain similarities can be detected between the slavery issue and the issue of women's roles. In each case, we find theological analogies. In each case, the biblical commands demonstrate "movement" with respect to the culture in which those commands were given. And in each case there are purpose clauses attached to some of the commands. But these similarities do not form a compelling argument for interpreting the two sets of texts in the same way. In the case of theological analogies, I have noted important ways in which Ephesians 5 and 1 Corinthians 11 are distinct from the other passages Webb references. Concerning preliminary movement and seed ideas, it is true that there are New Testament passages that point beyond certain social structures

103. Steven Richard Bechtler, *Following in His Steps: Suffering, Community, and Christology in 1 Peter*, SBLDS 162 (Atlanta: Scholars Press, 1998), 175.

104. Ibid.: "The concept of joint heirship recalls the mention of 1:4 of the inheritance that all Christians—without differentiation according to social roles—have gained as a result of their conversion. The husband's recognition that his wife is the weaker vessel, therefore, must be balanced by his acknowledgement that she is his equal in terms of the reception of God's grace." See also Wayne Grudem, *The First Epistle of Peter*, TNTC (Grand Rapids: Eerdmans, 1988), 145; idem, "Wives Like Sarah, and the Husbands Who Honor Them: 1 Peter 3:1–7," in *Recovering Biblical Manhood and Womanhood: A Response to Evangelical Feminism*, ed. John Piper and Wayne Grudem (Wheaton, IL: Crossway Books, 1991), 203–4.

105. Davids, "A Silent Witness," 226–27. He cites Balch's study, saying that "his evidence also indicates a virtually universal perception that women were to be ruled by men, usually with the assumption that they were inferior to men." See Balch, *Let Wives Be Submissive*, 27–29, 44–45.

of the first century. But we have no clear reasons for thinking that these texts point us beyond the *ethic* of the New Testament. Therefore, we can detect a movement beyond slavery that is inherent in the ethic of the New Testament. And we need not move beyond male headship, for the New Testament ethic prescribes it. We are happy to find movement when we compare the New Testament commands with the first-century culture, and we must recognize this to be "absolute movement," not "preliminary movement." Finally, regarding purpose/intent statements, the fact that these appear in both slavery and women's texts does not imply any significant connection between the two issues. The presence of a purpose statement does not necessarily imply a cultural component to the command. Therefore, we have to examine each issue separately and discern how the commands are to be applied today.

Webb seeks to build a cumulative case as he works his way through the various criteria. Since there is an element of truth in many places, the cumulative effect may seem compelling. However, as we closely analyze each criterion we begin to see some weaknesses. The similarities between the issues of slaves and women are superficial rather than substantive, and the logic that ties the two together is suspect. This chapter has dealt with various arguments that emphasize the similarities between the two. The next chapter will continue the hermeneutical discussion by analyzing four additional criteria.

6

Hermeneutical Considerations: Part 2

The last chapter dealt with three main arguments that Webb uses to bind together the slavery texts and the women's texts. Now we come to a discussion of an important *dis*similarity between the two, namely, basis in original creation. This is what I will take up first in this chapter, including the related matter of primogeniture. Then we must step back and deal with two broader hermeneutical questions: the relationship between creation and redemption, and the relationship between specific instructions and general principles.

Basis in Original Creation

Webb's discussion of original creation begins with a section on "patterns" in the creation account, and then moves specifically to the custom of primogeniture. As neutral examples, Webb points to nine issues that may be seen as "patterns" rooted in original creation, and his intention is to demonstrate that not all facets of the creation account are transcultural.[1] The first example *is* transcultural, the prohibition against divorce. Jesus refers back to creation in his statement against divorce in Matthew

1. William J. Webb, *Slaves, Women, and Homosexuals: Exploring the Hermeneutics of Cultural Analysis* (Downers Grove, IL: IVP, 2001), 124–27.

19:3–12 (Gen. 1:27; 2:24). Although the law permitted divorce, this was only because of the hardness of the human heart (Matt. 19:8). Webb states, "The social structure of lifelong marriage takes precedence over divorce regulations, since it reflects a higher moral ideal. In this instance, the creation pattern carries a strong transcultural force."[2]

Webb's conclusion is surely right that the pattern of marriage in original creation is transcultural. However, he should be clearer as to the reason why lifelong marriage takes precedence over divorce regulations. Webb says it is because "it reflects a higher moral ideal." I agree with this. And I assume Webb would agree with me when I say that Jesus' words in Matthew 19 are binding simply because they are the words of Jesus. But the fact that Webb states one and not the other gives us an insight into his thinking. Webb is looking for "a higher moral ideal" which may or may not be contained in the Bible itself. But if we recognize that the New Testament is God's final and authoritative word to his new covenant people,[3] then we can look at Matthew 19 and conclude that divorce is wrong *because Jesus says so*. And based on Jesus' words we can look back to the creation account and see that from the very beginning God's design for marriage has been lifelong faithfulness to one's spouse.[4]

Webb's next example is polygamy, which is closely related to divorce. He says, though, that because of the polygamy practiced by the patriarchs, the creation account has only a "mild transcultural force" with regard to this matter.[5] It is much more helpful, though, to see polygamy as a practice that was tolerated but never condoned, just as in the case of divorce.[6] The instances of polygamy found in the Bible do not constitute an endorsement of it. Therefore, the pattern of original creation provides

2. Ibid., 124.

3. See Wayne Grudem, "Should We Move Beyond the New Testament to a Better Ethic? An Analysis of William J. Webb, *Slaves, Women, and Homosexuals: Exploring the Hermeneutics of Cultural Analysis*," *JETS* 47 (2004): 301–7.

4. Thomas R. Schreiner, "Review of *Slaves, Women, and Homosexuals*," *JBMW* 7 (2002): 48. He says, "When we come to the issue of women in ministry, and this point cannot be stressed enough, the NT itself argues from the created order for differences in role (1 Cor. 11:8–9; 1 Tim. 2:13). . . . Hence, contrary to Webb, Jesus' appeal to creation in the matter of divorce and remarriage (Matt. 19:3–12) functions as the best parallel to the texts about women in ministry. For we see in the NT, the definitive revelation of the last days, an appeal to God's good creation supporting a different role for men and women."

5. Webb, *Slaves, Women, and Homosexuals*, 124.

6. Norman L. Geisler, *Baker Encyclopedia of Christian Apologetics* (Grand Rapids: Baker, 1999), s.v. "Polygamy."

more than a *mild* transcultural principle regarding polygamy. God's original design of one man and one woman speaks forcefully against both divorce and polygamy, which can be seen in the NT statements upholding monogamy.[7]

The Sabbath and the related matter of the length of a workweek are two other examples Webb provides in this section. He says that "Sabbath offers a good example of a creation pattern with a significant cultural component."[8] He goes on to describe the differences between now and then: "We live in an industrial, technological and informational society. The six-day work schedule was probably related to the agrarian setting of the original audience."[9] In a footnote, and at the end of his summary on the next page, Webb acknowledges that salvation history may have something to do with the shift in how we apply the Sabbath.[10] But his clear emphasis is on *cultural* factors that brought about change.

The issue of the Sabbath is not a simple one—certainly not as simple as an analysis of changing agricultural practices. It is true, as Webb points out, that God gave his people instructions concerning their cultivation of the land. Those instructions corresponded to the Sabbath principle of six periods of work followed by one period of rest. However, to call these directives "cultural" is to oversimplify the matter. The fact that these instructions do not apply directly to us does not mean that cultural factors are the sole (or even main) reason for this. Rather, it is in the development of salvation history that we find a much more illuminating answer to these questions. I will not try to defend a particular position here. But it is important to recognize that the answer lies not in the cultural factors of Old Testament agrarian practices, but in New Testament statements that elucidate the meaning and substance toward which the Old Testament Sabbath pointed. Therefore, it is overly simplistic, and thus misleading, to say that the pattern of Sabbath rest in the creation account is cultural. A more nuanced understanding of the issue would affirm that salvation

7. See Matt. 5:31–32; 19:4–6; Mark 10:2–8; Luke 16:18; 1 Cor. 7:2; 1 Tim. 3:2, 12; 5:9; Titus 1:6. Not all of these passages refer back to creation, but they all point to God's design for faithful monogamous marriage, which is first displayed in creation.

8. Webb, *Slaves, Women, and Homosexuals*, 126.

9. Ibid.

10. "Developments in salvation history (along with a movement away from an agrarian culture) have helped bring about a relinquishing or reworking of the Sabbath pattern" (ibid., 126n5). "The particular pattern may well be tied to salvation historical events and/or agricultural concerns that are time-bound and cultural" (ibid., 127).

history is by far the most significant factor in determining how to apply this creation pattern to our lives today.

Another cultural component, according to Webb, is the procreation command. God commanded the first couple, "Be fruitful and multiply and fill the earth and subdue it" (Gen. 1:28). Webb assumes that this command is at odds with any form of birth control, and therefore concludes that this must be a cultural component of the creation pattern and something we must significantly modify in our cultural context. We must ask, however, whether this procreation command means that everyone should have as many children as possible. That does not seem clear from the text. What is clear is the mandate to bear children, which is to be seen as a blessing from the Lord (Gen. 33:5; Ps. 127:3–5). We should not read this as an absolute mandate for all individuals to bear as many children as possible. First, this would mean that singleness is unacceptable. Second, it would imply that procreation is the primary (and possibly the sole) purpose of marriage.[11] It is better, therefore, to understand Genesis 1:28 as a statement of God's intent for marriage to be procreative. When taken in this straightforward way it does not constitute an absolute prohibition on birth control. Instead, it should be seen as a censure of those who would view childbearing as an inconvenience rather than a divine blessing.[12] Thus, in his treatment of the Sabbath issue and the procreation command, Webb's hermeneutic is reductionistic and simplistic. This weakness seems to be evident throughout the discussion of original creation.

The issue of singleness is related, as we have just seen. If the creation pattern establishes the expectation that all individuals marry and have children, then singleness clearly deviates from that pattern. Webb says, "If the creation material provides a tightly ordered paradigm for all of humanity to follow, one might get the impression that singleness was outside the

11. While procreation is definitely an important purpose of marriage, there are other important purposes that marriage serves. Mark Liederbach provides this helpful statement: "Scripture indicates that, in addition to procreation, God created marriage to meet other ends as well. Companionship through the development of a sacred marital bond (Gen. 2:18, 24), sexual pleasure (Prov. 5:15–23, Song of Songs), and marital fidelity (1 Cor. 7:1–9), to name but a few, are all biblically appropriate purposes for which God created the marriage sexual union" (Mark Liederbach's section labeled "Contraception," in Andreas J. Köstenberger and David W. Jones, *God, Marriage, and Family: Rebuilding the Biblical Foundation*, 2nd ed. [Wheaton, IL: Crossway, 2010], 122).

12. Ibid., 133–35. See quotations from Albert Mohler, "Can Christians Use Birth Control?," http://www.albertmohler.com/2006/05/08/can-christians-use-birth-control/; accessed February 1, 2012.

will of God."[13] Of course, he acknowledges that this is not so, citing New Testament verses that portray singleness as honorable and even preferable for some (Matt. 19:11; 1 Cor. 7:7–9, 25–35). Therefore, concerning this issue, "most Christians would view departure from creation pattern as an acceptable option."[14] But again, as in the case of the procreation command, we must ask whether the intent of the creation account is to command all individuals to be married. As Wayne Grudem points out, "to say that marriage is *good* does not imply that singleness is *bad*, or that marriage is *required* for every single individual, nor does the Genesis narrative imply those things (italics original)."[15]

Thus, in the case of the procreation command and singleness, Webb has assumed unlikely and hermeneutically simplistic interpretations of the creation account in an attempt to heighten the perceived tension between original creation and today's culture.[16] In this way he has set up reductionistic arguments that are easily dismantled.

This attempt becomes even more evident in the three remaining examples: farming as an occupation, ground transportation, and vegetarian diet.[17] These were facets of life in the garden of Eden, but these practices do not apply to all generations. Webb correctly concludes that we are not to require everyone to farm, to walk, or to eat only vegetables, just because that was the pattern in the garden. Indeed, we can determine relatively easily that these are not binding on subsequent generations. The Bible speaks of individuals who honored God in various occupations, indicating that farming is not the only acceptable way to make a living.[18] In the

13. Webb, *Slaves, Women, and Homosexuals*, 124.

14. Ibid.

15. Grudem, "Should We Move Beyond the New Testament to a Better Ethic?," 316.

16. For a more detailed articulation of this critique, see Grudem, "Should We Move Beyond the New Testament to a Better Ethic?," 314–18.

17. Webb, *Slaves, Women, and Homosexuals*, 124–25.

18. Consider Grudem's helpful statements concerning farming and ground transportation. With regard to farming as an occupation, he says, "A more sound application of this text is to say that God still expects human beings to gain food from the ground, but the diversity of occupations within Scripture shows that this never was an expectation or a requirement of every single person." Then regarding ground transportation, "We do not need Webb's redemptive-movement hermeneutic to know that the Bible never presents 'ground transportation' as the mode of transportation that people should use exclusively (think of all the journeys by boats in the Bible), nor is this pattern of transportation ever used elsewhere as a basis for commands to God's people, nor does the Bible ever command people to use only ground transportation" ("Should We Move Beyond the New Testament to a Better Ethic?," 315).

Bible, we also find alternative modes of transportation (e.g., by boat).[19] And we also know it is permissible to eat meat (e.g., Gen. 9:3). Therefore, it is not helpful to list these as creation patterns since biblical revelation itself clarifies that these practices were never intended to be transcultural. Thus, Webb's mention of farming, ground transportation, and vegetarianism make it appear that he is grasping for ways to minimize the weight of the creation account. He is searching for ways to lessen the force of those New Testament passages that cite the creation account as a basis for role distinctions between men and women.[20]

It is much more helpful to let Scripture interpret Scripture. In this way we can look at Jesus' words regarding divorce and conclude that the creation pattern of one man and one woman is an abiding expectation for marriage. In the case of the other creation patterns that Webb cites, we must examine each one according to the continuing revelation of Scripture to determine whether it is intended to be binding for other cultures. Thomas Schreiner states, "Complementarians, rightly understood, have never argued that every element of the creation narrative should be reproduced today. We have a canonical view of the Scriptures in which we see scripture as the interpreter of scripture, and the redemptive historical flow of the Bible is crucial."[21] In light of this, Webb's discussion of creation patterns is unhelpful, unenlightening, and hermeneutically weak. His point is moot since the complementarian understanding of 1 Timothy 2:13 and 1 Corinthians 11:8–9 does not assume that the creation account is binding in all of its details. The point is rather that certain things God established at creation *are* extremely significant, and the New Testament reveals those aspects to us.

Following the discussion of neutral examples, Webb then examines the features of the creation narrative that pertain to the relationship between man and woman. He first lists two aspects that "reflect an egalitarian spirit": the fact that both man and woman are created in God's image, and the creation mandate that is given to both of them.[22] Complementarians certainly agree that the creation narrative portrays a fundamental equality

19. For example, consider the use of watercraft by Noah, Jonah, Jesus, and Paul.

20. To read another redemptive-movement proponent who seeks to downplay the significance of Paul's reference to original creation, see R. T. France, *Women in the Church's Ministry: A Test Case for Biblical Interpretation* (Grand Rapids: Eerdmans, 1995), 67–68.

21. Schreiner, "Review of *Slaves, Women, and Homosexuals*," 48.

22. Webb, *Slaves, Women, and Homosexuals*, 127.

between male and female.[23] The question is whether or not that equality excludes male headship. Therefore, Webb must deal with the other elements of creation which indicate that equality and male headship are both present in creation in a complementary way. Webb provides six examples that "provide possible hints of patriarchy within the garden."[24] (1) The woman as helpmate; (2) the woman taken from Adam's rib; (3) the woman named by the man; (4) the man leaves and cleaves, not the woman; (5) God addresses the man first; (6) creation order—man first, then the woman. Webb minimizes these points in different ways, but recognizes the weight of the last one mentioned. "In view of our analysis of the creation story so far, it seems fair to say that this element of creation order supplies one of the strongest pieces of patriarchal data."[25] I will not quibble with the points Webb makes concerning the other features of the creation account. But the creation order, as Webb rightly recognizes, is extremely significant. He will return to this in the subsequent discussion of primogeniture.

Since the focus of this book is the comparison of the slavery issue and the issue of women's roles (or combination of issues), I have not given much attention to the third issue that Webb deals with extensively—homosexuality. But at this point the discussion is relevant. After citing the neutral patterns within creation, and then examining the patterns that relate specifically to the gender debate, Webb then comments on the issue of homosexuality as it relates to creation patterns. As we might expect, Webb minimizes the significance of creation order for the issue of homosexuality. He writes, "No biblical passages refer back to the creation material in a direct manner to make a point about homosexuality (although one Pauline text mentions creation within the immediate context, and an inference might be drawn)."[26] Only in the footnote, then, does he cite Romans 1. This comprises Webb's most extensive comment on Romans 1 in his entire book.

> Rom. 1:20, 25 explicitly refers to the original creation (cf., the allusions in 1:23). This provides the broader context for Paul's comments about

23. Raymond C. Ortlund Jr., "Male-Female Equality and Male Headship: Genesis 1–3," in *Recovering Biblical Manhood and Womanhood: A Response to Evangelical Feminism*, ed. John Piper and Wayne Grudem (Wheaton, IL: Crossway Books, 1991), 86–87.

24. Webb, *Slaves, Women, and Homosexuals*, 127.

25. Ibid., 130.

26. Ibid., 131.

> homosexual relationships (1:26–27). In view of these references to creation, it is likely that the original creation setting influenced his discourse on homosexuality. The expressions "natural relations" and "unnatural relations" (1:26–27) may allude to the original creation context as well as speaking about nature in general.[27]

It seems that Webb feels compelled at least to acknowledge these features of the text, but he minimizes them so as not to weaken his point. He says that it is "*likely* that the original creation setting influenced [Paul's] discourse on homosexuality," and that " 'natural relations' and 'unnatural relations' *may* allude to the original creation context." But this seriously minimizes a very important component of the text.

Webb concludes that other criteria in his book must be brought alongside the criterion concerning original creation. "Only as an interpreter establishes a dialogue between the creation story and other criteria can there be any emerging assurance of creation's continuing applicability or its needed discontinuance."[28] This is a telling move, for he ends up elevating his hermeneutical system above the clear and authoritative words of Romans 1:26–27. Rather than affirming the force of Paul's indictment against homosexuality which is rooted in the created order, Webb shifts the emphasis to the complex hermeneutical system involving his eighteen criteria.

Richard Hays offers some insights on Romans 1 that are relevant here. In an article responding to John Boswell, Hays writes, "The reference to God as creator [in verse 25] would certainly evoke for Paul, as well as for his readers, immediate recollections of the creation story in Genesis 1–3."[29] He also says, "Though he offers no explicit reflection on the concept of 'nature,' it is clear that in this passage Paul identifies 'nature' with the created order."[30] Similarly, C. E. B. Cranfield states, "the

27. Ibid., 131n15.

28. Ibid., 133.

29. Richard B. Hays, "Relations Natural and Unnatural: A Response to John Boswell's Exegesis of Romans 1," *Journal of Religious Ethics* 14 (1986): 191. He elaborates in an endnote, mentioning some lexical parallels between Rom. 1:23 and Gen. 1:26–28 (which demonstrate the irony in the fact that human beings, who were created to have dominion over the animals, are now worshiping animals), and also pointing out the allusion to Ps. 106:20 ("They exchanged the glory of God for the image of an ox that eats grass."). Hays then states, "Paul's description of Gentile idolatry thus achieves a 'double exposure' effect: humanity's turning away from God is both a reversal of the order of creation *and* a recapitulation of Israel's unfaithfulness in the wilderness" (212n6, italics original).

30. Ibid., 194.

decisive factor in Paul's use of [nature] is his biblical doctrine of creation. It denotes that order which is manifest in God's creation and which men have no excuse for failing to recognize and respect."[31] Observing these points, we should be able to recognize how critical this passage is for the issue of homosexuality. Paul here is condemning homosexual practice, and his reasoning is that it is contrary to God's creation design for man and woman. Heterosexuality is God's purpose for manhood and womanhood, not homosexuality.

Ultimately, we need not decipher various hermeneutical criteria in order to determine whether the prohibitions against homosexuality are transcultural. Rather, we simply need to read the text and understand that homosexual relations are contrary to God's design as revealed in creation. Webb fails to acknowledge the thrust of these verses and therefore plays down the importance of original creation. When that bias is removed, a very important principle emerges, namely, that some significant instructions are given to God's people which are rooted in creation and intended to be followed in every age and culture. Thomas Schreiner critiques Webb on this point, for Webb fails to recognize that "when it comes to divorce, homosexuality, and the women's issue, the NT argues from the created order."[32] The rationale given in the New Testament for the prohibition of homosexual behavior is that it contradicts God's created order. Similarly, the rationale given in the New Testament for the distinct roles of men and women is that it accords with God's created order.

While Webb's conclusion concerning homosexuality is to be commended, the means by which he reaches that conclusion makes his position prone to "further movement." As Kevin Vanhoozer observes, "others, such as Luke Johnson and Stephen Fowl, appeal to the very same logic of redemptive trajectory in order to legitimate same-sex relations."[33] Thus,

31. C. E. B. Cranfield, *The Epistle to the Romans*, vol. 1, ICC (Edinburgh: T & T Clark, 1975), 126. See also Douglas J. Moo, *The Epistle to the Romans*, NICNT (Grand Rapids: Eerdmans, 1996), 115; Thomas R. Schreiner, *Romans*, BECNT (Grand Rapids: Baker, 1998), 94–96.

32. Schreiner, "Review of *Slaves, Women, and Homosexuals*," 49. He also marvels at Webb's limited treatment of Rom. 1:26–27, "How one can write a book on the issue of hermeneutics and homosexuality, and refer to this text on only three pages (according to the index) and provide very little exposition of its meaning is nothing short of astonishing" (48).

33. Kevin J. Vanhoozer, "Into the Great 'Beyond': A Theologian's Response to the Marshall Plan," in *Beyond the Bible: Moving from Scripture to Theology*, I. Howard Marshall (Grand Rapids: Baker, 2004), 90. See Luke Timothy Johnson, *Scripture and Discernment: Decision Making in the Church* (Nashville: Abingdon, 1996), 144–48; Stephen E. Fowl, *Engaging Scripture: A Model for Theological Interpretation* (Malden, MA: Blackwell, 1998), 119–26.

it may appear to some that Webb has presented a persuasive egalitarian argument and at the same time upheld heterosexual marriage. This is certainly the case regarding what he affirms and denies. But it must be acknowledged that the logic of his position makes it susceptible to the impetus to condone the homosexual lifestyle. A much stronger defense against this impetus is the creation design in which Paul roots his condemnation of same-sex relations in Romans 1:26–27.

In this way, the issue of original creation highlights two very important weaknesses in Webb's system. On the one hand, original creation differentiates the slavery issue and the gender issue, which Webb attempts to tie together throughout his book. While Webb sees the two as fundamentally similar, he fails to recognize the significance of the fact that slavery is never rooted in creation, whereas gender roles are. On the other hand, basis in original creation plays an important role in the discussion of gender roles and homosexuality, affirming distinct roles for men and women and condemning homosexual relations.

Primogeniture

Now we move on to Webb's treatment of primogeniture, which is of fundamental importance for his argument against the transcultural status of 1 Timothy 2:12–13. His statement of this criterion is as follows: "A component of a text may be transcultural, if it is rooted in the original-creation material, and, more specifically, its creative order."[34] This criterion specifically deals with the logic of Paul's statement in 1 Timothy 2:13 that "Adam was formed first, then Eve," and his use of this fact to ground the instruction in the previous verse, "I do not permit a woman to teach or to exercise authority over a man; rather, she is to remain quiet." Webb writes, "While we do not know for certain what Paul sees as the logical relationship between creation order (1 Tim. 2:13) and the restrictions on women teaching (1 Tim. 2:11–12), the most plausible explanation is that it is based upon, or is an extension of, primogeniture customs."[35]

Next, he cites three complementarian writers who refer to firstborn customs in relation to either 1 Timothy 2:13 or 1 Corinthians 11:8.[36] The por-

34. Webb, *Slaves, Women, and Homosexuals*, 134.

35. Ibid.

36. Ibid., 134–35.

trayal of the complementarian position, however, is somewhat misleading. First, he quotes John Piper and Wayne Grudem, "The contextual basis for this argument [from 1 Tim. 2:13—i.e., male authority based upon the man being created before the woman] in the book of Genesis is *the assumption throughout the book that the 'firstborn' in a human family has the special responsibility of leadership in the family*."[37] It is important to consider the context in which Piper and Grudem make this statement. This is part of their chapter that surveys various matters in a question-answer format, and the question they are addressing here is as follows: "Paul seems to base the primary responsibility of man to lead and teach on the fact that he was created first, before woman (1 Timothy 2:13). How is this a valid argument when the animals were created before man, but don't have primary responsibility for leading him?"[38] The statement quoted by Webb was meant by Piper and Grudem to show that this question would have never entered the minds of those in Moses' day or Paul's day.[39] Therefore, the emphasis is not on primogeniture as a transcultural principle, but simply as a reality of the ancient mind-set that helps us better understand the historical background.

Webb then quotes from Craig Blomberg's commentary on 1 Corinthians: "People in the ancient world familiar with *the privileges that firstborn sons retained (of dynastic succession, inheritance, etc.)* would not have found Paul's argument unusual."[40] As in the quote from Piper and Grudem, Blomberg is responding to the challenge that if the order of creation implies hierarchy of authority, then the animals would have authority over humans. Blomberg responds, "But Paul is not arguing from Genesis 1 but from Genesis 2. He is not claiming that order *always* implies rank, merely that it does in the one part of the one creation account to which he refers."[41] Thus Blomberg makes the point that the original readers would not have been confused by Paul's reasoning.

37. John Piper and Wayne Grudem, eds., *Recovering Biblical Manhood and Womanhood: A Response to Evangelical Feminism* (Wheaton, IL: Crossway Books, 1991), 74. The brackets and italics belong to Webb.

38. Ibid.

39. Webb understands this point and does not raise the question concerning the priority of animals in creation. He summarizes primogeniture logic by stating, "The first within any 'creative order' receives special prominence over others in that order" (*Slaves, Women, and Homosexuals*, 135). But see R. T. France, *Women in the Church's Ministry*, 67, who raises the question of the animals, although he does not pursue it.

40. Craig Blomberg, *1 Corinthians*, NIVAC (Grand Rapids: Zondervan, 1994), 216. Italics belong to Webb.

41. Ibid.

Finally, Webb quotes from Thomas Schreiner, from the first edition of *Women in the Church*. Webb's quotation from Schreiner is as follows:

> It seems the unclarity [of logic in 1 Tim. 2:13] is in the eye of the beholder, for the thrust of the verse has been deemed quite clear in the history of the church. The creation of Adam first gives the reason why men should be the authoritative teachers in the church. James Hurley notes that the reasoning would not be obscure to people of Paul's time, for *they were quite familiar with primogeniture*.[42]

Again, the point is simply to recognize that the original recipients of this instruction would have easily understood the rationale because of the customs of primogeniture.

Webb does not state explicitly how he thinks complementarians view primogeniture customs. But the implication that seems to come through in this section is that primogeniture customs are extremely important to the complementarian position. And it may even appear from Webb's discussion that complementarians are in favor of continuing those practices today (or at least that they should be if they want to be consistent in their application of Scripture). This can be seen in his point that Christians no longer apply firstborn customs today, where he says, "it is interesting that those who appeal to primogeniture in affirming the transcultural status of 1 Timothy 2:13 say very little about the sustained application of their primogeniture texts for our lives."[43] In these ways, Webb's presentation of this issue is misleading, for Webb has misunderstood and wrongly

42. Thomas R. Schreiner, "An Interpretation of 1 Timothy 2:9–15: A Dialogue with Scholarship," in *Women in the Church: A Fresh Analysis of 1 Timothy 2:9–15*, ed. Andreas J. Köstenberger, Thomas R. Schreiner, and H. Scott Baldwin (Grand Rapids: Baker, 1995), 136. Brackets and italics are Webb's. In the second edition of *Women in the Church*, the section quoted by Webb is expanded to include these sentences: "Egalitarians often say that the argument from the order of creation does not work because it would also imply that animals have authority over humans since they were created first. This objection is not compelling. For it is obvious in Genesis that only human beings are created in God's image (Gen. 1:26–27) and that they are distinct from animals. Paul, as a careful reader of the Hebrew narrative, under the inspiration of the Spirit, detected significance in the order of creation of the roles of men and women" ("An Interpretation of 1 Timothy 2:9–15," in *Women in the Church: An Analysis and Application of 1 Timothy 2:9–15*, ed. Andreas J. Köstenberger and Thomas R. Schreiner, 2nd ed. [Grand Rapids: Baker Academic, 2005], 106). See also the work of James Hurley, to which Schreiner refers and in which we find again a response to the question of animals ruling over humans. James B. Hurley, *Man and Woman in Biblical Perspective* (Grand Rapids: Zondervan, 1981), 208–9.

43. Webb, *Slaves, Women, and Homosexuals*, 142.

conveyed how complementarians use the background feature of primogeniture in their discussions of creation order. Thomas Schreiner states the matter clearly:

> In referring to primogeniture, complementarian scholars are scarcely suggesting that the cultural practice of primogeniture should be enforced today, nor do they think that Paul is endorsing primogeniture per se. Nor would they deny the many examples from the Old Testament, adduced by Webb, in which primogeniture was overturned. Instead, they appeal to primogeniture to explain that the notion of the firstborn having authority would be easily understood by Paul's readers.[44]

Complementarians would certainly agree with many of Webb's points concerning primogeniture customs. Webb makes three main points. First, he provides many biblical examples in which a younger sibling was chosen over the firstborn, something we all surely recognize. Second, he makes the point that primogeniture is tied to the ancient world, another point on which complementarians are happy to agree. Webb has studied these customs extensively, and it is interesting to read his findings. Third, he asserts that believers today no longer apply these firstborn customs. Here, again, there is agreement. It seems that Webb must have missed the intent of complementarians in citing primogeniture, for he goes to such great lengths to prove the cultural limitations of it.

It is important to examine the connection (or lack thereof) between primogeniture and the instruction in 1 Timothy 2:12. First, we must recognize that primogeniture practices are not commanded. Paul is not instructing (here or elsewhere) that we should give special honor to firstborns. Rather, the instruction is that women should not teach or have authority over men. Second, we have to recognize that the basis given for this instruction is not the custom of primogeniture. Paul does not say that women shouldn't teach or have authority over men because honoring the firstborn is a biblical principle that applies to this issue. Rather, Paul refers specifically to an historical event. He cites a specific detail of the creation narrative, namely, that God formed Adam first, and then Eve.

These points demonstrate how tenuous Webb's conclusion is, for his argument is that the cultural component of primogeniture (1 Tim. 2:13)

44. Schreiner, "An Interpretation of 1 Timothy 2:9–15," in *Women in the Church*, 2nd ed., 107.

implies a cultural limitation on the instruction regarding women (1 Tim. 2:12). Webb views primogeniture as a *principle* that Paul *applies* to a particular situation. He states later in the book, "The apostle Paul applies the primogeniture principle in his culture. But his application does not equal the principle itself."[45] In this way, Webb derives a transcultural principle from the culturally bound customs of primogeniture. He states the abstracted universal principle as "Grant honor to whom honor is due."[46] Then, in the context of 1 Timothy 2, which addresses the matter of teaching, the application of this principle should include both genders: "choose teachers/leaders who are worthy of high honor within the congregation."[47]

In this way, Webb's reasoning begins with the cultural component of primogeniture, which is related to the statement of 1 Timothy 2:13. He thoroughly demonstrates the cultural nature of this ancient mind-set and the fact that it does not apply today. Then he abstracts a general principle from this custom, and finally applies that principle to the matter of teaching and leadership in the church. But Paul is not using the *principle* of primogeniture and *applying* it to a specific issue in the church. Rather, he is citing a *historical event* which has great theological significance, and he uses it to ground a clear *instruction* for the church. Thus the fact that primogeniture is cultural cannot legitimately be used to say that Paul's instruction in 1 Timothy 2:12 is cultural. It is a very fragile connection, indeed.

It is in this section of the book that Webb proceeds to question whether the patriarchy seen in the creation narrative was really present in the garden. In his evaluation of this criterion, he responds to the question of "how cultural features could possibly be found in the garden before the influence of culture."[48] This is an important question, for Paul's appeal is not to primogeniture per se but to creation order itself. Therefore if Webb wishes to prove that 1 Timothy 2:13 is culturally bound, he must show that a reference to creation order is somehow also a direct reference to primogeniture customs.[49] As we will see, this is not an easy hurdle for him to overcome. He offers three explanations. "First, the whispers of

45. Webb, *Slaves, Women, and Homosexuals*, 237.

46. Ibid., 141.

47. Ibid., 145.

48. Ibid., 142.

49. Note, this is different from the complementarian position, which simply cites primogeniture as an indication that Paul's original readers would have easily understood the statement of 1 Tim. 2:13.

patriarchy in the garden may have been placed there in order to anticipate the curse."[50] He cites the craftiness of the serpent as another literary foreshadowing of the curse, for he assumes that craftiness could not exist in the pre-fall garden. "Second, Eden's quiet echoes of patriarchy might be a way of describing the past through present categories."[51] Here he refers to prophetic descriptions that accommodate the present audience so as not to foster confusion. "Third, given the agrarian base to primogeniture logic, the patriarchy of the garden may reflect God's anticipation of the social context into which Adam and Eve were about to venture."[52] An agrarian society is naturally patriarchal, Webb explains, because the women must rely on the men for provision.

In a paper responding to Wayne Grudem, Webb states that "my cultural/transcultural analysis of the creation accounts and my primogeniture perspective is *supplemental* (not *instrumental*) to a RMH [redemptive-movement hermeneutic]. If you do not like my approach to the creation account, then simply place it aside and work with a RMH from your own alternative creation-account vantage point (italics original)."[53] He also seeks to make this point in the last chapter of his book, "What If I Am Wrong?" In that chapter he is not questioning whether he is wrong concerning the entirety of his system, but instead is examining the specific matter of 1 Timothy 2:13. He recognizes that 1 Timothy 2:13 is a weak link in the chain of his overall argument, and he tries to assess what his conclusions would be if he happened to be wrong on this point.

Hypothetically conceding the point, he says, "If one accepts a transcultural dimension to the garden's patriarchy, the most that can be said is that *man should have some kind of greater honor or prominence than woman*. Paul applied the principle of the Genesis text within his day and culture. But Paul's use of the Genesis text in restricting women from teaching is an application of the principle, not the principle itself" (italics original).[54] It is the *primogeniture* principle that Webb has in mind here. As I stated above, Paul is not using the principle of primogeniture

50. Webb, *Slaves, Women, and Homosexuals*, 142–43.

51. Ibid., 143.

52. Ibid., 144.

53. William J. Webb, "A Redemptive-Movement Hermeneutic: Responding to Grudem's Concerns" (paper presented at the annual meeting of the Evangelical Theological Society, San Antonio, TX, November 17, 2004), 10.

54. Webb, *Slaves, Women, and Homosexuals*, 237.

and applying it to a particular situation. Rather, he is citing a significant historical event as the basis for a command to the church. In our attempt to derive a principle from the creation order, it would be a mistake to do so mainly through the lens of a cultural custom such as primogeniture.

Based on this, Webb comes up with a principle of *greater honor*. But that is not the way the New Testament uses the historical data concerning creation order. In fact, we should say based on the truth of Galatians 3:28 that men *should not* receive greater honor than women. And the significance of creation order does not contradict this, for it is cited as a means of demonstrating God's design for the *roles* of men and women. The fact that Adam was created first is not used to say that men should receive greater honor than women. Instead, Paul cites this fact as a basis for the differing roles of men and women (1 Tim. 2:13; 1 Cor. 11:8).

Webb develops an alternative view that he labels "ultra-soft patriarchy," based on the possibility that the Genesis material is transcultural. Again we see Webb's rationale concerning primogeniture. "At least in an analogous way, the creative-order argument by Paul reflects primogeniture customs that accentuate a kind of social-honor logic within that culture. If one sees primogeniture as transcultural, surely it still leaves open the question of whether the degree or weight of creative-order deference should be viewed as cultural."[55] Therefore, in Webb's mind, if one retains this social-honor principle of primogeniture, then it would involve "granting men a certain level of *symbolic* honor for their firstborn status within the human family (italics original)."[56] He maintains that the redemptive-movement hermeneutic would still push us to affirm an equality of roles in the home and church. But if it turns out that he's wrong concerning primogeniture, the only difference would involve this symbolic honor for men.[57]

The problem, again, is that Webb makes the primogeniture principle the determining factor rather than what the New Testament texts actually state. The fact is that later biblical revelation shows that the creation material is significant in relation to the roles of men and women in the home and church. Webb's focus on primogeniture customs diverts his discussion from the specific matter of creation order. The two issues are related, but

55. Ibid., 242.

56. Ibid., 243.

57. Grudem rightly points out that "the only two options [Webb's] system will allow are *both thoroughgoing egalitarian options*" ("Should We Move Beyond the New Testament to a Better Ethic?," 335; italics original).

they are not synonymous. Thus, primogeniture serves as a kind of red herring that leads us away from the logic of the pertinent New Testament texts. Primogeniture, as complementarians have explained, is helpful in understanding the historical backdrop of Paul's statements in 1 Timothy 2:13 and 1 Corinthians 11:8. But the weight of those statements is not found in the *principle* of primogeniture. The significance of the creation material for Paul's inspired instructions to the church is that God's design from the very beginning has been for men and women to fulfill different (and complementary) roles in the home and church. And the order in which God created the man and the woman is indicative of this design.

Creation versus Redemption

Webb's next criterion is "Basis in New Creation," and on this point we will hear from some other redemptive-movement proponents as well. Webb cites five Pauline passages that describe the new-creation community. I will quote them with Webb's interpretive comments.[58] "For we were all baptized by one Spirit into one body—whether Jews or Greeks, slave or free—and we were all given the one Spirit to drink" (1 Cor. 12:13). "There is neither Jew nor Greek, slave nor free, male nor female . . . in Christ Jesus" (Gal. 3:28). "His [Christ's] purpose was to create in himself one new man [i.e., one new humanity] out of the two [Jew and Gentile]" (Eph. 2:15). "You were taught, with regard to your former way of life, to put off your old self [identity in the old humanity/society] which is being corrupted by its desires . . . and to put on the new self [identity in the new humanity/society], created to be like God in true righteousness and holiness" (Eph. 4:22–24). "Here [in the new society in Christ] there is no Greek or Jew, circumcised or uncircumcised, barbarian, Scythian, slave or free" (Col. 3:11). Webb concludes from these verses that "new-creation patterns should be given prominence over the old-creation patterns."[59]

Krister Stendahl, many years earlier, stressed this same point. In his discussion of Galatians 3:28 he says "it should be noted that this statement [Gal. 3:28] is directed against what we call the order of creation, and consequently it creates a tension with those biblical passages—Pauline and non-Pauline—by which this order of creation maintains its place in

58. Webb, *Slaves, Women, and Homosexuals*, 146–47. Webb quotes from the NIV.
59. Ibid., 147.

the fundamental view of the New Testament concerning the subordination of women."[60] He goes on to develop this by emphasizing the tension between creation and redemption. "If one counters that this would lead to a conflict with the order of creation, and hence must be wrong, we must say that it does indeed lead to such a conflict, and that is precisely what it should do and intends to do."[61] As Stendahl draws out some implications from his observations, he reflects on the matter of continuity and discontinuity between creation and redemption. He uses the following historical illustration to stress our current need to emphasize that which is new.

> When Marcion and the Gnostics stressed what was new in Christ, their radicalism led them to affirm a discontinuity between the old and the new, between the Creator and the Redeemer. This overstatement should, however, not blind us to the validity of their emphasis on the actual newness in Christ and in the church, even if the orthodox theologians, in their defense of the continuity, were compelled to stress the order of creation and the "not yet" aspect of this newness.[62]

Stendahl asserts that in certain situations, such as Corinth, there is the need for an emphasis on the old. In other situations, such as Galatia, there is the need for an emphasis on the new. He concludes that our current situation calls for the latter, for "we need badly the reminder of that which is new. We are not in danger of overstating that. We need help to see the forces toward renewal and re-creation. A mere repetition of Paul's reminder of the order of creation is not our most crying need."[63]

Richard Longenecker also develops this notion of a tension between creation and redemption. As he discusses the tension in 1 Corinthians 11:2–16, he asserts, "What Paul appears to be saying, in effect, is that though he has argued on the basis of creation for the subordination of women in worship, on the basis of redemption he must also assert their equality."[64] He also observes that in the Household Codes, as well as in 1 Corinthians 11:2–16, "Paul seems to be attempting to bring together two important theological categories: the redemptive category of new life

60. Stendahl, *The Bible and the Role of Women*, 32.

61. Ibid., 34.

62. Ibid., 36–37.

63. Ibid., 37.

64. Richard Longenecker, *New Testament Social Ethics for Today* (Grand Rapids: Eerdmans, 1984), 80–81.

in Christ wherein freedom, mutuality, and equality are prominent, and the category of what God has done by means of creation wherein order, submission, and subordination are features."[65] In Longenecker's view, this tension is not just something we perceive, but something that was present in Paul's own thinking. This extended quotation captures the thrust of Longenecker's point.

> When circumstances within the churches urged on [Paul] a more moderate course, he seems at times to have argued more from the categories of creation and curse than from the categories of eschatological redemption in Christ. At such times he appears, when judged from our present Christian perspective, almost chauvinistic. But we should not blame Paul too severely for failing to resolve all the tensions or solve all the difficulties, particularly since we seem to have done very little better in resolving them ourselves. On the contrary, we should applaud him for what he did do: he began to relate the theological categories of creation and redemption, most often emphasizing the latter; and he began to apply the gospel principles of freedom, mutuality, and equality to the situations of his day—including that of the place and status of women. In so doing, he set a pattern and marked out a path for Christian thought and action after him to follow.[66]

Thus, in the view of Webb, Stendahl, and Longenecker, there is a tension between creation and redemption, with a clear biblical emphasis on redemption. We are urged to heed this biblical emphasis by moving further along the trajectory that upholds freedom, mutuality, and equality over against order, submission, and subordination.

An important question surfaces at this point, and both Webb and Longenecker address it. The question concerns the destination of this path. Where is it taking us? Are there any limits that guide this pathway to freedom, mutuality, and equality? This question is particularly relevant in relation to homosexuality. If the freedom that accompanies redemption can be used to trump the order of creation, then one must ask whether this can happen in an open-ended way, or only in certain respects. Webb raises this question and responds by asserting that "Galatians 3:28 and the other Pauline clusters [1 Cor. 12:13; Eph. 2:15; 4:22–24; Col. 3:11] set

65. Ibid., 85.
66. Ibid., 87.

definite limits to the modification."[67] The fact that Paul mentioned certain categories—Jew and Greek, slave and free, male and female—shows the newness of redemption applied in certain ways but not necessarily in every imaginable way. Webb clarifies concerning the issue of homosexuality: "New-creation theology does not intend for 'male and female' intimacy and complementary relations to degenerate into homosexual relations, that is, no relations between men and women."[68] Longenecker frames the question in terms of "how we correlate the theological categories of creation and redemption."[69] He answers,

> Because of creation there are differences between the sexes which exist for the blessing of both men and women and for the benefit of society. Paul does not argue for anything like unisexuality or some supposed androgynous ideal. Heterosexuality is presupposed in all of his letters as having been ordained by God, and he has nothing but contempt and condemnation for homosexual practices. Yet Paul also lays emphasis on redemption in such a way as to indicate that what God has done in Christ transcends what is true simply because of creation.[70]

So for both of these scholars, there is the desire to move beyond the confines of creation theology as it relates to the roles of men and women, while maintaining the clear creation design of heterosexuality. It is commendable that Webb and Longenecker are constrained by God's Word to uphold the biblical prohibitions against homosexuality, but it is doubtful that the developmental hermeneutic can be passed along to another generation without allowing "further movement" on that issue. This is a major concern with the way that these writers view a tension between creation and redemption.

Another critique of this position is that it confuses creation and the curse. It is certainly appropriate and necessary to see a painful tension between *fallen* creation and redemption. This is the tension that we experience every day as believers, and it is the reality that Ephesians 4:22–24 speaks of (one of the "new-creation" texts cited by Webb). We must put off the old self and put on the new self. The tension between these two is not

67. Webb, *Slaves, Women, and Homosexuals*, 149.
68. Ibid., 150.
69. Longenecker, *New Testament Social Ethics for Today*, 92.
70. Ibid.

between *creation* and redemption, but rather between *sin* and redemption. An additional tension is seen in this statement when we compare it with what Paul says in Colossians 3:9–11 (Webb also cites Col. 3:11 as another "new-creation" text). For there the old self/new self contrast is stated in the indicative rather than the imperative, and thus we see the dynamic that we experience in this age, namely, the "already" and the "not yet." We have *already* put off the old self and put on the new self (Col. 3:9–10), but we are painfully aware this has *not yet* happened to the full extent that is intended. Hence, we are commanded to continually put off the old self and put on the new self (Eph. 4:22–24).[71]

Therefore when we think about two eras of history that are in tension with one another, the primary dichotomy exists between the fallen old age and the new age of redemption that has been inaugurated but not yet consummated. Comparing and contrasting creation itself with redemption may be legitimate in a secondary sense, as I will discuss below. But it is surely confusing and misleading to suppose there is a fundamental and ongoing strain between the two. Ben Witherington, in responding to Stendahl's view that Galatians 3:28 is directed against the order of creation,[72] observes that "Paul nowhere else in his letters indicates such distinctions are obliterated in Christ."[73] Then Witherington quotes his former instructor, Andrew Lincoln, as saying, "All this should immediately make us suspicious of any interpretation of Paul which makes a sharp distinction between creation and new creation . . . in Paul, redemption presupposes creation and includes creation (cf. Rom. 8:18ff., Col. 1:20, Eph. 1:10), and Christ as Lord is mediator both of creation and redemption (cf. 1 Cor. 8:6)."[74] In this way we should observe a significant cohesion between the realms of creation and redemption rather than drawing a sharp distinction between the two.[75]

71. F. F. Bruce, *The Epistles to the Colossians, to Philemon, and to the Ephesians*, NICNT (Grand Rapids: Eerdmans, 1984), 357: "This tension between the indicative and the imperative, between the 'already' and the 'not yet,' is common in the Pauline letters; it is summed up in the admonition: 'Be what you are!'—Be in practice what the calling of God has made you."

72. See Stendahl, *The Bible and the Role of Women*, 32.

73. Ben Witherington III, "Rite and Rights for Women—Galatians 3:28," *NTS* 27 (1981): 598.

74. Ibid. The quote is from an unpublished paper by Andrew Lincoln.

75. Albert Wolters provides this helpful comment on how we ought to understand the relationship between creation and redemption: "In the words of John Calvin, we must distinguish between 'the order of creation' and 'the order of sin and redemption,' which relate to each other as health relates to sickness-and-healing" (*Creation Regained: Biblical Basics for a Reformational Worldview* [Grand Rapids: Eerdmans, 1985], 48). Notice that the distinction is not between creation and redemption,

The standard egalitarian argument has been that male headship is simply a result of the fall. On this reasoning, one need not assert any tension between creation and redemption, for male headship is not part of the pre-fall creation. It is, rather, a product of sin, which is erased in the work of redemption.[76] Webb develops this argument in the discussion of his fifth criterion, "Basis in Fall or Curse." In responding to complementarians who understand the curse as introducing a distortion of male headship, Webb writes, "It is just as easy to work from the assumption that hierarchy and submission were a part of the pain that entered into a previous relationship of mutuality and equality."[77] He says later, "If hierarchy was introduced into human relationships post-Fall as a part of the curse, then there is no need to sustain hierarchy as part of gender relationships today. A redemptive approach to the curse would be to restore equality, not to perpetuate hierarchy."[78] If this was the extent of Webb's argument, he would not need to give new-creation patterns prominence over old-creation patterns.[79] He could simply emphasize the need to restore the

---

but between creation and sin. Redemption, then, is the restoration of the creation order. See also Cornelis P. Venema, "Calvin's Doctrine of the Last Things: The Resurrection of the Body and the Life Everlasting," in *Theological Guide to Calvin's Institutes: Essays and Analysis*, ed. David W. Hall and Peter A. Lillback (Phillipsburg, NJ: P&R Publishing, 2008), 460: "According to Calvin, the knowledge of God as Redeemer can be understood only within the framework of the doctrine of creation. The eternal Son through whom all things were made is the One through whom all things are being redeemed. Redemption, accordingly, amounts to nothing less than the restoration of all things to proper order through the mediation of Christ and the work of his Spirit." We could add here that redemption will be *more than* the restoration of all things to proper order, but it should be agreed that it will not be *less than* that or involve something that is in tension with it.

76. Richard S. Hess, "Equality with and without Innocence: Genesis 1–3," in *Discovering Biblical Equality: Complementarity without Hierarchy*, ed. Ronald W. Pierce and Rebecca Merrill Groothuis (Downers Grove, IL: IVP, 2004), 94–95: "There is neither explicit nor implicit mention of any authority or leadership role of the man over the woman, except as the sad result of their sin in the Fall and their ensuing judgments. Even then, such hierarchy is not presented as an ideal, but rather as a reality of human history like that of the weeds that spring from the earth. The resolution of this conflict in equality and harmony cannot be found in these chapters but looks forward to a future redemption." Also see Aida Besançon Spencer, *Beyond the Curse: Women Called to Ministry* (Nashville: Thomas Nelson Publishers, 1985), 36–37; Rebecca Merrill Groothuis, *Good News for Women: A Biblical Picture of Gender Equality* (Grand Rapids: Baker Books, 1997), 123; Judy L. Brown, *Women Ministers According to Scripture* (Kearney, NE: Morris Publishing, 1996), 51, 55; Gilbert Bilezikian, *Beyond Sex Roles: A Guide for the Study of Female Roles in the Bible* (Grand Rapids: Baker, 1985), 55 and 226n12. For a response to this argument that male headship is a result of the fall, see Wayne Grudem, *Evangelical Feminism and Biblical Truth: An Analysis of More Than 100 Disputed Questions* (Sisters, OR: Multnomah, 2004), 108–10. He says, "This is a fundamental claim of every egalitarian writer I know" (108).

77. Webb, *Slaves, Women, and Homosexuals*, 115.

78. Ibid., 119.

79. Ibid., 147. Quoted above.

equality of the original creation prior to the fall. But it seems that he wants to go one step further for the sake of argument. He recognizes that his assessment of the creation material may be a weak link in his system, as evidenced by the specific point on which he asks, "What if I am wrong?"[80] Therefore, he continues the discussion in his next two criteria pertaining to original creation, which I have discussed earlier in this chapter. It is commendable that Webb wrestles seriously with the elements of the creation narrative that point to God's pre-fall design for the distinct roles of men and women. He does not brush them off quickly, but recognizes that they exist and attempts some new explanations for why they appear before the fall. I have outlined these explanations in the previous section of this chapter, and it seems that the novelty of these hypotheses highlights the difficulty of denying male headship before the fall. It is certainly a stretch to acknowledge "whispers of patriarchy" in the garden and yet claim that they were not there in actuality.[81] So Webb first defends the standard egalitarian assumption that male headship is a result of the fall. But then he goes on to defend the egalitarian position even if this point is not true. He does so (1) by suggesting that the elements of original creation are not necessarily transcultural[82] and (2) by asserting that new-creation patterns should take precedence over old-creation patterns.[83]

The position of Stendahl and Longenecker is slightly different, for they do not seek to diminish the fact that the original creation possesses clear aspects of leadership and submission. They do not argue that male headship is only a product of sin. Instead, they focus on the priority of redemption over against creation. As evident in the quotations above,

80. Ibid., 236. He asks this question concerning his interpretation of 1 Tim. 2:13, which refers back to the order of creation. Thus, the issue at stake is whether Adam's priority in creation constitutes a transcultural principle of male leadership.

81. Ibid., 142–45.

82. This he does in criteria 6 and 7, "Basis in Original Creation, Section 1: Patterns" and "Basis in Original Creation, Section 2: Primogeniture" (ibid., 132–45).

83. This he does in criterion 8, "Basis in New Creation" (ibid., 145–52). Stanley Grenz, like Webb, holds that male headship is a result of the fall. But he also takes the next step, as Webb does, to assert that even if male headship was an aspect of creation, it still need not apply today. He writes, "Even if God had built this principle into creation from the beginning (which we have already indicated is not the case), this would not necessarily require that the Church continue to practice male leadership and female subordination. Christ did not establish the Church merely to be the mirror of original creation but to anticipate the eschatological new community. We are to live in accordance with the principles of God's new creation and thereby reflect the character of the triune God" (Stanley J. Grenz, "Anticipating God's New Community: Theological Foundations for Women in Ministry," *JETS* 38 [1995]: 604).

both Stendahl and Longenecker assert a very real tension between the two realms. Terrence Teissen rightly objects to Longenecker: "My major point of discomfort with Longenecker's proposal is the disjunction it introduces between creation and redemption and the suggestion that there is an unresolved tension in Paul's own ethical teaching that later Christians must resolve."[84] This reveals a fundamental problem for any redemptive-movement or developmental hermeneutic, for we must not assume that God's Word contains tensions we must resolve. The grave danger in such an assumption is the elevation of our contemporary subjective ideals above the authoritative instruction of the Bible.

It is much better to view the realms of creation and redemption as complementary, rather than disjunctive. As David Clowney points out, "In Ephesians 5, the husband's headship (a nurturing role, but apparently also one of primary accountability) is grounded by Paul simultaneously in creation and redemption, by his claim that the mystery of marriage, quoted from Genesis, means Christ and the church."[85] Clowney also sees this in 1 Timothy 2:11–15 and 1 Corinthians 11:3–16 in the same way. "In these passages, Paul argues for his conclusions by appeal to the order of creation, transformed in Christ."[86] Wayne Grudem also makes this point that male headship is part of the new creation in Christ. He cites, for instance, Colossians 3:18, "Wives, submit to your husbands, as is fitting *in the Lord*." And he adds, "In fact, Paul's commands as an apostle for the NT church *are* part of the 'new-creation' in Christ, and therefore 'I do not permit a woman to teach or exercise authority over a man' *is also part of that new creation*, because it is part of the teaching of the NT for the church" (italics original).[87] In this way, we should recognize the New Testament ethic as the final and authoritative ethic of the new creation in Christ. And the movement of redemption will not take us *beyond* creation in any way that involves tension with creation. On the contrary, redemption

84. Terrance Tiessen, "Toward a Hermeneutic for Discerning Universal Moral Absolutes," *JETS* 36 (1993): 206.

85. David Clowney, "The Use of the Bible in Ethics," in *Inerrancy and Hermeneutic: A Tradition, A Challenge, A Debate*, ed. Harvey M. Conn (Grand Rapids: Baker, 1988), 230.

86. Ibid. He contrasts this with the issue of slavery, which is not rooted in creation or redemption. He writes, "it seems to be apostolic teaching that, from the creation to consummation, men and women have differing roles to play with regard to authority and responsibility in family and church life. In contrast to the abolition of slavery, an abolition of those differences cannot be a fuller expression of basic principles laid down in the New Testament" (230–31).

87. Grudem, "Should We Move Beyond the New Testament to a Better Ethic?," 329.

will renew and restore the beauty of creation. In the area of male-female relationships, this will involve a restoration of the equality and complementarity of original creation, in which men and women delight in the respective roles God has assigned to them.

Finally in this section, it should be clarified in what ways redemption *does* go beyond creation. Redemption is not *merely* a restoration of creation—it is not limited to that. The new heaven and new earth will exceed the garden of Eden in beauty and splendor and glory. My point, though, is that the trajectory of redemption will not lead us to something that violates the order of God's original good creation. In other words, redemption will be more than a restoration of creation, but it will not be less than that or something that is in tension with it. Therefore, the way in which redemption *goes beyond* creation will be consistent with the patterns of creation.

Richard Hove provides some helpful insights in clarifying this point. First, after quoting Richard Longenecker and Stanley Grenz, Hove acknowledges that they are right in their claim that redemption transcends creation. Hove writes, "For example, in the consummate age believers will have resurrection bodies (1 Cor. 15) and people will 'neither marry nor be given in marriage' (Matt. 22:30)."[88] But then Hove makes a critical point that trajectory advocates seem to miss, namely, that we now live between the ages and therefore "cannot assume that consummated Christian ethics are the norm for today, in every respect, when we are not yet in the consummate age."[89] Thus, it is certainly appropriate to see redemption taking us beyond creation in certain respects, but it would be an over-realized eschatology to assume that all of those developments will happen in this age. The question, then, is how we are to discern God's ethical guidelines for us during this overlap of the ages. Hove responds, "The answer to this question is that God's Word both prescribes and describes life between the ages. Texts such as Ephesians 5, Colossians 3, 1 Timothy 2, etc., are given to this end."[90]

Second, Hove agrees that the new era is significantly different from the old (e.g., Paul's emphasis on freedom [Gal. 5], mutuality [1 Cor. 7], and equality). However, we cannot read the New Testament writers as

88. Richard Hove, *Equality in Christ? Galatians 3:28 and the Gender Dispute* (Wheaton, IL: Crossway, 1999), 101n23.

89. Ibid.

90. Ibid.

introducing "a sharp break with creation." He says, "On the contrary, Paul views the present redemption as including the restoration of creation (cf. Col. 3:10)."[91] And third, Hove points to the clear fact, which I have discussed at length, that "when Paul deals with sexual roles he often grounds his teaching by appealing to the created order (e.g., 1 Cor. 11:8; Eph. 5:31; 1 Tim. 2:13). This in itself should make one wary of affirming that sexual roles in the present are a radical break with sexual roles at creation."[92] These points should certainly give us pause when a writer appeals to redemption in order to minimize principles that are rooted in creation.

Specific Instructions versus General Principles

Redemptive-movement advocates appeal also to the tension between specific instructions and general principles. The point is built on a sound principle of hermeneutics: we must interpret Scripture with Scripture. R. T. France states this principle by saying, "It is a good rule to interpret Scripture in the light of Scripture, and to interpret the more obscure in the light of the clearer."[93] On this point we certainly agree. However, when it comes to deciding which passages are more obscure and which are clearer, divergent opinions emerge. The following statement by F. F. Bruce has been quoted by many egalitarians. He comments on Galatians 3:28, "Paul states the basic principle here; if restrictions on it are found elsewhere in the Pauline corpus, as in 1 Cor. 14:34f . . . or 1 Tim. 2:11f, they are to be understood in relation to Gal. 3:28, and not *vice versa*" (italics original).[94] Longenecker cites this statement by Bruce as a fundamental point that must inform our treatment of the New Testament gender passages. "We must, we have argued, first of all take our stand with the gospel proclamation and its principles (i.e., with the confession of Galatians 3:28) and seek to understand these passages [Col. 3:18–4:1; Eph. 5:21–6:9; 1 Cor. 11:2–16] from that perspective, and not vice versa."[95] The general principle of Galatians 3:28 is given clear priority over the specific instructions given elsewhere.

91. Ibid.

92. Ibid.

93. R. T. France, *Women in the Church's Ministry*, 70.

94. F. F. Bruce, *The Epistle to the Galatians: A Commentary on the Greek Text*, NIGTC (Grand Rapids: Eerdmans, 1982), 190.

95. Longenecker, *New Testament Social Ethics for Today*, 85.

In accord with the hermeneutical principle stated above, egalitarians contend that Galatians 3:28 is the clearer verse, and the other passages are more obscure. This is what R. T. France states emphatically, "The above discussion suggests that 1 Timothy 2:8–15 (no less than 1 Corinthians 14:34–35) falls rather firmly into the category of the more obscure!"[96] W. Ward Gasque writes similarly, "*Galatians 3:28 is the necessary theological starting place for any discussion of the role of women in the church.* Here is an unequivocal statement of absolute equality in Christ in the church. . . . Other texts must not be used to undermine this fundamental theological affirmation" (italics original).[97]

So on the one hand egalitarians have trumpeted Galatians 3:28 as the fundamental truth through which the other passages must be interpreted. On the other hand, complementarians are accused of using 1 Timothy 2 as the starting point that takes precedence over Galatians 3:28.[98] Andreas Köstenberger responds to this accusation in a balanced way. He first agrees that 1 Timothy 2 cannot simply be asserted as the fundamental teaching on gender issues. But then he observes that "generally writers are less aggressive in arguing that 1 Timothy 2 is a 'paradigm passage' than those who assign central importance to Gal. 3:28."[99] And he observes that "it is often those writers focusing on Gal. 3:28 who isolate 1 Timothy 2 as the only passage of its kind in the NT, thus dichotomizing between different kinds of gender passages of the NT and seeking to marginalize and relativize 1 Timothy 2."[100] Such a stark dichotomy is unneeded and unhelpful, and that applies to those on either side of the debate. Complementarians should not write off Galatians 3:28,[101] nor should egalitarians use Galatians 3:28 to silence the passages that give specific instructions for gender roles.

96. R. T. France, *Women in the Church's Ministry*, 70. See also David M. Scholer, "Feminist Hermeneutics and Evangelical Biblical Interpretation," *JETS* 30 (1987): 417–18.

97. W. Ward Gasque, "Response," in *Women, Authority, and the Bible*, ed. Alvera Mickelsen (Downers Grove, IL: IVP, 1986), 189.

98. See Scholer, "Feminist Hermeneutics," 417–18, who writes facetiously, "For example, 'everybody' knows that 1 Tim. 2:11–12 is the 'clear' text through which all other texts on women in the Church are to be read." Also see Klyne Snodgrass, "Galatians 3:28: Conundrum or Solution?," in *Women, Authority, and the Bible*, ed. Alvera Mickelsen (Downers Grove, IL: IVP, 1986), 164–65.

99. Andreas J. Köstenberger, "Gender Passages in the NT: Hermeneutical Fallacies Critiqued," *WTJ* 56 (1994): 275n63.

100. Ibid.

101. I believe Richard Hove's work is a good example of a complementarian who takes Galatians 3:28 very seriously, seeking to understand the verse in its context, and even acknowledging that the verse *does* have social implications (*Equality in Christ?*, 121–24).

The question that we must wrestle with is how to put these various passages together in a coherent way. If Galatians 3:28 emphasizes equality, whereas other passages (1 Tim. 2; 1 Cor. 11, 14; Eph. 5; Col. 3) emphasize role distinctions, then how are we to understand the unified biblical message concerning gender issues? We should first recognize that not all think this is possible. Many see a disjunction that is irreconcilable. They cannot comprehend how one person could write these seemingly contradictory statements, and therefore they search for other explanations. For instance, it may be that Paul's views had changed from the time he wrote Galatians to the time he wrote his other letters.[102] Or it may be that Paul wrote Galatians 3:28, while 1 Timothy 2 and 1 Corinthians 14:34–35 were written later by other individuals.[103] Yet another explanation is that there may have been an unresolved tension in Paul's own mind.[104]

Most evangelical feminists, however, do not resort to these explanations. Their contention is simply that we should begin with Galatians 3:28 (and other statements like it) as the starting place for the gender issue, and then with that as our foundation move to the other passages that seem to command distinct roles for men and women. Gretchen Gaebelein Hull, for instance, compares the issue to reconciling God's love with the Imprecatory Psalms or the Canaanite Wars. She says that she puts these passages to one side, "But I do *not* throw out the known truth 'God is love,' simply because some passages about the nature of

102. Hans Dieter Betz, *Galatians*, Hermeneia (Philadelphia: Fortress Press, 1979), 200: "While Paul admits the radical implications in Galatians, he has obviously changed his position in 1 Corinthians, and it may not be accidental that the whole matter is dropped in Romans."

103. For instance, L. Legrand, "There Is Neither Slave Nor Free, Neither Male Nor Female: St. Paul and Social Emancipation," *Indian Theological Studies* 18 (1981): 156, who writes, "The parallelism between 1 Cor. 14:35–37 and 1 Tim. 2:11–12 suggests that, if 1 Cor. 14:35–36 is to be taken as an interpolation, it finds its setting in the same deutero-pauline circles which produced the Pastoral Epistles, in the eighties. Also see Gordon D. Fee, *The First Epistle to the Corinthians*, NICNT (Grand Rapids: Eerdmans, 1987), 699–702, who considers 1 Cor. 14:34–35 to be inauthentic.

104. Paul K. Jewett, *Man as Male and Female: A Study in Sexual Relationships from a Theological Point of View* (Grand Rapids: Eerdmans, 1975), 112. He asserts that Paul's thinking about women "reflects both his Jewish and Christian experience. . . . So far as he thought in terms of his Jewish background, he thought of the woman as subordinate to the man for whose sake she was created (1 Cor. 11:9). But so far as he thought in terms of the new insight he had gained through the revelation of God in Christ, he thought of the woman as equal to the man in all things, the two having been made one in Christ, in whom there is neither male nor female" (Gal. 3:28).

God puzzle me (italics original)."[105] In the same way, she contends, we should put aside the "hard passages" about women. "Therefore we may legitimately put these Scripture portions aside for the very reason that they *remain* 'hard passages'—hard exegetically, hard hermeneutically, and hard theologically (italics original)."[106] W. Ward Gasque makes a similar point, and is very transparent about how one's starting point affects the conclusion.

> The Egalitarian View also takes these texts seriously [1 Cor. 11:2–16; 14:33–35; 1 Tim. 2:11–15; Eph. 5:22–33; 1 Peter 3:1–7], but it does not begin with these. It points out that if you leave these texts to the side until the end of the discussion, you will come out with a different conclusion. If you look at these texts first, you have basically programmed yourself to come to the Traditional View; but if you put these texts aside for the time being and first study all else that the Bible has to teach theologically about the role of men and women—in society and in the created order, in the Old Testament people of God and the New Testament people of God, in the church and the home—then you come to a different position.[107]

There is a serious hermeneutical problem with this dichotomy, as is evidenced in the above quotation, for it increases subjectivism rather than diminishes it. If one simply needs to find the verses that confirm his or her preconceived notions about a particular matter, and can then bring in the other passages only at the end of the discussion, then the presuppositions of the interpreter become dangerously influential. Of course, we would all acknowledge that our presuppositions will always be influential to some extent. But our goal should be to diminish that influence rather than increase it.

John Piper and Wayne Grudem recognize the danger in this. In responding to the suggestion that hotly debated texts should not be allowed any significant influence in the matter of manhood and womanhood, they state, "we are all biased and would very likely use this principle of

105. Gretchen Gaebelein Hull, *Equal to Serve: Women and Men in the Church and Home* (Old Tappan, NJ: Fleming H. Revell, 1987), 188.

106. Ibid., 189. She cites 1 Cor. 11:2–16; 14:33b–36; and 1 Tim. 2:8–15 as the three "hard passages," and then adds Col. 3:18; Eph. 5:22–24; and 1 Peter 3:1–6. On the other hand, she then mentions Gal. 3:28; 2 Cor. 5:17; John 1:12; and Rom. 8:17, commenting that "*all these clear teachings add up to the larger truth of the equality of all believers, and we do not ever throw that out*" (188, italics original).

107. W. Ward Gasque, "The Role of Women in the Church, in Society, and in the Home," *Crux* 19 (September 1983): 4.

interpretation to justify neglecting the texts that do not suit our bias while insisting that the ones that suit our bias are crystal clear."[108] They go on to say, "Our procedure should be rather to continue to read Scripture carefully and prayerfully, seeking a position that dismisses no texts but interprets all the relevant texts of Scripture in a coherent way."[109] David Scholer, an egalitarian, also recognizes this dilemma. He says, "What I want to stress is that from a hermeneutical point of view the question of where one enters the discussion is really an open question to which no canonical text speaks with clarity."[110] We would all agree that we should attempt to give each passage its due weight in our conclusions. Our goal should be to understand each text on its own terms, in its own context, and then to integrate them as best we can.

The problem with using Galatians 3:28 as a starting point is that it so easily and so quickly becomes a slogan for gender equality,[111] while it remains unclear whether Paul intended it in such a way. Köstenberger critiques Gasque for his statement, "In Galatians 3:28, Paul opens wide the door for women, as well as for Gentiles and slaves, to exercise spiritual leadership in the church."[112] Köstenberger asks "whether this is *really* Paul's point in the text's context or an implication drawn by Gasque himself," and he suggests "it would be advisable to distinguish more clearly between historical exegesis and contemporary application (italics original)."[113]

Köstenberger goes on to examine Galatians 3:28 in its context, tying it together with Galatians 3:16, 26, 29. He concludes, "In the context of the divine promise to Abraham, Paul's point is that in the one Son of the promise, Jesus Christ, all believers are indiscriminately heirs of God's promise to Abraham. There is no discrimination in that promise between Jew or Gentile, slave or free, male or female, as Paul proceeds to

108. Piper and Grudem, *Recovering Biblical Manhood and Womanhood*, 82.

109. Ibid. See also the helpful article by Paul Felix, "The Hermeneutics of Evangelical Feminism," *Master's Seminary Journal* 5 (1994): 133–36. These pages include his discussion of "The Principle of an Interpretive Center" and "The Principle of the Analogy of Faith."

110. Scholer, "Feminist Hermeneutics," 417–18. Just before this statement, however, he makes a case that "1 Tim. 2:11–12 is a far more difficult, less clear text than Gal. 3:28" (417).

111. For instance, see Richard Hove's response to Rebecca Groothuis' book, *Good News for Women*. Hove examines the references to Gal. 3:28 in her book and summarizes, "Virtually every reference Groothuis makes to this verse is accompanied by a statement regarding equality" (*Equality in Christ?*, 126).

112. Gasque, "Response," 192.

113. Köstenberger, "Gender Passages in the NT," 276.

develop in chapter four of Galatians."[114] This is Hove's conclusion as well: "Sandwiched between verses 26 and 29, Galatians 3:28 describes God's people in the new covenant. . . . As predicted by the Old Testament, the new covenant is now known by its universal call; *all* are invited, whether Jew or Greek, slave or free, male or female."[115] With these observations from the context of Galatians, egalitarians should be careful not to use this verse too forcefully in the gender debate. Yes, it is a significant verse that should influence our understanding of gender roles in the body of Christ, but it must be understood in its own context and alongside other pertinent texts.

On the one hand, egalitarians elevate the importance and relevance of Galatians 3:28, and on the other hand they seek to obscure the clarity of other passages, such as 1 Timothy 2. Thomas Schreiner demonstrates this point by citing several egalitarians.

> Egalitarians back away from verse 13 because it calls into question the exegetical edifice they have built to justify women teaching men. For example, Mary Evans says that the relevance of verse 13 for verse 12 is unclear, and that verse 13 merely introduces the next verse about Eve. Gordon Fee asserts that the verse is not central to Paul's argument. Timothy Harris says that the verse "is difficult to understand on any reading." Craig Keener thinks that the argument here is hard to fathom. David Scholer protests that the text is unclear and that Paul cites selectively from Genesis. Steve Motyer says that logic and justice are nullified if the complementarian position of verses 13–14 is accepted.[116]

Admittedly, there are difficult exegetical issues in 1 Timothy 2. For instance, what does it mean that "she will be saved through childbearing"? Nevertheless, the text contains a clear command in verse 12 and a clear ground for that command in verse 13. Therefore, Schreiner says of the egalitarian writers just cited, "It seems that unclarity is in the eye of the beholder, for the thrust of the verse [vs. 13] has been deemed quite clear in

114. Ibid., 277.

115. Hove, *Equality in Christ?*, 91. See also Ronald Y. K. Fung, *The Epistle to the Galatians*, NICNT (Grand Rapids: Eerdmans, 1988), 176: " 'In Christ Jesus' emphasizes that Paul views the elimination of these antitheses from the standpoint of redemption in Christ, while the context clearly shows that the primary emphasis of the verse is on *unity* in Christ rather than on equality" (italics original).

116. Schreiner, "An Interpretation of 1 Timothy 2:9–15," in *Women in the Church*, 2nd ed., 106.

the history of the church. The creation of Adam first gives a reason why men should be the authoritative teachers in the church."[117]

In addition to this, Köstenberger finds it interesting that "the same commentators who view Gal. 3:28, a passage that is clearly part of a polemical context, as a paradigmatic passage for gender roles, tend to be the ones who seek to limit the applicability of 1 Timothy 2, a passage that is much less clearly polemical but rather seems to be self-consciously and explicitly grounded on antecedent OT Scripture."[118]

Finally, Grudem highlights a key difference between the specific instructions to which complementarians appeal for their position, and the general principles to which egalitarians appeal. On the one hand, "The passages that prohibit women from being elders and from teaching or having authority over men in the assembled church are not isolated passages. They occur in the heart of the main New Testament teachings about church office and about conduct in public worship."[119] On the other hand, "egalitarian claims that all church leadership roles should be open to women are based not on any direct teaching of Scripture but on doubtful inferences from passages where this topic is not even under discussion."[120]

My attempt thus far in this section has been to illustrate how egalitarians use general principles (specifically the general principle of Gal. 3:28) as a starting point in establishing their view of gender equality, and to cite some of the complementarian responses to this practice. The point is not to suggest that Galatians 3:28, or any of the other texts highlighted by egalitarians, should be ignored. Nor am I recommending that 1 Timothy 2, or any other particular text, should be used as a "starting point." My hope is simply that we would not drive a wedge between general principles and specific instructions. When we come to the gender debate, all the relevant passages should be incorporated into our discussion and each text should be studied in its context and brought alongside the others.

Having surveyed the broader landscape of egalitarianism on this issue, I will now interact with William Webb, who lists this as one of his

117. Ibid.

118. Köstenberger, "Gender Passages in the NT," 277–78. He also responds to the view that passages such as 1 Cor. 14:33b–36 and 1 Tim. 2:11–15 were "necessitated by specific problems" (quoted from Snodgrass, "Galatians 3:28: Conundrum or Solution?," 180). Köstenberger responds, "The question arises whether or not Gal. 3:28, too, could be seen as 'necessitated by specific problems' in the Galatian church" (274).

119. Grudem, *Evangelical Feminism and Biblical Truth*, 362.

120. Ibid., 365.

eighteen criteria. His thirteenth criterion is "Specific Instructions Versus General Principles," and he states the criterion in this way: "A component of a text may be culturally relative if its specific instructions appear to be at odds with the general principles of Scripture."[121] He considers this a "moderately persuasive criteria," and we must note that he is using this principle in a more nuanced way than other egalitarians. He is not asserting that Galatians 3:28 simply trumps the other texts. In fact, he doesn't even mention Galatians 3:28 in his treatment of this criterion.[122] Rather, he is adding this principle to his arsenal, as it were, in order to push us further along the trajectory of redemptive movement. His assumption is that "*specific statements within Scripture are more likely to be culturally confined in some aspect than general statements*" (italics original).[123]

Webb then appeals to the slavery debate of the nineteenth century, because in that debate the same dichotomy emerged between specific instructions and general principles. I have discussed in chapter 1 the nature of this distinction as it was used by abolitionists. Webb summarizes the point in this way, "Slave owners in the United States valued the concession-based *specifics* of Scripture and argued their case primarily from those verses. . . . Abolitionists, on the contrary, began with the *broad principles* of Scripture and showed that slavery should be repealed on the basis of love and the ethics of equality in God's kingdom and in Jesus' new community" (italics original).[124] This is a valid and interesting observation from the slavery debate. At first it seems to give much credence to the trajectory hermeneutic in that the contemporary fight to end patriarchy is identified with the nineteenth-century fight to end slavery.

But a couple things should be noted. First, while many abolitionists did employ this strategy in arguing their case, it was by no means the only way that individuals used the Bible to oppose slavery. Other arguments were made, some of which were sound appeals to specific biblical texts without resorting to immutable principles. Second, the move to immutable principles in the slavery debate may have aided the abolitionists in certain respects, but it did not serve to uphold the authority of the Bible. As Mark

121. Webb, *Slaves, Women, and Homosexuals*, 179.

122. He has discussed Galatians 3:28 in criterion 2, "Seed Ideas," 83–91, and criterion 8, "Basis in Original Creation," 145–52. He also mentions it in criterion 10, "Opposition to Original Culture," 160, 162.

123. Ibid., 179.

124. Ibid., 180.

Noll notes, "This move led directly or indirectly to the theological liberalism of the last third of the twentieth century."[125] Therefore, we should be careful not to accept an argument uncritically, even if it was used for a very noble cause. Thus, the fact that a distinction between specific instructions and general principles was present in abolitionist arguments cannot be taken as a compelling reason to do the same in the gender debate.

Webb's second illustration has to do with gleaning laws (cf. Lev. 19:9–10; 23:22), which made provision for the poor. He makes the helpful point that while the principle of these instructions is still applicable, the manner in which we carry it out will most likely be different.[126] Webb qualifies his point, "While this example does not illustrate the tension that sometimes arises between the general and specific features of Scripture (as with slavery above), it does support the basic general-specific dictum: general statements within Scripture are more likely to be transcultural than specific statements."[127]

This illustration appears again in criterion 17, in which Webb offers a diagram of his ladder of abstraction.[128] As I discussed in my last chapter, in the section on purpose/intent statements, Webb's ladder of abstraction is helpful. The problem, however, is the manner in which one moves up the ladder. On the matter of gleaning laws, Webb rightly abstracts the principle inherent in these instructions. There is a transcultural principle that we should help the poor, and there is ultimately the principle of loving one's neighbor. But the way in which Webb "moves up the ladder" with respect to civil government and wifely submission is questionable.[129] Thus, Webb

125. Mark A. Noll, "The Bible and Slavery," in *Religion and the American Civil War*, ed. Randall M. Miller, Harry S. Stout, and Charles Reagan Wilson (New York: Oxford University Press, 1998), 51. He then explains, "Reasoning that led to liberal theological conclusions was prominent in the United States from the 1840s and became even more so in the decades after the war. But it was never the only alternative to the Reformed, literal hermeneutic. The prominence of liberal reasoning, however, made it extraordinarily difficult for orthodox alternatives. These alternatives faced the task of supplanting an approach to Scripture that, by contributing to the Christianization of the nation, had become part of the national myth. But especially on the application of the Bible to slavery, they also bore the burden of demonstrating that efforts to relativize individual texts seeming to affirm slavery did not at the same time subvert biblical authority itself."

126. He cites William W. Klein, Craig L. Blomberg, and Robert L. Hubbard Jr., *Introduction to Biblical Interpretation* (Dallas: Word Publishing, 1993), 411, who use the same illustration. Speaking of the gleaning laws, they write, "Such principles would scarcely help the vast majority of urban poor in our world today. Instead, those who seek to apply this text must find new ways to prevent the wasting or hoarding of surplus food in our world."

127. Webb, *Slaves, Women, and Homosexuals*, 181.

128. Ibid., 210.

129. See my section, "Purpose/Intent Statement," in chapter 5.

is correct that with certain biblical instructions we will need to move up the ladder of abstraction in our attempt to apply the instruction to our own lives today. And in this way general biblical principles will guide us in our application of specific instructions. However, Webb is wrong to use certain general statements to minimize the specific instructions concerning manhood and womanhood.

In the case of slavery, we can discern statements that undermine the practice and eventually brought about its abolition.[130] And in this way it is legitimate to point to general principles that complement those statements. The key difference, though, between this issue and the gender issue, is that slavery is not commanded, and it is never rooted in the order of creation. Therefore, we need not drive a wedge between general principles and specific instructions, for the specific instructions concerning slavery are not commanding slavery. On the other hand, the specific instructions concerning gender roles are clear commands and are rooted in the order of creation, and therefore to posit that general principles somehow undermine *these* commands is to insert an unnecessary and harmful tension into the Bible's message.

As Webb discusses the impact of this criterion on the issue of women's roles, he says, "It would appear that the broad ethical principles of justice, love, fairness, compassion, etc. offer a rationale for change to, or at least further improvements in, the kind of treatment that women received in the biblical text."[131] We should recognize that this is a step beyond the argument that Galatians 3:28 teaches gender equality and eliminates role distinctions. What Webb is saying here is even a step higher on the ladder of abstraction. He is not appealing to a particular text, but rather to the broad principles of justice, love, fairness, compassion, etc. This is more akin to the arguments from moral intuition that were marshaled by some abolitionists, arguments that were well intentioned but ultimately undercut the Bible's authority.[132] Similarly, Webb is appealing to general

130. See chapter 2.

131. Webb, *Slaves, Women, and Homosexuals*, 181.

132. See my section in chapter 1, "The Biblical Debate over Slavery." See J. Albert Harrill, *Slaves in the New Testament: Literary, Social, and Moral Dimensions* (Minneapolis: Fortress Press, 2006), 166, 175–76. He describes the moral-intuition hermeneutics in this way: "Direct observation of nature, not the verbal inspiration of Scripture, was considered to be the basis of knowledge, conscience the medium of observation. If, as in observation of the evils of slavery, conscience is found to conflict with certain passages in the Bible, conscience took priority as a more secure access to God's higher law" (175).

principles in a way that seems to put his moral intuition above biblical revelation. In fairness to him, it is doubtful that he intends to diminish the authority of the Bible in the least. He does not even classify this criterion as persuasive, but only moderately persuasive. However, this move will have the unintended effect of placing one's own perception of justice and fairness above the ethical instructions presented in the Bible.

Webb claims that complementarians (the "soft patriarchy" position, in Webb's terminology) also utilize this criterion, although perhaps unwittingly. He says they move "away from certain biblical texts in their own journey from hard to soft patriarchy," by which he is referring to the complementarian position that women are equal to men in essence and dignity and importance. Apparently Webb believes that the movement from hard patriarchy (I assume he means the position that women are inferior to men) to soft patriarchy must involve the elevation of certain general principles above specific instructions. He cites the first chapter of *Recovering Biblical Manhood and Womanhood*, but without any specific comment.[133] However, it does not require an appeal to broad general principles to establish the essential equality of male and female. One needs only to cite Genesis 1:27, "So God created man in his own image, in the image of God he created him; male and female he created them." Other passages and principles may be used, as John Piper does in his chapter,[134] but this does not involve a tension between general principles and specific instructions. The troublesome aspect of Webb's suggestion is that it places general principles *over against* certain instructions in such a way that those instructions are effectively silenced.

This becomes more precarious as Webb moves finally to the issue of homosexuality. He immediately acknowledges that advocates for the homosexual lifestyle often use this same reasoning. He refers to the book by Letha Scanzoni and Virginia Mollenkott titled *Is the Homosexual My Neighbor? A Positive Christian Response.*[135] Webb summarizes the argument of the book: "From the broad principle of loving one's neighbor Scanzoni

133. John Piper, "A Vision of Biblical Complementarity: Manhood and Womanhood Defined According to the Bible," in *Recovering Biblical Manhood and Womanhood*, ed. Piper and Grudem, 26–55.

134. For instance, he says that "mature masculinity gives appropriate expression to the Golden Rule in male-female relationships (Matt. 7:12)" (ibid., 37).

135. Letha Dawson Scanzoni and Virginia Ramey Mollenkott, *Is the Homosexual My Neighbor? A Positive Christian Response*, rev. ed. (San Francisco: HarperCollins, 1994).

and Mollenkott infer that a Christian response should ultimately be one that accepts homosexuality as an appropriate alternative form of sexual expression."[136]

Webb's response to this book is very gracious and very helpful in many ways. He urges us to love and minister to homosexuals while telling them the truth about sin and the forgiveness that comes through Christ. I wholeheartedly agree with these points, and I am grateful for Webb's winsome treatment of this delicate issue. Nevertheless, Webb's stance against homosexual behavior is severely weakened by the way he juxtaposes general principles and specific instructions. He seeks to distance himself from Scanzoni and Mollenkott, but his rationale is not compelling. The reasons he gives for why we should not adopt the hermeneutic developed in *Is the Homosexual My Neighbor?* are reasons I could cite for why we should not adopt the egalitarian use of Galatians 3:28. Webb writes, "To the question, 'Is the homosexual my neighbor?' we should answer with a resounding 'Yes!' But having given that answer, it hardly affirms the acceptance of homosexuality."[137] He is correct. But Webb does not demonstrate why his use of this principle is any different from Scanzoni and Mollenkott. Similarly, our response to the questions, "Is the woman my neighbor?" or "Is Galatians 3:28 transcultural?" or "Should we uphold justice and fairness?" should be a resounding "Yes!" But that hardly denies the biblical pattern of manhood and womanhood clearly taught in other passages.

As he concludes his discussion of this criterion, Webb makes a couple additional points. He tries to distinguish between the "women/slavery issues" and the homosexual issue by saying that the slavery issue and the gender issue "involve options that are on a graded scale," whereas "we see that a person either practices homoerotic acts or does not; thus, incremental assessment is not part of the equation."[138] He then makes the point that a person's conclusions on slavery or gender roles do not threaten the person's position in Christ's kingdom. "Compared to the homosexual issue, the spectrum of alternatives in the slavery/women issues does not call into question one's salvation or eternal destiny."[139] These points are odd, and somewhat out of place in this section, for they do not give any

136. Webb, *Slaves, Women, and Homosexuals*, 182. He cites Scanzoni and Mollenkott, *Is the Homosexual My Neighbor?*, 1–11, 23.

137. Webb, *Slaves, Women, and Homosexuals*, 182.

138. Ibid., 184.

139. Ibid.

concrete reason why general principles take precedence over instructions concerning gender roles but not instructions concerning homosexuality. These points offer certain dissimilarities between the issues, but they do not specifically relate to the criterion under discussion. Additionally, the issue of gender roles is not as "incremental" as Webb makes it out to be. It may be true that there is a spectrum of positions, each with its particular nuances (as is true in the debate over homosexuality), but when we get to the bottom of the matter there are those who believe that 1 Timothy 2:12 still means that in the church women should not teach or have authority over men, and there are those who deny that the verse still applies in this way. And concerning marriage, there are those who believe Ephesians 5:22–33 still prescribes male headship and wifely submission, and there are those who deny this. Therefore, Webb's attempt to turn the discussion into a sliding scale of positions muddles the discussion and diminishes the importance of the pivotal texts.

The criterion of specific instructions versus general principles reveals an attempt by egalitarians to minimize certain texts that contradict their conclusions. This reveals the subjective tendency to emphasize passages and principles that favor one's presuppositions and to minimize those texts that teach otherwise. This criterion also drives an arbitrary wedge into Scripture, by setting certain principles over against certain instructions. Finally, it makes Webb's system, as well as the arguments of other egalitarians, susceptible to those who seek to condone the homosexual lifestyle. It is good that Webb has not taken this step, but he has not provided an adequate foundation for future generations who would utilize his hermeneutical method.

Conclusion

This chapter has dealt with four additional matters. First, I interacted with Webb concerning the important issue of original creation. The significance of original creation is seen in all three components of Webb's book, *Slaves, Women, and Homosexuals.* In comparing the slavery issue and the issue of women's roles, we see an extremely important difference, for slavery is never rooted in the order of creation while gender roles are. And a similarity can be seen in the instructions concerning gender roles and homosexuality, for these instructions find their basis in creation.

Male headship and wifely submission, as well as the prohibition against homosexuality, are all rooted in God's creation design for manhood and womanhood. The second section of this chapter dealt with the closely related issue of primogeniture. This is a cultural custom which gives us an insight into the minds of those who would have originally heard the instructions of 1 Timothy 2:11–15. But the cultural nature of primogeniture itself does not undermine the transcultural nature of Paul's instructions. Paul was not appealing to primogeniture per se, but to the specific order of creation, "For Adam was formed first, then Eve" (1 Tim. 2:13). This is the ground for his instruction in the previous verse; he is not basing it on a cultural practice that calls for greater honor to be attributed to the firstborn.

The second half of this chapter contained a discussion of two broader hermeneutical questions: the relationship between creation and redemption, and the relationship between specific instructions and general principles. On the question of creation and redemption, I contended that the two realms should be viewed as harmonious and cohesive, rather than disjunctive. Certainly there are ways in which redemption transcends creation, but this will not happen in a way that creates tension between the two. In the area of manhood and womanhood, redemption will restore the beauty of gender equality and complementarity that was present in the garden before the fall. Finally, on the issue of specific instructions and general principles, we must be wary of subjective tendencies to elevate the passages or principles that fit our preconceived notions while suppressing the texts that challenge them. This tendency easily raises our own intuitions above the authoritative revelation of God's Word. Instead, we must seek to examine every pertinent text, understanding it in its own context, and then seek to understand how the various passages fit together in a coherent whole.

CONCLUSION

The comparison of New Testament slavery passages and women's passages is a fascinating study. We have been faced with difficult hermeneutical questions, and my hope is that this book will serve to clarify at least some of those questions.

SLAVERY

The issue of slavery in the Bible is certainly complex, and an examination of the New Testament slavery passages does not yield easy or simple solutions. We can look back to the nineteenth-century debate over slavery and see the difficulty for abolitionists to convince others that the Bible does not support slavery but rather undermines it.[1] Some of these abolitionist arguments were sound appeals to the Bible, and yet they failed to convince, largely, it seems, because of the racist presupposition that resided in so many minds and hearts. Other abolitionist arguments distinguished between specific instructions and general principles and eventually led to more liberal views of Scripture. These were the arguments that resemble the trajectory approach, for they used the *spirit* of certain passages to override the *letter* of other texts, as those texts had been understood.

However, as we examine the specific commands to slaves and other comments on slavery in the Bible, we see that the institution, in fact, does not receive biblical support or sanction. While we do not find a clear condemnation of slavery, neither do we find it commended.[2] The New Testament writers assume the reality of slavery and speak to masters

1. This discussion is found in chapter 1, in the section on the "Nineteenth-Century Slavery Debate."

2. See chapter 2, the section "Why Does the New Testament Not Condemn the Institution of Slavery?"

and slaves in their specific roles, but there is nothing that positively supports the institution of slavery. In addition to this, we observe that references to creation are absent from the slavery passages, which marks the crucial distinction between these passages and the passages dealing with gender roles.

In the three texts where a ground clause undergirds a command to slaves (Eph. 6:8; Col. 3:24; 1 Peter 2:19–20), the ground involves a reference to God looking kindly on those who obey Him. There is nothing in these passages that establishes slavery as a God-ordained institution. Rather, instructions are given to slaves and masters in their respective positions without explicit comment on the morality of slavery itself. In 1 Timothy 6:1 and Titus 2:10, which contain purpose clauses, slaves are exhorted to obey so that they might adorn the reputation of Christianity rather than tarnish it. In this way, these two verses resemble 1 Peter 3:1 and Titus 2:5, which state similar purposes for wifely submission.

After close examination of the New Testament slavery passages, we do not detect a "biblical" case favoring the institution of slavery. This is in contrast with those in the past who have defended slavery from the Bible. It is also in contrast with certain egalitarian writers who assert that such a biblical case for slavery exists, and thus argue that we must move beyond the biblical teaching on slavery *and the biblical teaching on gender roles.*

Women

A comparison of the slavery passages with the women's passages reveals critical differences between the two.[3] Most notable are the repeated references to creation found in 1 Timothy 2:13, 1 Corinthians 11:8–9, Ephesians 5:31, and most likely 1 Corinthians 14:34 in its reference to "the Law." Also significant are the Christological and theological analogies of Ephesians 5:22–33 and 1 Corinthians 11:3. William Webb seeks to trivialize these analogies by comparing them to other "theological" analogies that are connected to slavery, monarchy, primogeniture, and right-handedness.[4] But important differences have been blurred. In the

3. See chapter 4 for a summary of the exegetical conclusions and comparison of the two sets of passages.

4. William J. Webb, *Slaves, Women, and Homosexuals: Exploring the Hermeneutics of Cultural Analysis* (Downers Grove, IL: IVP, 2001), 186–87. See my discussion of 1 Corinthians 11 and Ephesians 5 in chapter 3, and also my discussion of theological analogy in chapter 5.

slavery passages where a theological analogy is used (Eph. 6:5–9; Col. 3:22–4:1; 1 Peter 2:18–25), the example given is not intended as a basis for the institution of slavery. Rather, Paul and Peter offer examples that illustrate appropriate behavior. In contrast with those passages, Ephesians 5:22–33 and 1 Corinthians 11:3 are offering much more than an illustration of appropriate behavior. They are making profound statements about the reality of how God designed us. Indeed, there is an intentional parallel between God's relationship with his Son, Christ's relationship with his church, and a husband's relationship with his wife.

Hermeneutics

Following the exegesis of chapters 2 and 3, and the summary and comparison of chapter 4, I moved to the hermeneutical discussion related to a redemptive-movement hermeneutic. I did not interact with every one of Webb's eighteen criteria but chose eight that seemed particularly relevant to the focus of this book. In the case of theological analogies, Webb's discussion is helpful with respect to the slavery passages. For he says, "When the biblical text addresses human sociological structures, there is a significant possibility that the theological analogy is intended to motivate behavior within existing structures without necessarily endorsing the structures themselves as transcultural."[5] This is precisely what is going on in the slavery texts. However, this principle cannot be applied to Ephesians 5 and 1 Corinthians 11, since these are not *mere* analogies, but rather describe significant aspects of God's nature that are to serve as a pattern for male-female relationships. Also, the comparisons Webb makes between these texts and other "theological analogies" are highly suspect.

Preliminary movement and seed ideas are the two criteria I dealt with next. While there are New Testament passages that point beyond certain social structures of the first century, this does not give us warrant to move beyond the *ethic* of the New Testament. In particular, we can detect in the ethic of the New Testament a movement beyond the institution of slavery. On the other hand, though, we must not move beyond biblical gender roles, for the New Testament ethic prescribes them. Purpose/intent statements is another criterion Webb uses to build his case for a trajectory hermeneutic. But it is not clear that purpose/intent statements necessarily

5. Webb, *Slaves, Women, and Homosexuals*, 187.

imply that a text is cultural. In particular, it is not clear that the purpose of 1 Peter 3 can no longer be fulfilled in our day.

Issues related to creation are pivotal to this study, and the next three criteria relate to it. Basis in original creation is a compelling reason to assume the transcultural application of the gender passages. Webb attempts to minimize this by pointing to several aspects of original creation that are *not* transcultural. However, his discussion assumes unlikely and hermeneutically simplistic interpretations of the creation account in an attempt to heighten the perceived tension between original creation and today's culture. But his reasoning fails to address the issue at hand since the complementarian understanding of 1 Timothy 2:13 and 1 Corinthians 11:8–9 does not assume that the creation account is binding in all of its details. The point is rather that certain things God established at creation *are* extremely significant, and the New Testament reveals those aspects to us. In this way, basis in original creation is extremely significant for the gender passages. Slavery is never rooted in creation, but gender roles are. This is also important in relation to the issue of homosexuality, for this is prohibited based on God's creation design for manhood and womanhood (Rom. 1:26–27).[6]

Primogeniture is closely related to the issue of original creation, and it is a pivotal point for Webb. Webb argues that the cultural nature of primogeniture customs points to the cultural nature of 1 Timothy 2:13. But complementarians refer to primogeniture only to point out how the original readers of 1 Timothy would have understood this statement. When we examine the text itself, we see that Paul is appealing to the order of creation, not to the custom of primogeniture. He cites the specific order in which God created the man and the woman, and he uses this to ground his instruction that women are not to teach or exercise authority over men. The third criterion related to creation is the relationship between creation and redemption. On this question I acknowledged that there are ways in which redemption transcends creation. However, we must recognize that the New Testament reveals how this will be so, and the authoritative instructions of the New Testament include guidelines for the differing roles of men and women. We would need clear textual warrant for overturning the design for manhood and womanhood revealed in creation, but what we find rather are appeals to creation in order to uphold gender

6. Webb minimizes the significance of this passage, as I discussed in chapter 6.

differences (e.g., 1 Tim. 2:13; 1 Cor. 11:8–9). Thus, concerning the matter of manhood and womanhood, redemption cannot be viewed as moving beyond creation in any way that would contradict or create tension with the order of creation.

Last of all is the criterion that juxtaposes specific instructions and general principles. Here Galatians 3:28 is asserted by many egalitarian writers as the clear gospel principle that must supersede the specific instructions of passages such as 1 Timothy 2. But we need not drive a wedge between the two. Asserting this tension between certain biblical principles and specific biblical instructions is not only unnecessary, it can be extremely harmful. For instance, in the debate over homosexuality, this same dichotomy is used to condone behavior that is clearly condemned in Scripture. Webb distances himself from such arguments, but his system is susceptible to this line of thinking.[7] A significant problem with distinguishing general principles and specific instructions and using the first to minimize the latter, is that it makes the interpretive task more subjective, and thus diminishes the authority of the Bible. It allows a person to emphasize the principles that fit his or her presuppositions and to undermine the texts that are at odds with those presuppositions. We must strive, rather, to understand how each passage fits into the unified message of the Bible. And we must allow each passage to challenge and refine any assumptions we may have absorbed from sources other than the Bible.

What Is at Stake?

This study has not been an abstract, academic endeavor for me. As a pastor, I am zealous to teach and preach and lead in such a way that individuals are inspired and instructed to glorify God in every aspect of their lives, not least of which is the area of manhood and womanhood. By pursuing the model of marriage presented in Ephesians 5, husbands and wives vividly display Christ's relationship to his church and thus proclaim the gospel to those around them. Single individuals and young people will also glorify God as they grow into godly men and godly women who recognize their God-ordained roles in the home and church and affirm and encourage those roles as they are played out in the marriages around

7. See discussion in chapter 6.

them. I desperately want our church and other churches to recognize the beauty of what God has done in creating us male and female.

As a husband, I am very aware of the ways in which I fall short of the biblical model of manhood. But I have also begun to experience the delights of living with my wife in a way that honors God and brings both of us great satisfaction. As I grow and mature in my role as the sacrificial leader of our home, and as Stacy supports and encourages my leadership, we are discovering the joy of our complementary, God-given roles.

Finally, as a father, I want to pass on to our children a clear vision of manhood and womanhood. In the moral confusion of our culture, I want my son and two daughters to know what it means to be a man and what it means to be a woman. I want them to know that there is a difference between the two, and that it is a wonderful and noble thing to grow into the roles that God has set out for each of them. I desire that our daughters one day will know what to look for in a prospective husband, and that our son will know what to look for in a prospective wife.

Therefore, there is much at stake in this debate—for the church, for marriages, and for families. The debate over gender roles has not diminished, and I do not see any end in sight. But we must not grow weary in defending the beautiful portrait of gender complementarity presented in the Bible. For by minimizing this aspect of Scripture, we put ourselves at great risk of looking more and more like the world, and we also miss out on many joys God intends for his people. May we rather submit ourselves to the teaching of God's Word, no matter how countercultural it may be, and discover the joy of affirming and conforming to God's plan for manhood and womanhood.

Postscript: The Continuing Discussion

The redemptive-movement hermeneutic continues to develop, and it will continue to be an important subject of discussion. In this postscript I will summarize some of the relevant publications that have appeared in the last few years.

Four Views on Moving Beyond the Bible to Theology

An important work was published in 2009 which highlights the significance of these matters. *Four Views on Moving Beyond the Bible to Theology* includes chapters by Walter Kaiser, Daniel Doriani, Kevin Vanhoozer, and William Webb.[1]

What is most intriguing to me in this book is to see two egalitarians, Kaiser and Webb, presenting opposing hermeneutical approaches for their conclusions. I will give a general overview of the book and then focus on comparing and contrasting Kaiser and Webb.[2]

General Overview

The book consists of the presentation of four hermeneutical models, each followed by responses from the three other contributors. Following

1. Gary T. Meador, ed., *Four Views on Moving Beyond the Bible to Theology* (Grand Rapids: Zondervan, 2009).

2. This material is from an article I wrote for *The Journal for Biblical Manhood and Womanhood*, "Two Egalitarian Paths toward the Same Destination," 15, 1 (Spring 2010). Used by permission.

this section of the book there are three "reflection" chapters, offered by Mark Strauss, Al Wolters, and Christopher Wright.

Walter Kaiser presents a principlizing model of biblical interpretation. A key aspect of this approach is using the Ladder of Abstraction, which Kaiser defines as "a continuous sequence of categorizations from a low level of specificity up to a high point of generality in a principle and down again to a specific application in the contemporary culture" (24). He illustrates this by citing the Old Testament prohibition against muzzling an ox (Deut. 25:4) and showing how Paul applies that principle to the matter of financially supporting pastors in the church (1 Cor. 9:9–12; 1 Tim. 5:18).

Kaiser then addresses various issues in order to demonstrate the use of a principlizing model. He discusses euthanasia, women and the church, homosexuality, slavery, abortion, and embryonic stem cell research. In each case he seeks to show that principles within the Word of God are sufficient for our instruction concerning these matters. There is no need to *go beyond* the Bible.

Daniel Doriani commends a redemptive-historical model for hermeneutics. The focus here is on the progressive development and christocentricity of the Bible. Doriani strongly affirms the authority, sufficiency, and perspicuity of Scripture and the need for interpreters to be both technically skilled and spiritually sensitive. On the matter of Scripture's authority he states, "If Scripture says something I do not prefer, then so much the worse for my preferences" (77).

Doriani discusses two specific ways in which one may go beyond the sacred page. First, casuistry can be used to answer questions that are not addressed specifically in the Bible. Quoting Thomas Merrill, Doriani defines casuistry as the " 'art of resolving particular cases of conscience through appeal to higher general principles,' especially when one must act at a time when principles seem to be in conflict or when a new problem has emerged" (100). Second, we must go beyond the sacred page by asking the right questions, specifically having to do with duty, character, goals, and worldview (103). Doriani applies this approach to issues such as gambling, wedding planning, architecture, and women in ministry.

Kevin Vanhoozer presents a drama-of-redemption model for understanding Scripture. This position is similar to the redemptive-historical model, but with an emphasis on our role as performers in the theodrama that continues to unfold. We hold a script, but it is also incumbent on us to improvise in response to the unexpected situations that we encounter. Vanhoozer applies his method to the theology of Mariology and the contemporary issue of transsexuality.

William Webb advances a redemptive-movement hermeneutic. He begins his chapter by qualifying what he means by moving beyond the Bible. He states that in one sense "we should never move beyond the Bible for it contains the sacred and cherished covenant with the God we have come to love deeply" (215). By moving beyond the Bible he means moving beyond the *concrete specificity* of the Bible, or the *time-restricted elements* of the Bible, or an *isolated* or *static* understanding of the Bible (215). In this essay Webb summarizes his previous points concerning slavery and also develops his hermeneutical model in relation to two additional matters: war and corporal punishment.

Slavery and the Gender Debate

Now I will focus on a few of the points made by Kaiser, Doriani, and Webb that specifically relate to slavery and the gender debate. The fascinating thing to see here is the drastically different (and opposing!) ways in which Kaiser and Webb defend the egalitarian stance. Doriani's complementarian position helps to highlight these differences. Webb believes we must move beyond the "concrete specificity" of the Bible in order to arrive at abolitionism and egalitarianism. Kaiser sees both of these positions inherent in the biblical statements themselves.

Kaiser, through an interesting word study, concludes that Gen. 2:18 should read "I will make a power corresponding to the man" (Kaiser's translation, page 30) rather than "I will make him a helper fit for him" (ESV). He then offers this alternative translation as a possible explanation for Paul's wording in 1 Cor. 11:10, "For this reason, a woman ought to have power/authority [Gk. *exousia*] on her head" (Kaiser's translation, page 31). As for 1 Cor. 14:33b–35, he says that it "actually comes from a letter addressed to Paul from the Corinthian church and therefore is not normative teaching" (32). Then on the pivotal text of 1 Timothy 2, Kaiser suggests that Paul is basing his instructions not on the "orders of creation" but on the "orders of education." He bases this on the fact that Paul does not employ his usual word for "to create" (*ktizō*) in verse 13. Rather, he uses the word "to form" (*eplasthē*), which can carry the meaning of "shaping or molding educationally, spiritually" (35). Therefore, "since the woman had not as yet been taught, she was all the more easily 'tricked'" (35). Kaiser's reading of 1 Timothy 2, then, is that women should be taught and then allowed to teach and exercise authority over men. Thus, one need not go beyond the Bible to see the principles of egalitarianism.

Kaiser also addresses the issue of slavery, drawing a sharp distinction between biblical debt slavery and pagan slavery. He surveys various passages in the Pentateuch and shows the gracious nature of these instructions in comparison with the slavery found in pagan society. Then he points to Philemon as a conclusive biblical statement against pagan slavery. "Alas, despite the clarity of Paul's statements, many do not believe the Bible ever finally took a stand against all forms of involuntary, that is, pagan, slavery" (42). It is at this point that Webb will sharply disagree with Kaiser.

Doriani defends a complementarian reading of 1 Timothy 2. One must conclude that the prohibition in this text is either temporary (the egalitarian position) or partial (the complementarian position). Doriani seeks to show that the prohibition is permanent but partial. "Women should learn the faith and share their knowledge in some settings, as Paul says in Titus 2:4. But they should not become primary public instructors and defenders of the faith in the local church's pastoral positions, as Paul envisioned them in his instruction to Timothy. This division of gender roles has been God's design from the beginning. So there is no reason to go beyond/against the plain sense of 1 Timothy 2 if we seek Paul's guidance for the role of women in the church" (112–13).

Doriani also compares the question of gender roles to the issue of slavery. He acknowledges that "the Bible does make concessions to cultural realities," noting that "biblical law regulates and undermines the institution of slavery but does not forbid it" (118). Male leadership, however, is no such concession. As Doriani presents in his survey of biblical history, the principle of male leadership is present throughout the Bible and not a conclusion based on "a mere heap of texts" (118). Earlier in the chapter he also appeals to 1 Cor. 7:21, 23 and Philemon 11–21, concluding (less emphatically than Kaiser) that "Paul's opposition to slavery is not stated in the form of a frontal assault on the institution, but he clearly wants Christians to avoid or escape it if they can" (83). He then makes the critical observation that the way the Bible addresses slavery and the way it presents male leadership are fundamentally different. They are not parallel, as Webb asserts (and also John Stackhouse, *Finally Feminist*, which Doriani interacts with briefly). Rather, "the parallel is between male leadership of marriage and parental leadership of children. Both are grounded in creation," "continue after the fall," and "are reaffirmed after Christ accomplishes redemption" (83).

Webb, in his responses to Kaiser and Doriani, uses a significant amount of space to critique their statements about slavery. He first takes issue with Kaiser's stark contrast between biblical debt slavery and pagan slavery. Webb asserts, "Debt slavery was part of the pagan scene, and permanent chattel slavery was part of the biblical scene at least for non-Hebrew slaves" (65). His more important criticism of Kaiser has to do with Philemon. Where Kaiser sees abolitionism, Webb sees nothing of the sort. He presents seven arguments for a non-abolitionist reading of Philemon and then, in a move reminiscent of his book, asks "What if I'm wrong?" with regard to one detail of his argument (68).

It seems that Kaiser finds a solution to the slavery question too simply, and Webb presents it as overly difficult. Webb minimizes the liberating features of these texts, and in doing so appears to strengthen the appeal of his hermeneutical system. If the Bible does not point beyond slavery in the concrete specificity of certain texts, then the redemptive-movement hermeneutic may be our only hope of arriving at an abolitionist ethic. But if texts such as 1 Corinthians 7:21 and Philemon do provide pointers beyond slavery, then we need not move beyond the ethic of the NT. Rather, we can embrace this NT ethic which, itself, points beyond slavery.

In response to Doriani, Webb's criticisms are similar. He argues against the idea that 1 Corinthians 7:21 provides any support for abolitionism and reasserts the same concerning Philemon. For Webb there is simply no way of getting from the biblical text to an abolitionist ethic without the use of his redemptive-movement hermeneutic. "These texts are not simply there to regulate society, as Doriani suggests. We need to celebrate the *incremental redemptive movement* of both Old and New Testament slavery texts and permit their underlying spirit to carry us to an abolitionist position—using a logical and theological extension of Scripture's redemptive spirit found within the slavery texts themselves" (137, emphasis original).

It is interesting that Webb does not discuss any of the gender passages in his chapter. He does not want his hermeneutical model to be equated with egalitarianism, as he states in his response to Doriani. Webb claims that "there are leading evangelicals who endorse a redemptive-movement hermeneutic approach (contra Doriani) and yet maintain some sort of contextually configured hierarchy, generally of a soft or light version, for today" (133–34, citing Darrell Bock, Craig Blomberg, and Mark Strauss). Nonetheless, Webb has made his views clear in *Slaves, Women, and Homosexuals*, and it seems to be a fundamental aim of his hermeneutic to uphold egalitarianism and undermine complementarianism.

There are many things I sincerely appreciate about Webb's work. He is helpful in raising difficult questions that require a sensitive response. He certainly gives any reader much to ponder concerning those potentially troubling passages of Scripture. In addition to this, it is Webb's desire to provide skeptics with an apologetic for the Scriptures, an intention that is to be commended.

The way in which Webb's system comes together, however, seems misguided. As Al Wolters points out in his reflection chapter, it is curious that, "according to [Webb's] scheme, the same text can have contradictory meanings" (307). He is referring to 1 Timothy 2:12, which Webb agrees prohibits women from teaching or having authority over men, at least in the "concrete specificity" of the text. But then the redemptive movement of the text reveals that the opposite is the case: women are free to teach and exercise authority over men. Wolters says, "In this way [Webb] can have his cake (hold to contemporary values) and eat it too (claim faithfulness to Scripture)" (307). This, I believe, goes to the heart of the problem with the redemptive-movement hermeneutic. Webb desires to root his egalitarianism in the text of Scripture, but knows he must avoid the exegetical issues that Kaiser cannot successfully tackle. Thus, he concedes the complementarian exegesis and then moves beyond the "concrete specificity" of what the passage is saying. I believe this move will unavoidably loosen one's foundation in the text.

Doriani's response to Webb is helpful in seeing the differences between the redemptive-movement hermeneutic and a nuanced complementarian reading of the slavery issue and the gender debate. The question is not whether there is redemptive movement, but rather how much. "We agree that there is movement in the teaching on slavery and that there is not movement on homosexuality; we disagree about gender roles" (260).

We will have to watch in the years to come to see whether egalitarians will move in a unified way to adopt Webb's approach, or if many will continue to advance the more "traditional" egalitarian approach represented by Kaiser. The two scholars find themselves on different paths as they seek the same destination. Which path will egalitarianism take into the future?

Corporal Punishment in the Bible: A Redemptive-Movement Hermeneutic for Troubling Texts[3]

Recently, Webb has published a book that applies the redemptive-movement hermeneutic to another hot-button issue—spanking.

Overview

The introductory chapter of the book is titled, "A Troubled Christian Soul." Webb laments the "unsettling juxtaposition of values" that seems to exist between the Bible and our contemporary ideals. We are appalled by stories of parents beating and bruising and scarring their children, but "the Bible does not view the leaving of marks and bruises from a beating as abusive" (20). In fact, the Bible presents the leaving of marks as virtuous, Webb asserts. From this unsettling juxtaposition arises a troubled soul . . . and a book to wrestle with this tension.[4]

At the end of the introduction, Webb summarizes the central question addressed in the book: "*Should Christians using a grammatical-historical hermeneutic add (or not add) a component of redemptive-movement meaning and application as they read the corporal punishment texts?*" (22, italics original). The claim is that the redemptive-movement hermeneutic is not a new concept at all, but rather can be a helpful "subcomponent" of the grammatical-historical approach.

In chapter 1, Webb juxtaposes the contemporary pro-spanking position with the corporal punishment texts in the Bible, arguing that contemporary advocates of spanking have moved beyond the Bible in their understanding of spanking. In other words, they have unwittingly made a move similar to the trajectory approach by softening the corporal punishment commands. The problem is they haven't gone far enough.

3. This material is from a review I wrote for *Themelios* 37, 2 (2012). Used by permission.

4. In a footnote, Webb cites another book of his which is forthcoming and deals with yet another set of troubling texts. William J. Webb, *Brutal, Bloody and Barbaric: War Texts That Trouble the Soul* (Downers Grove, IL: IVP, forthcoming).

According to Webb, the consistent position is to eliminate all corporal punishment.

James Dobson and Focus on the Family are cited in this discussion, but Webb says that his "strongest disagreements lie with biblical scholars such as Andreas Köstenberger, Al Mohler, Wayne Grudem and Paul Wegner, who have recently published on this subject" (27). The rest of chapter 1 deals with seven ways in which spanking advocates have moved beyond what the Bible says. They are as follows: "(1) age limitations, (2) the number of lashes or strokes, (3) the bodily location of the beating, (4) the resultant bruising, welts and wounds, (5) the instrument of discipline, (6) the frequency of beatings and offenses punishable, and (7) the emotive disposition of the parent" (28). In each of these areas Webb draws a stark contrast between what the Bible teaches and what contemporary pro-spankers teach.

Chapter 2 explains the redemptive-movement hermeneutic and uses the slavery texts as a means of doing so. Some of this material is adapted from the discussion in *Slaves, Women, and Homosexuals.* Chapter 3 makes the case for a redemptive-movement interpretation of the corporal punishment texts. To do so, Webb describes how corporal punishment was exercised in ancient Egypt, ancient Babylon, and ancient Assyria. He then compares this with ancient Israel and illustrates the redemptive movement that has taken place in the biblical commands. Two other important facets of this chapter are abstracted meaning and purpose meaning. These points were also discussed in *Slaves, Women, and Homosexuals.*

Webb then asks the question in chapter 4, "What about adult corporal punishment?" He examines the "heavy knife" or "meat cleaver" text of Deuteronomy 25:11–12. These verses describe a unique situation in which two men are fighting and the wife of one of them tries to rescue her husband by seizing the other man by his private parts. In such an event, the woman's hand is to be cut off. Webb contrasts this with corporal mutilation in other ancient Near Eastern cultures, seeking to demonstrate that even Deuteronomy 25:11–12, as harsh as it may sound, is an example of redemptive movement. The redemptive movement, however, is only incremental. "In no way do the concrete specifics of what we encounter in Deuteronomy 25:11–12 represent an ultimate ethical application in terms of how to treat human beings within a fallen-world context where punishments are necessary" (114). We must continue the trajectory of this incremental movement in order to arrive at an ultimate ethic. Webb suggests applying this in terms of finding penalties that provide some kind of restitution to those who have been wronged. "Punishments that can in some way lessen or redeem damages are far better than punishments that create more damage within an already damaged world" (114).

Webb's study of corporal punishment concludes with the practical question of whether or not parents should spank their kids. He elaborates on the question this way: "*Having already journeyed beyond the concrete-specific teaching of the Bible about 'beating with the rod' (the seven ways) to a gentler and kinder form of discipline (two-smacks-max)—a journey that embraces the redemptive spirit of Scripture—should that same redemptive spirit logically carry Christians to use alternative-discipline methods only?*" (119, italics original). Many of the arguments in this final chapter have to do with the assertion that noncorporal forms of discipline are more humane. Webb makes a significant hermeneutical point by comparing the corporal punishment question to the abolition of slavery. Slavery should be abolished, not merely softened. "In a similar way, a logical extension or trajectory of the redemptive spirit with the corporal punishment texts means the abolition of physical beatings and bodily mutilations altogether. Softer and gentler beatings are good but do not offer the fullest expression of redemptive movement" (127).

A lengthy and very helpful postscript to the book shares the "unplanned parenting journey" of Webb and his wife, Marilyn. This is the practical outworking of the hermeneutical conclusions. It was moving to read of the Webbs' experiences in their own family, and it was extremely helpful to read of the wise methods they have used for training up their children.

Webb's Helpful Insights

On that note, let me mention the things I appreciated about this book. I have enjoyed reading all of Webb's books and articles because he forces me to ask difficult questions that I might otherwise be inclined to ignore. He challenges my assumptions and therefore forces me to think more deeply about those assumptions. I am in debt to him for spurring me on in this way.

It is also helpful to see the redemptive nature of Israel's laws in contrast with the harsher punishments of other cultures. I am grateful to Webb for the research he has done regarding these things. It is very enlightening.

And as I just mentioned, the postscript is immensely practical and useful for parents. Although I do not agree with his hermeneutical conclusions, there is a lot of practical wisdom for parenting here. This has stimulated my thinking about various methods of discipline we use in our own home with our three young children.

Critique from Other Scholars

The main critique that has been brought against Webb on this issue is that he does not adequately account for differences of genre in Scripture. Andreas Köstenberger, in the second edition of *God, Marriage, and Family,* responds to a paper that Webb presented on this topic.[5] In Webb's book, he includes an appendix that interacts with Köstenberger's critiques. One of Köstenberger's three critiques is as follows:

> Webb failed to account adequately for the genre distinctions between legal Torah texts and wisdom literature, treating these different types of texts on equal terms. However, while both are part of sacred Scripture, one should not interpret a legal text from Deuteronomy or Leviticus in the same way as a passage in Proverbs or Psalms. The proverbial nature of wisdom literature does not require strict literalism but rather provides universal principles about the disciplining of children. In contrast to certain legal stipulations, OT wisdom is perennially relevant rather than something to be relegated to a now-passé stage in the development of biblical ethics.[6]

Walter Kaiser responds similarly in *Four Views on Moving Beyond the Bible to Theology.* In his response to Webb's chapter, Kaiser writes:

> Webb takes a handful of spanking texts from the book of Proverbs but forgets the well-known hermeneutical instructions for interpreting

5. Andreas J. Köstenberger with David W. Jones, *God, Marriage, and Family: Rebuilding the Biblical Foundation*, 2nd ed. (Wheaton, IL: Crossway, 2010), 342–43. The paper that Köstenberger is responding to is William J. Webb, "Rod, Whip and Meat Cleaver: Spanking Kids and Cutting Off a Wife's Hand" (presentation at the annual ETS meeting, November 2007).

6. *God, Marriage, and Family*, 343.

> proverbial types of literature. . . . To take a proverb and demand that it is to be understood as a literal word with no exceptions, but universally applicable to all in all situations is to run counter to the literary genre and its own rules of interpretation. . . . However, once again Webb searches the Bible topically (not staying with chair-teaching passages in context) and gathers teachings on all sorts of corporal punishment, from Exod. 21:20–21 (slave passage) to punishments meted out by judges in the courts (Deut. 25:1–3), and lumps them (not to mention apocryphal material from Sirach) all together with proverbial material on raising and disciplining children. This is no way to do Bible study![7]

Daniel Doriani also raises the question of genre:

> [W]hile I appreciated Webb's remarks about the progress of the OT compared to its culture, about the purpose of discipline, and about the "abstracted meaning" of the texts (reminiscent of Kaiser's principlizing), I had two questions: Had Webb sufficiently accounted for the fact that many of his CP texts are civil/penal code, not family law? And is "redemptive movement" most suited to serve as the dominant paradigm for analyzing CP?"[8]

Webb conducts a fascinating study of many passages that can be very troubling, indeed. However, his conclusions are suspect because of the lack of clarity regarding various genres of Scripture. This seems to be another example of Webb wanting to have his cake and eat it too (see Al Wolters' quote above). He desires to embrace the popular values of our time (anti-spanking) and also maintain fidelity to the Bible. Again, there is danger in this hermeneutical system which loosens our foothold in the authority of Scripture.

The Seven Ways

I agree with the critiques given by Köstenberger, Kaiser, and Doriani. I think they put their finger on one of the key weaknesses in Webb's whole system. He lumps passages together without accounting for the different parts of Scripture in which they are found. He also misconstrues the pro-

7. *Four Views*, 252–53.
8. Ibid., 259.

verbial material.[9] These problems are very evident in chapter 1 of Webb's book, where he identifies seven ways "that pro-spankers go beyond the specific teachings about corporal punishment found in the Bible."[10]

Webb deals first with age limitations. Those today who advocate spanking also recommend guidelines for how and when to administer spankings. This includes suggestions of the age range of children for whom spankings are appropriate. Webb, however, counters with the observation that the Bible gives no age limitations for corporal punishment.

> The instructions for beating children in Scripture do not stand alone; they intersect with at least three other spheres of corporal punishment: slaves, fools, and Torah violators. For each of these categories the adult application of the rod or whip was a normative biblical virtue. The Deuteronomy text that establishes physical beatings as a broad-based punishment for Torah infractions (Deut. 25:1–3) was in all likelihood applied as early as twelve to fourteen years of age. The Exodus text that supports beating slaves (Ex. 21:20–21) may well have applied to all slaves regardless of age.[11]

He also cites verses from Proverbs that speak of corporal punishment for the "fool," and asserts that these could include children as well as adults.

Pulling all of these texts together in this way is unwarranted. Webb is correct in observing that the Bible does not give us explicit age limitations for the use of corporal punishment with children. But he is incorrect to suggest that individuals would be disobedient to the instructions of the Bible if they were to limit spankings to certain ages. This is what Webb asserts. "Given this larger biblical context, the idea of primarily spanking preschoolers, tapering off from there and eliminating all spankings for teenagers, while appearing reasonable to contemporary readers, is simply not biblical at the level of what the Bible explicitly teaches."[12]

If we interpret these passages correctly, however, we must acknowledge that the Bible does not teach *anything* explicitly regarding the

9. Webb critiques Paul Wegner, among others, throughout this discussion. I would submit that Wegner's position is far stronger, for he deals with the proverbial material in a way that is appropriate to how it is intended. See Paul D. Wegner, "Discipline in the Book of Proverbs: 'To Spank or Not to Spank,'" *JETS* 48, 4 (2005): 715–32.

10. *Corporal Punishment*, 28

11. Ibid., 30.

12. Ibid.

specific question of age limitations. It could be helpful if those who advocate spanking make a distinction here. The use of corporal punishment in the discipline of children *is* taught in the Bible. But many of the specifics are not explicitly taught. Therefore, recommendations regarding some of the details of spanking are based more generally on the wisdom we glean from the whole of what the Bible says about parenting.[13]

Webb goes too far in the other direction, giving the impression that obeying the clear instructions of Scripture would mean administering harsh beatings to our children all the way into their adulthood. If we are convinced by his portrayal of the biblical landscape on this issue, then it becomes plain that we must somehow "move beyond" what the Bible says. But what do Deuteronomy 25:1–3 and Exodus 21:20–21 have to do with corporal punishment for children? Very little, in my opinion. They may have superficial aspects in common, but the passages from the Mosaic Law should be interpreted in their own context, whereas the passages from Proverbs should be understood within the genre of wisdom literature. And even within Proverbs, we must consider the distinction between disciplining the "fool" and disciplining one's own child. There is the overlapping matter of corporal punishment, but we are dealing with two very different situations.

The second issue Webb addresses is the number of lashes or strokes. He refers to the pro-spanking position as "two-smacks-max." In contrast, the Bible sets the limit at forty. "Within a broader theology of corporal punishment the maximum limit on strokes or lashes is clearly set at forty (not two) strokes for Torah infractions (Deut. 25:3)."[14] Again, the comparison is unhelpful and confusing. Deuteronomy 25:3 is dealing with a legal matter among adults in the context of the Mosaic Law. The verses in Proverbs concerning parenting do not give all the specifics for how to exercise corporal punishment. For godly and knowledgeable teachers to make certain recommendations about these details seems to be perfectly legitimate and not outside the bounds of biblical teaching. Webb makes it seem like the Bible gives crystal-clear answers to these questions. But he can only import these answers from irrelevant contexts. In reality, the Bible is silent on age limitations and number of lashes.

13. Eph. 6:4 is an important verse for consideration.
14. Ibid., 34.

The arguments are similar in other categories. Webb discusses the "bodily location of the beatings" and "resultant bruises, welts and wounds." He draws from verses that *do not* speak directly to the situation of parents disciplining their children, and he concludes that the back (not the buttocks) is the biblical place for administering corporal punishment with children and that the Bible advocates leaving bruises on children.[15]

This same confusion is seen in the chapter on adult corporal punishment. The chapter focuses on the "heavy knife (hand amputation) text" of Deuteronomy 25:11–12. Here we have another passage from the Mosaic Law, but Webb makes us feel like we would have to enforce this instruction if it were not for the redemptive-movement hermeneutic. Redemptive *history* is a more important consideration on this point than redemptive *movement*.[16]

Webb does raise many fascinating questions with which we must wrestle. I certainly have not addressed them all in this short response. But one should read Webb carefully and critically to discern whether his assertions hold when he describes what the Bible teaches. Each corporal punishment passage should be understood in its context, and the Proverbs should be read in light of their unique genre.

Other Publications

Webb has cited another book of his that is forthcoming, *Brutal, Bloody, and Barbaric: War Texts That Trouble the Soul* (IVP). So we will all have the opportunity to see the redemptive-movement hermeneutic applied to yet another controversial topic.

The redemptive-movement, or trajectory, model has also been evident in books from a couple of other authors worth noting. Kenton Sparks advocates trajectory theology in *God's Word in Human Words: An Evangelical Appropriation of Critical Biblical Scholarship*.[17] He speaks of "trumping the Bible," but in a biblical way. "When we legitimately trump the Bible with newer insights, as the church did in the case of circumcision, and as was eventually done in the case of Galileo's astronomy and in the case of

15. Proverbs 20:30 does not specify who is administering this punishment or who is receiving it. But see Wegner's helpful discussion of this passage, "To Spank or Not to Spank," 726–27.

16. See Thomas R. Schreiner, "Review of *Slaves, Women, and Homosexuals*," *JBMW* 7 (2002): 46.

17. Kenton L. Sparks, *God's Word in Human Words: An Evangelical Appropriation of Critical Biblical Scholarship* (Grand Rapids: Baker, 2008), 285–99.

slavery, we should recognize at once that this need not involve disrespect for the Word of God."[18]

Sparks mentions Kevin Giles, William Webb, R. T. France, and I. Howard Marshall as advocates of this approach. He interacts with Marshall's book *Beyond the Bible: Moving from Scripture to Theology* and also the response by Kevin Vanhoozer found in that volume. Sparks clearly sides with Marshall. He summarizes Vanhoozer's objections in this way: "Vanhoozer is not at all keen, for instance, on Marshall's argument that the Canaanite genocide, or the biblical slave laws, or the imprecatory psalms, reflect sub-Christian ethical viewpoints."[19] Sparks responds,

> [T]o my mind the real difficulty with Vanhoozer's objection is that it simply does not come to grips with the profound ethical and theological diversity in the canon. In my opinion, if there is a basic and fundamental theological division emerging among evangelical scholars at this juncture in history, it is the division between those like Marshall who recognize this diversity, and those like Vanhoozer who more or less want to deny it.[20]

This shows the significance of this discussion, not only for the gender debate, but for the ramifications it will have on the future of evangelical theology. Sparks points out that,

> Although Vanhoozer offers numerous and pointed criticisms of his book, in the end he affirms that Marshall's work is within the orbit of evangelical theology. Moreover, Vanhoozer confesses that the church must discover a theological approach that can go beyond the Bible *biblically*. This task is perhaps the most important theological challenge that faces contemporary evangelical theology. (italics original)[21]

Paul Copan also promotes the redemptive-movement model in his recent book, *Is God a Moral Monster? Making Sense of the Old Testament God*.[22] He refers approvingly to Webb's book, *Slaves, Women,*

18. Ibid., 295.
19. Ibid., 297.
20. Ibid., 298.
21. Ibid.
22. Paul Copan, *Is God a Moral Monster? Making Sense of the Old Testament God* (Grand Rapids: Baker, 2011), see especially pages 62–65.

and Homosexuals, and he summarizes the points regarding all three issues. "While such a redemptive movement operates for women and servants/slaves in Scripture, the same cannot be said for homosexual activity. This action is consistently viewed negatively—a departure from God's creational design-plan."[23] Copan's use of this model shows its apologetic attractiveness for evangelicals. Copan is writing in response to the New Atheism, which takes shots at the atrocities of the God of the Old Testament.

Webb, in his *Corporal Punishment* book, cites this as one of the reasons for using only noncorporal methods for children. Our Christian witness is at stake. In the face of the New Atheists, we must help them to see the Scriptures in light of redemptive movement.

> The new atheism movement and its high-profile representatives like Richard Dawkins have made it their business to discredit Christians through casting high-beam spotlights on certain unsightly passages in the Bible. We must introduce non-Christians to a redemptive-movement understanding of the biblical text and help them read the corporal punishment texts through an ancient-world lens. Such a witnessing act gives them a deeper opportunity to believe that God may have in fact had something to do with the writing of Scripture.[24]

In these various ways, the discussion concerning redemptive movement continues. Over time we will begin to discern more clearly the fruit of this hermeneutical model.

23. Ibid., 63.
24. Webb, *Corporal Punishment*, 136.

Select Bibliography

Books

Abzug, Robert H. *Passionate Liberator: Theodore Weld and the Dilemma of Reform*. New York: Oxford University Press, 1980.

Balch, David L. *Let Wives Be Submissive: The Domestic Code in 1 Peter*. SBLMS 26. Chico, CA: Scholars Press, 1981.

Barnes, Albert. *An Inquiry into the Scriptural Views of Slavery*. Philadelphia: Parry & McMillan, 1855.

Bartchy, S. Scott. *MALLON CHRESAI: First Century Slavery and the Interpretation of 1 Corinthians 7:21*. Missoula, MT: Scholars Press, 1973.

Bechtler, Steven Richard. *Following in His Steps: Suffering, Community, and Christology in 1 Peter*. SBLDS 162. Atlanta: Scholars Press, 1998.

Beck, James R., and Craig L. Blomberg, eds. *Two Views on Women in Ministry*. 2nd ed. Grand Rapids: Zondervan, 2005.

Bilezikian, Gilbert. *Beyond Sex Roles: A Guide for the Study of Female Roles in the Bible*. Grand Rapids: Baker, 1985.

Bloesch, Donald G. *Is the Bible Sexist? Beyond Feminism and Patriarchalism*. Westchester, IL: Crossway, 1982.

Channing, William E. *Slavery*. Boston: James Munroe, 1835.

Cheever, George B. *The Guilt of Slavery and the Crime of Slaveholding: Demonstrated from the Hebrew and Greek Scriptures*. Boston: John P. Jewett, 1860.

Clouse, Bonnidell, and Robert G. Clouse. *Women in Ministry: Four Views*. Downers Grove, IL: IVP, 1989.

Copan, Paul. *Is God a Moral Monster? Making Sense of the Old Testament God*. Grand Rapids: Baker, 2011.

Cosgrove, Charles H. *Appealing to Scripture in Moral Debate: Five Hermeneutical Rules*. Grand Rapids: Eerdmans, 2002.

Elliot, E. N., ed. *Cotton Is King, and Pro-Slavery Arguments Comprising the Writings of Hammond, Harper, Christy, Stringfellow, Hodge, Bledsoe, and*

Cartwright on This Important Subject. 1860. New York: Negro Universities Press, 1969.

Fiorenza, Elisabeth Schüssler. *Discipleship of Equals: A Critical Feminist Ekklēsia-logy of Liberation*. New York: The Crossroad Publishing Company, 1993.

_________. *In Memory of Her: A Feminist Theological Reconstruction of Christian Origins*. New York: The Crossroad Publishing Company, 1994.

Foh, Susan T. *Women and the Word of God: A Response to Biblical Feminism*. Phillipsburg, NJ: Presbyterian and Reformed, 1980.

Fowl, Stephen E. *Engaging Scripture: A Model for Theological Interpretation*. Malden, MA: Blackwell, 1998.

France, R. T. *Women in the Church's Ministry: A Test Case for Biblical Interpretation*. Grand Rapids: Eerdmans, 1995.

Giles, Kevin. *The Trinity and Subordinationism: The Doctrine of God and the Contemporary Gender Debate*. Downers Grove, IL: IVP, 2002.

_________. *Women and Their Ministry: A Case for Equal Ministries in the Church Today*. East Malvern, Australia: Dove Communications, 1977.

Grenz, Stanley, and Denise Muir Kjesbo. *Women in the Church: A Biblical Theology of Women in Ministry*. Downers Grove, IL: IVP, 1995.

Groothuis, Rebecca Merrill. *The Feminist Bogeywoman: Questions and Answers about Evangelical Feminism*. Grand Rapids: Baker, 1995.

_________. *Good News for Women: A Biblical Picture of Gender Equality*. Grand Rapids: Baker Books, 1997.

Grudem, Wayne. *Evangelical Feminism: A New Path to Liberalism?* Wheaton, IL: Crossway Books, 2006.

_________. *Evangelical Feminism and Biblical Truth: An Analysis of More Than 100 Disputed Questions*. Sisters, OR: Multnomah, 2004.

Harrill, J. Albert. *The Manumission of Slaves in Early Christianity*. Hermeneutische Untersuchungen. zur Theologie 32. Tübingen: J. C. B. Mohr, 1995.

_________. *Slaves in the New Testament: Literary, Social, and Moral Dimensions*. Minneapolis: Fortress Press, 2006.

Harris, Murray J. *Slave of Christ: A New Testament Metaphor for Total Devotion to Christ*. Downers Grove, IL: IVP, 2001.

Hays, Richard B. *The Moral Vision of the New Testament: Community, Cross, New Creation; A Contemporary Introduction to New Testament Ethics*. San Francisco: HarperSanFrancisco, 1996.

Hove, Richard. *Equality in Christ? Galatians 3:28 and the Gender Dispute*. Wheaton, IL: Crossway, 1999.

Hurley, James B. *Man and Woman in Biblical Perspective*. Grand Rapids: Zondervan, 1981.

Jewett, Paul K. *Man as Male and Female: A Study in Sexual Relationships from a Theological Point of View.* Grand Rapids: Eerdmans, 1975.

Johnson, Luke Timothy. *Scripture and Discernment: Decision Making in the Church.* Nashville: Abingdon, 1996.

Kassian, Mary A. *The Feminist Gospel: The Movement to Unite Feminism with the Church.* Wheaton, IL: Crossway, 1992.

_________. *The Feminist Mistake: The Radical Impact of Feminism on Church and Culture.* Wheaton, IL: Crossway, 2005.

_________. *Women, Creation, and the Fall.* Westchester, IL: Crossway, 1990.

Keener, Craig S. *Paul, Women, and Wives: Marriage and Women's Ministry in the Letters of Paul.* Peabody, MA: Hendrickson, 1992.

Kidd, Reggie M. *Wealth and Beneficence in the Pastoral Epistles: A "Bourgeois" Form of Early Christianity?* SBLDS vol. 122. Atlanta: Scholars Press, 1990.

Knight, George W., III. *The Role Relationship of Men and Women: New Testament Teaching.* Chicago: Moody Press, 1985.

Köstenberger, Andreas J. *Studies on John and Gender: A Decade of Scholarship.* Studies in Biblical Literature, vol. 38. New York: Peter Lang, 2001.

Köstenberger, Andreas J., and David W. Jones. *God, Marriage, and Family: Rebuilding the Biblical Foundation.* 2nd ed. Wheaton, IL: Crossway, 2010.

Köstenberger, Andreas J., and Thomas R. Schreiner, eds. *Women in the Church: An Analysis and Application of 1 Timothy 2:9–15.* 2nd ed. Grand Rapids: Baker Academic, 2005.

Köstenberger, Andreas J., Thomas R. Schreiner, and H. Scott Baldwin, eds. *Women in the Church: A Fresh Analysis of 1 Timothy 2:9–15.* Grand Rapids: Baker, 1995.

Kroeger, Catherine Clark, and Richard Clark. *I Suffer Not a Woman: Rethinking 1 Timothy 2:11–15 in Light of Ancient Evidence.* Grand Rapids: Baker, 1992.

Longenecker, Richard N. *New Testament Social Ethics for Today.* Grand Rapids: Eerdmans, 1984.

Lowance, Mason, ed. *Against Slavery: An Abolitionist Reader.* New York: Penguin Books, 2000.

_________. *A House Divided: The Antebellum Slavery Debates in America, 1776–1865.* Princeton, NJ: Princeton University Press, 2003.

Marshall, I. Howard. *Beyond the Bible: Moving from Scripture to Theology.* Grand Rapids: Baker Academic, 2004.

_________. *The Role of Women in the Church.* Leicester: IVP, 1984.

Mickelsen, Alvera. *Women, Authority, and the Bible.* Downers Grove, IL: IVP, 1986.

Mollenkott, Virginia R. *Women, Men, and the Bible.* Rev. ed. New York: Crossroad, 1988.

Patterson, Orlando. *Slavery and Social Death: A Comparative Study*. Cambridge, MA: Harvard University Press, 1982.

Pierce, Ronald W., and Rebecca Merrill Groothuis, eds. *Discovering Biblical Equality: Complementarity without Hierarchy*. Downers Grove, IL: IVP, 2004.

Piper, John, and Wayne Grudem, eds. *Recovering Biblical Manhood and Womanhood: A Response to Evangelical Feminism*. Wheaton, IL: Crossway Books, 1991.

Scanzoni, Letha Dawson, and Virginia Ramey Mollenkott. *Is the Homosexual My Neighbor? A Positive Christian Response*. Rev. ed. San Francisco: HarperCollins, 1994.

Sparks, Kenton L. *God's Word in Human Words: An Evangelical Appropriation of Critical Biblical Scholarship*. Grand Rapids: Baker, 2008.

Spencer, Aida Besançon. *Beyond the Curse: Women Called to Ministry*. Nashville: Thomas Nelson Publishers, 1985.

Stendahl, Krister. *The Bible and the Role of Women: A Case Study in Hermeneutics*. Translated by Emilie T. Sander. Philadelphia: Fortress Press, 1966.

Stewart, John W., and James H. Moorhead, eds. *Charles Hodge Revisited: A Critical Appraisal of His Life and Work*. Grand Rapids: Eerdmans, 2002.

Swartley, Willard M. *Slavery, Sabbath, War and Women: Case Issues in Biblical Interpretation*. Scottdale, PA: Herald Press, 1983.

Tise, Larry E. *Proslavery: A History of the Defense of Slavery in America, 1701–1840*. Athens: The University of Georgia Press, 1987.

Verner, David C. *The Household of God: The Social World of the Pastoral Epistles*. Chico, CA: Scholars Press, 1981.

Webb, William J. *Corporal Punishment in the Bible: A Redemptive-Movement Hermeneutic for Troubling Texts*. Downers Grove, IL: IVP, 2011.

________. *Slaves, Women, and Homosexuals: Exploring the Hermeneutics of Cultural Analysis*. Downers Grove, IL: IVP, 2001.

Weld, Theodore. *The Bible Against Slavery: or, An Inquiry into the Genius of the Mosaic System, and the Teachings of the Old Testament on the Subject of Human Rights*. Pittsburgh: United Presbyterian Board of Publication, 1864.

Witherington, Ben. *Women in the Earliest Churches*. SNTSMS 59. Cambridge: Cambridge University Press, 1988.

Wolters, Albert M. *Creation Regained: Biblical Basics for a Reformational Worldview*. Grand Rapids: Eerdmans, 1985.

ARTICLES

Clines, David J. A. "What Does Eve Do to Help? and Other Readerly Questions to the Old Testament." *Journal for the Study of the Old Testament*, 94. Sheffield: Sheffield Academic Press, 1990.

Giles, Kevin. "The Biblical Argument for Slavery: Can the Bible Mislead? A Case Study in Hermeneutics." *EQ* 66 (1994): 3–17.

———. "A Critique of the 'Novel' Contemporary Interpretation of 1 Timothy 2:9–15 Given in the Book, *Women in the Church*. Part I." *EQ* 72 (2000): 151–67.

———. "A Critique of the 'Novel' Contemporary Interpretation of 1 Timothy 2:9–15 Given in the Book, *Women in the Church*. Part II." *EQ* 72 (2000): 195–215.

———. "The Ordination of Women: On Whose Side Is the Bible?" In *Force of the Feminine: Women, Men and the Church*, ed. Margaret A. Franklin, 38–48. Sydney: Allen & Unwin, 1986.

———. "Women in the Church: A Rejoinder to Andreas Köstenberger." *EQ* 73 (2001): 225–45.

Grudem, Wayne. "Should We Move Beyond the New Testament to a Better Ethic? An Analysis of William J. Webb, *Slaves, Women, and Homosexuals: Exploring the Hermeneutics of Cultural Analysis*." *JETS* 47 (2004): 299–346.

Guelzo, Allen C. "Charles Hodge's Antislavery Moment." In *Charles Hodge Revisited: A Critical Appraisal of His Life and Work*, ed. John W. Stewart and James H. Moorhead, 299–325. Grand Rapids: Eerdmans, 2002.

Gundry-Volf, Judith M. "Christ and Gender: A Study of Difference and Equality in Gal. 3, 28." In *Jesus Christus als die Mitte der Schrift: Studien zur Hermeneutik des Evangeliums*, ed. Christof Landmesser, Hans-Joachim Eckstein, and Hermann Lichtenberger, 439–77. Beihefte zur Zeitschrift für die neutestamentliche Wissenschaft und die Kunde der älteren Kirche, Band 86. Berlin: Walter de Gruyter, 1997.

———. "Gender and Creation in 1 Corinthians 11:2–16: A Study in Paul's Theological Method." In *Evangelium, Schriftauslegung, Kirche: Festschrift für Peter Stuhlmacher zum 65. Geburtstag*, ed. Jostein Ådna, Scott Hafemann, and Otfried Hofius, 151–71. Göttingen: Vandenhoeck & Ruprecht, 1997.

Haas, Guenther. "The Kingdom and Slavery: A Test Case for Social Ethics." *Calvin Theological Journal* 28 (1993): 74–89.

———. "Patriarchy as an Evil That God Tolerated: Analysis and Implications for the Authority of Scripture." *JETS* 38 (1995) 321–36.

———. "Slave, Slavery." In *Dictionary of the Old Testament: Pentateuch*. Edited by T. Desmond Alexander and David W. Baker. Downers Grove, IL: IVP, 2003.

Hamilton, James M., Jr. "What Women Can Do in Ministry: Full Participation within Biblical Boundaries." Paper presented at the Wheaton Theology Conference, Wheaton, IL, April, 2005.

Harrill, J. Albert. "Slave." In *Eerdmans Dictionary of the Bible*. Edited by David Noel Freedman. Grand Rapids: Eerdmans, 2000.

________. "Slavery." In *Dictionary of New Testament Background*. Edited by Craig A. Evans and Stanley E. Porter. Downers Grove, IL: IVP, 2000.

________. "The Use of the New Testament in the American Slave Controversy: A Case History in the Hermeneutical Tension between Biblical Criticism and Christian Moral Debate." *Religion and American Culture* 10 (2000): 149–86.

Köstenberger, Andreas J. "Gender Passages in the NT: Hermeneutical Fallacies Critiqued." *WTJ* 56 (1994): 259–83.

________. "Women in the Church: A Response to Kevin Giles." *EQ* 73 (2001): 205–24.

Moo, Douglas J. "1 Timothy 2:11–15: Meaning and Significance." *TrinJ* 1 NS (1980): 62–83.

________. "The Interpretation of 1 Timothy 2:11–15: A Rejoinder." *TrinJ* 2 NS (1981): 198–222.

Niccum, Curt. "The Voice of the Manuscripts on the Silence of Women: The External Evidence for 1 Cor. 14:34–5." *NTS* 43 (1997): 242–55.

Noll, Mark A. "The Bible and Slavery." In *Religion and the American Civil War*, ed. Randall M. Miller, Harry S. Stout, and Charles Reagan Wilson, 43–73. New York: Oxford University Press, 1998.

Osborne, Grant R. "Hermeneutics and Women in the Church." *JETS* 20 (1977): 337–52.

Padgett, Alan. "Wealthy Women at Ephesus: 1 Timothy 2:8–15 in Social Context." *Interpretation* 41 (1987): 19–31.

Patterson, Orlando. "Paul, Slavery and Freedom: Personal and Socio-Historical Reflections." *Semeia* 83/84 (1998): 263–79.

Payne, Philip B. "Fuldensis, Sigla for Variants in Vaticanus, and 1 Cor. 14:34–5." *NTS* (1995): 240–62.

________. "Libertarian Women in Ephesus: A Response to Douglas J. Moo's Article, '1 Timothy 2:11–15: Meaning and Significance.'" *TrinJ* 2 NS (1981): 169–97.

Rupprecht, Arthur A. "Attitudes on Slavery Among the Church Fathers." In *New Dimensions in New Testament Study*, ed. Richard N. Longenecker and Merrill C. Tenney, 261–77. Grand Rapids: Zondervan, 1974.

________. "Slave, Slavery." In *Dictionary of Paul and His Letters*. Edited by Gerald F. Hawthorne and Ralph P. Martin. Downers Grove, IL: IVP, 1993.

________. "Slave, Slavery." In *The Zondervan Pictorial Encyclopedia of the Bible*. Edited by Merrill C. Tenney and Steven Barabas. Grand Rapids: Zondervan, 1975.

Sanders, Carl. "The 19th Century Slave Debate: An Example of Proto-Redemptive-Movement Hermeneutics?" Paper presented at the annual meeting of the Evangelical Theological Society, San Antonio, TX, November 18, 2004.

Sanders, Laura L. "Equality and a Request for the Manumission of Onesimus." *Restoration Quarterly* 46 (2004): 109–14.

Scholer, David M. "Feminist Hermeneutics and Evangelical Biblical Interpretation." *JETS* 30 (1987): 407–20.

_________. "1 Timothy 2:9–15 & the Place of Women in the Church's Ministry." In *Women, Authority & the Bible*, ed. Alvera Mickelsen, 193–219. Downers Grove, IL: IVP, 1986.

Schreiner, Thomas R. "Review of *Slaves, Women, and Homosexuals*," *JBMW* 7 (2002): 41–51.

Scorgie, Glen G. "Tracing the Trajectory of the Spirit: Gender Egalitarians and Biblical Inerrancy." Paper presented at the meeting of the Far West Region of the Evangelical Theological Society, La Mirada, CA, April 19, 2002.

Scroggs, Robin. "Paul and the Eschatological Woman." *JAAR* 40 (1972): 283–303.

_________. "Paul and the Eschatological Woman: Revisited." *JAAR* 42 (1974): 532–37.

Stendahl, Krister. "Women in the Churches: No Special Pleading." *Sounding* 53 (1970): 374–78.

Stowers, Stanley K. "Paul and Slavery: A Response." *Semeia* 83/84 (1998): 295–311.

Thompson, David L. "Women, Men, Slaves, and the Bible: Hermeneutical Inquiries." *CSR* 25 (1996): 326–49.

Tiessen, Terrance. "Toward a Hermeneutic for Discerning Universal Moral Absolutes." *JETS* 36 (1993): 189–207.

Vanhoozer, Kevin J. "Into the Great 'Beyond': A Theologian's Response to the Marshall Plan." In *Beyond the Bible: Moving from Scripture to Theology*, by I. Howard Marshall, 81–95. Grand Rapids: Baker, 2004.

Ware, Bruce A. "Male and Female Complementarity and the Image of God." In *Biblical Foundations for Manhood and Womanhood*, ed. Wayne Grudem, 71–92. Wheaton, IL: Crossway, 2002.

Webb, William. "Balancing Paul's Original-Creation and Pro-Creation Arguments: 1 Corinthians 11:11–12 in Light of Modern Embryology." *WTJ* 66 (2004): 275–89.

_________. "Bashing Babies against the Rocks: A Redemptive-Movement Approach to the Imprecatory Psalms." Paper presented at the annual meeting of the Evangelical Theological Society, Atlanta, November 20, 2003.

_________. "Gender Equality and Homosexuality." In *Discovering Biblical Equality: Complementarity without Hierarchy*, ed. Ronald W. Pierce and Rebecca Merrill Groothuis, 401–13. Downers Grove, IL: IVP, 2004.

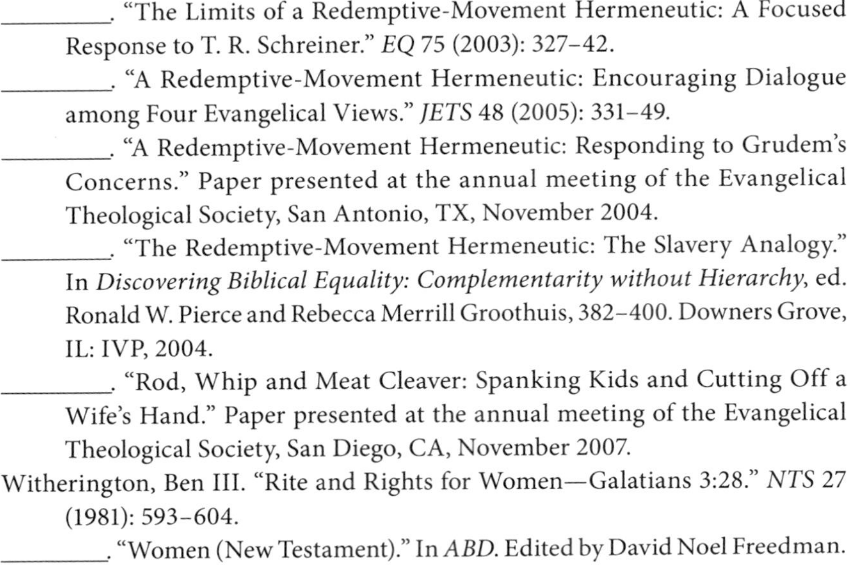

________. "The Limits of a Redemptive-Movement Hermeneutic: A Focused Response to T. R. Schreiner." *EQ* 75 (2003): 327–42.

________. "A Redemptive-Movement Hermeneutic: Encouraging Dialogue among Four Evangelical Views." *JETS* 48 (2005): 331–49.

________. "A Redemptive-Movement Hermeneutic: Responding to Grudem's Concerns." Paper presented at the annual meeting of the Evangelical Theological Society, San Antonio, TX, November 2004.

________. "The Redemptive-Movement Hermeneutic: The Slavery Analogy." In *Discovering Biblical Equality: Complementarity without Hierarchy*, ed. Ronald W. Pierce and Rebecca Merrill Groothuis, 382–400. Downers Grove, IL: IVP, 2004.

________. "Rod, Whip and Meat Cleaver: Spanking Kids and Cutting Off a Wife's Hand." Paper presented at the annual meeting of the Evangelical Theological Society, San Diego, CA, November 2007.

Witherington, Ben III. "Rite and Rights for Women—Galatians 3:28." *NTS* 27 (1981): 593–604.

________. "Women (New Testament)." In *ABD*. Edited by David Noel Freedman. New York: Doubleday, 1992.

Index of Scripture

2 Corinthians

Galatians

Index of Subjects and Names